CINELITERACY
Film Among the Arts

CINELITERACY
Film Among the Arts

Charles Eidsvik

The University of Georgia

RANDOM HOUSE
NEW YORK

For Richard Balkin

First Edition

9 8 7 6 5 4 3 2 1

Copyright © 1978 by Charles Eidsvik

Library of Congress Cataloging in Publication Data

Eidsvik, Charles, 1943–
   Cineliteracy: film among the arts.
   Bibliography: p.
   Includes index.
   1. Moving-pictures—Aesthetics. 2. Art and
moving-pictures. I. Title.
PN1995.E44   791.43'01   77–19071
ISBN 0–394–32065–4

Text design: Meryl Sussman Levavi

Cover art: C. Gianakos

Manufactured in the United States of America

PERMISSIONS
ACKNOWLEDGMENTS

Portions of the following works have been reprinted by permission.

Rudolf Arnheim, *Visual Thinking*. Copyright © 1969 by The Regents of the University of California; reprinted by permission of the University of California Press.

André Bazin, *What Is Cinema?* Copyright © 1967 by The Regents of the University of California; reprinted by permission of the University of California Press.

C. G. Crisp, *François Truffaut*. Copyright © 1972 by Praeger Publishers, Inc. Reprinted by permission of the publisher.

John Dos Passos, *U.S.A.: The 42nd Parallel*. Copyright, 1946 by John Dos Passos and Houghton Mifflin Company. Reprinted by permission of Elizabeth Dos Passos and the publisher.

Lawrence Durrell, *Justine*. Copyright © 1957 by Lawrence Durrell. Reprinted by permission of the publishers, E. P. Dutton.

George Garrett, "Don't Make Waves," in *Man and the Movies*, ed. W. R. Robinson. Copyright © 1967 by The Louisiana State University Press. Reprinted by permission of the publisher.

John Gassner (ed.), Introduction to *A Treasury of the Theatre: From Ibsen to Ionesco*. Copyright © 1963 by Simon and Schuster, Inc. Reprinted by permission of the publisher.

Helmut and Alison Gernsheim, *L. J. M. Daguerre: The History of the Diorama and the Daguerreotype*, 2nd rev. ed. Copyright © 1968 by Dover Publications, Inc. Reprinted by permission of the publisher.

David Grimsted, *Melodrama Unveiled*. Copyright © 1968 by The University of Chicago Press. Reprinted by permission of the publisher.

Erving Goffman, *The Presentation of Self in Everyday Life*. Copyright © 1959 by Erving Goffman. Reprinted by permission of Doubleday & Company, Inc.

E. H. Gombrich, *Art and Illusion: A Study in the Psychology of Pictorial Representation*, 2nd ed., The A. W. Mellon Lectures in the Fine Arts, Bollingen Series XXXV, 5. Copyright © 1969 by The Trustees of the National Gallery of Art. Quotations from pp. 172 and 345 and illustrations 275, 276, 282, 287, and 288 reproduced by permission of Princeton University Press, Princeton, N.J.

Edward T. Hall, *The Hidden Dimension*. Copyright © 1969 by Edward T. Hall. Reprinted by permission of Doubleday & Company, Inc.

Norman N. Holland, *The Dynamics of Literary Response*. Copyright © 1968 by Norman N. Holland. Reprinted by permission of the author and Oxford University Press, Inc.

James Joyce, *Ulysses*. Copyright, 1914, 1918 by Margaret Caroline Anderson. Copyright renewed, 1942, 1946 by Nora Joseph Joyce. Copyright, 1934 by Modern Library, Inc. Copyright renewed, 1961 by Lucia and George Joyce. Reprinted by permission of Random House, Inc.

Garth Jowett, "The First Motion Picture Audiences," *The Journal of Popular Film*, vol. III, no. 1, Winter 1974. Copyright © 1974 by *The Journal of Popular Film*. Reprinted by permission of the Journal.

Jan Kott, *Shakespeare Our Contemporary*, trans. Boleslaw Taborski. Copyright © 1964, 1965, 1966 by Doubleday & Company, Inc. Reprinted by permission of the publisher.

John LeCarré, *Call for the Dead*. Copyright © 1962 by Walker and Company. Reprinted by permission of the publisher.

ACKNOWLEDGMENTS

vi

André Malraux, *Museum Without Walls*, trans. Stuart Gilbert and Francis Price. Copyright © 1967 by Martin Secker & Warburg, Ltd. Reprinted by permission of Doubleday & Company, Inc.

George Orwell, *Down and Out in Paris and London*. Harcourt, Brace and World, Inc. Copyright, 1933 by George Orwell. Copyright renewed, 1960 by Sonia Pitt-Rivers. Reprinted by permission of Brandt & Brandt.

Frank Rahill, *The World of Melodrama*. Copyright © 1967 by The Pennsylvania State University Press. Reprinted by permission of the publisher.

Geoffrey Reeves, "Finding Shakespeare on Film: From an Interview with Peter Brook," *Tulane Drama Review*, vol. XI, no. 1, Fall 1966. Copyright © 1966 by *Tulane Drama Review*. Reprinted by permission of *The Drama Review*.

Henri Pierre Roché, *Jules and Jim*, trans. Patrick Evans. Copyright © 1963 by Calder and Boyars, Ltd. Reprinted by permission of the publisher.

Charles Thomas Samuels, *Encountering Directors*. Copyright © 1972 by G. P. Putnam's Sons. Reprinted by permission of the publisher.

Susan Sontag, *Styles of Radical Will*. Copyright © 1966, 1967, 1968, 1969 by Susan Sontag. Reprinted with the permission of Farrar, Straus & Giroux, Inc.

August Strindberg, Introduction to *Miss Julie*, trans. Elizabeth Sprigge. Copyright © 1957 by Elizabeth Sprigge. Reprinted by permission of Ruth Lumley-Smith.

François Truffaut, *Jules and Jim*, trans. Nicholas Frye. Copyright © 1968 by Lorrimer Publishing, Ltd. Reprinted by permission of the publisher.

Paul Valéry, *The Art of Poetry*, trans. Denise Folliot, vol. 7, *The Collected Works of Paul Valéry*, ed. Jackson Mathews, Bollingen Series XLV. Copyright © 1958 by Bollingen Foundation. Selection from p. 63 reprinted by permission of Princeton University Press, Princeton, N.J.

Richard Wasson, "Marshall McLuhan and the Politics of Modernism," *Massachusetts Review*, vol. XIII, no. 4, Autumn 1972. Copyright © 1972 by *Massachusetts Review*. Reprinted by permission of the Review.

Richard Wilbur, "A Poet and the Movies," in *Man and the Movies*, ed. W. R. Robinson. Copyright © 1967 by The Louisiana State University Press. Reprinted by permission of the publisher.

Tennessee Williams, Production Notes to *The Glass Menagerie*. Copyright 1945, 1948 by Tennessee Williams and Edwina D. Williams. Reprinted by permission of Random House, Inc.

William Carlos Williams, *Collected Earlier Poems*. Copyright 1938 by New Directions Publishing Corporation. Reprinted by permission of New Directions Publishing Corporation.

A brief portion of Chapter 10 was previously published in *Literature/Film Quarterly*, vol. I, no. 2, Spring 1973. Copyright © 1973 by Salisbury State College. I gratefully acknowledge permission from the editors of the Quarterly to reprint this material in greatly revised form.

PREFACE

Cineliteracy is intended to be, among other things, an overview of the languages of film. It is at the same time an attempt to provide an aesthetic of the cinema from the perspective of the film-viewing experience. As such, the discussion is necessarily eclectic, often borrowing as much from cultural anthropology, for instance, as it does from the literature of film aesthetics and film criticism. And as the subtitle, "Film Among the Arts," suggests, I investigate the various relationships between the cinema and other narrative, dramatic, and pictorial arts, showing in particular how the traditions, conventions, and experiments intrinsic to one medium are adapted to, and so transformed by, another medium with its own conventions and inherent limitations and possibilities. In this way I hope to provide the readers of this book with the essential critical structures and vocabulary necessary to analyze their own experiences with film.

I begin in Part One with a general description of how movies work. My emphasis is on neither the technology nor the technique of film making, but rather on how movies involve viewers in imaginative experience. From an opening discussion of the foundations of imaginary experience and aesthetic response and the contributions of culture to both, I go on to examine the primary artifices and conventions of film making and characterization and caricature as they affect viewer response. My approach throughout the book, but especially in Part One where I lay the conceptual groundwork for the book, has been interdisciplinary. Not only am I indebted to pioneering film theorists such as Sergei Eisenstein, Rudolf Arnheim, André Bazin, Siegfried Kracauer, and Jean Mitry, but I have availed myself of recent theories and research in anthropology, sociology, and general aesthetic theory. For instance, my discussion of the characteristics of narrative play owes much to Johan Huizinga's *Homo Ludens*, and many other of my central themes and concepts derive from the works of E. H. Gombrich (the relationships between perception, imagination, and thought), Erving Goffman and Edward T. Hall (the cultural components of communication), and Ray L. Birdwhistell (the nature of nonverbal communication in relation to a culture's total structure of communication).

Part Two deals with the cultural contexts that influence film experience. Here I describe the quite different kinds of expectations involved in film response and trace the cultural components of these expectations to the beginnings of urban industrialization. In my analysis of popular art and modernism in theater, literature, painting, and of course film, I deal with influence, economics, and aesthetic symbiosis. My intent is to show how apparently divergent aesthetics have converged in the cinema, how arts as seemingly different as vaudeville and cubist painting have come together to create our contemporary aesthetic milieu. By sorting out the cultural and historical processes through which works of art as well as our expectations with regard to them have come into being, I have attempted both to elucidate different kinds of film experience and to help others broaden their responses to films.

Film experience has both functional and cultural components, but it has an idealistic side, too. When we watch a film or criticize it, we do so partly in terms of what we want films to be or think they should be. Part Three analyzes film in terms of its future possibilities. In these chapters I argue that antiliterary and antitheatrical conceptions of cinema are beside the point, since films, in becoming films, transform whatever they borrow into something quite new, and that literature, and theater even more so, have a great deal to offer film.

Like the mainstream of cinema itself, *Cineliteracy* is aimed at a general audience rather than at specialists. Although I hope specialists will find a considerable amount of new theory in this book and will find it pertinent to critical debate about film theory, I have avoided frequent references to existing film theory. I have also avoided discussing films that are not regularly shown in rerun houses, art cinemas, film societies, or on public television.

I have taken a pragmatic approach to illustrations, using production stills whenever they correspond to actual shots in films and whenever they were available. Frame enlargements—especially when taken from 16 mm projection prints—reproduce badly in books and give little indication of how their originals look on the screen, so I have kept their number to a minimum.

A writer cannot escape the fact that all communication is based on convention, loose agreements about what stands for what. In this book I usually refer to the film viewer as "he." I do so for brevity's sake and because the masculine convention is deeply embedded in English. This generic use of the masculine pronoun is to be understood as referring to women as well as men.

I wish to thank my editors, Richard Garretson, Deborah Drier, and James Kemp, for their assistance in creating this book, and my wife, Anne, for her tolerance of a project that became a five-year obsession. I greatly appreciate the invaluable help of those who reviewed the manuscript of this book during its preparation, particularly Dudley Andrew and Frank McConnell. Without their evaluations, constructive criticisms, and recommendations, this book would never have attained its present form. I, however, am solely responsible for any shortcomings that it may now contain.

I would also like to thank the following organizations and individuals for granting me permission to reproduce illustrations and photographs: United Artists, Inc.; New World Pictures; Contemporary Films/McGraw-Hill; Cinema 5; New Yorker Films; Janus Films; Metro-Goldwyn-Mayer, Inc.; The National Film Board of Canada; Twentieth Century-Fox, Inc.; The Roy Export Company Establishment; Arthur Cantor, Inc.; Lord Michael Birkett; John Whitney; Christopher Kertesz; The Basel Kunstmuseum; Dover Publications, Inc.; Princeton University Press; The Museum of Modern Art.

CHARLES EIDSVIK

CONTENTS

CINELITERACY
Film Among the Arts

PART ONE

How Movies Work

Movies are perhaps the most carefully scrutinized of all the modern arts. The cinema is eighty years old, and film criticism has been with us for about sixty of those years. Books, journals, and newspapers have, especially in the last decade, inundated us with commentary on films. We should therefore, one would think, have a pretty fair grasp of the cinema's aesthetics by now. But we do not. Although the historical and technical sides of film making have received intensive study, answers to the most basic question about the movies—how do they work?—have evaded us. Why? Certainly not because knowledge is unavailable. Rather, in our approach to the problem of how movies affect viewers, that is, what makes film a potent and vital art form, we must be introspective, aware of recent information from the physical and social sciences, and willing to deal openly with the larger cultural contexts within which the cinema functions. To attempt such a broad task is inevitably to wander beyond the bounds of personal expertise, and probably to risk making a fool of oneself. Yet the task must be started somewhere, and so in the following pages I have attempted to sort out the basics from which an understanding of film experience can proceed. Part One approaches film experience from a structural perspective, describing the essential features of film experience.

For a film to affect viewers strongly—that is, for it to work—several things must happen simultaneously. Each of these is a cornerstone of film experience, and thus of film aesthetics. First, the viewer must engage in playful imaginative and perceptual speculation about the film in front of him. To understand what he sees on the screen, he must apply his knowledge of those cultural languages that film uses as a perceptual base. He must also be willing to let his imagination go along with the film. For the imagination to function efficiently, images must be structured to make imaginative sense in relation to each other. If this is to occur, images must be devised and organized within a particular frame of reference; essentially they must proceed according to conventions or rules. The cinema itself provides some such conventions; narrative traditions provide the rest. These conventions operate at both the perceptual and the imaginative levels, and though they are structured according to the demands of fiction, they are validated by the human dimension of film, as enacted by its characters. The characters in films convince viewers to take the film experience as imaginatively valid; together, the characters and the settings they inhabit create fictive social worlds within which the viewer's imagination can roam. It is the human element in films, more than any other, that determines the overall meaning (as distinguished from the effect) of the film experience. But unless each basic component of the film experience works well, no single virtue can make a film involving.

In this part, each basic component of film experience is treated in a separate chapter. The chapters are brief and suggestive rather than exhaustive; they are meant to raise issues rather than define the limits of each problem. Chapter 1 examines the initial and essential act of volition that engages the viewer in imaginative and perceptual speculation and on which all narrative experience is based. Chapter 2 takes up the environment in which this act occurs, the movie theater. This chapter considers the perceptual and psychological situation of the viewer, and discusses the ways in which the theatrical viewing situation makes perceiving and imagining easier. Chapter 3 examines perception further, looking into the dialectic between perception, the organization of our perceptual environments, and the structures of social life—each of which is a factor in film experience. Chapter 4 explores the basic structures of the imagination, and the processes by which art evokes imaginative response. Chapters 5 and 6 relate the generalized discussions of the previous chapters to the specific situation of the cinema, showing how the cinema uses both perceptual and narrative conventions to make film viewing a coherent experience. And Chapter 7 discusses the human element in film: actors, characterization, and their effects.

Central to each chapter is the assumption that movie viewing is an active experience involving all of our perceptual and imaginative faculties. We cannot understand films unless we understand that film viewing is not something that happens to us, but something we *do,* actively and with all our mental equipment. If Part One helps clarify what we do when we watch a film, as well as what movies do when we watch them, it will have provided a basis from which film criticism can proceed.

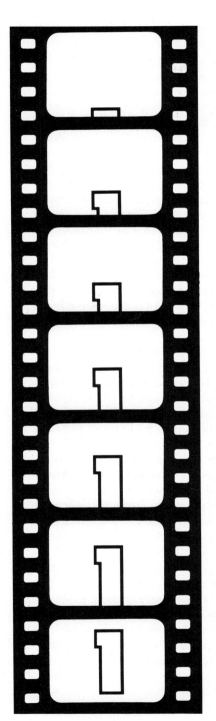

ART, NARRATIVE, AND PLAY
The Foundations of Imaginary Experience

What is the cinema? What is the cinema's place among the arts? In order to speak to these two questions, one must from the outset recognize two facts: first, that movies are a narrative dramatic form, one that demands the viewer's attention for a substantial, though limited, period of time; and second, that in order to work as a narrative form, movies must invoke a "play mood" in the viewer. As I shall show in subsequent chapters, the cinema has unique means for accomplishing both narrativity and the spirit of play. But the conditions of narrativity and playfulness are not in themselves unique to the cinema; they are conditions on which all narrative arts, including written fiction and theater, depend. Though narrativity and playfulness may appear to be obvious attributes of movies, their implications are complex and important. Therefore, before turning to a direct examination of the cinema, I must first outline the situation that allows movies to exist at all.

WHAT IF?

All narratives, no matter in what medium, are essentially suppositional; they function by invoking the subjunctive mood of the viewer's or reader's imagination. The basic tactic of all narratives is to ask implicit questions that can be answered only by imaginative means. Once the viewer or reader goes along with a set of (usually unstated) questions that can be dealt with only hypothetically—through the imagination—his attention will be engaged in a world of implied suppositions. The initial act in any narrative is to invite the viewer or reader to ask silently, "What if . . . ?" Everything that follows "what if" functions either as an assumption or a supposition following from the assumption. Once the viewer or reader begins assuming and supposing, he locks into the assumption-laden and supposition-enacting world of narrative, bringing everything he "knows" to bear on the problems of that world. Once the viewer or reader takes up the mood of "what if?" further questions are generated: more "what ifs?" and "and ifs?" and "what thens?" and "how longs?" All art that works does so because it gets its audience to ask questions, and thereby to become involved. But the narrative arts work by putting their questions in a form that has no "correct" answers except in the imagination; their initial questions are not questions at all, but rather ploys to engage the viewer's or reader's mind.

Let us look at a preliminary and crude example. What if there were a man named Rick, an expatriate American, running a café frequented by expatriates in wartime Casablanca, which is part of Occupied France and, therefore, nominally run by the Vichy government but really under the thumb of the Gestapo? What if Rick and his piano-playing black sidekick, Sam, had escaped from Paris just before the Germans occupied it? What if Rick had an ambiguous past, which included gunrunning for the Spanish Loyalists? What if Rick's true love had failed to accompany him out of Paris? What if she were to show up with her husband at Rick's café? What if the husband were a Resistance hero, whom the Gestapo wanted to silence? And what if Rick, by chance, had *two* exit visas that would allow escape to freedom? What would happen? Who would get the visas? What would be the consequences? Throw the questions, assumptions, and entire suppositional complex together, and one has a simplified description of the classic film *Casablanca*.

Once the suppositional process begins, it generates its own life, becoming functionally an organic web. Every additional assumption creates further consequences and further questions. The viewer accustomed to the roles played by Humphrey Bogart, Claude Rains, and Sidney Greenstreet brings assumptions about their characters with him; the viewer accustomed to the 1940s Hollywood film brings assumptions about cinematography, dramatic structure, and music. Once involved, the viewer can become intrigued with even a single still from the film (1–1). Greenstreet usually played charming but unscrupulous characters; what does he want from Sam? What will the piano playing tell about the story? Who are the people in the café at the

1–1. *Casablanca* (1942, Michael Curtiz).

moment? what will they do? Because there are questions implicit in every moment of the film, the viewer rivets his eyes to the screen, tunes his ears, lets his imagination play, and searches for clues that will allow him to anticipate and discern the film's "meaningful"—that is, consequential—structure of events.

The events in *Casablanca* are, of course, sheer fiction. But fiction, fantasy, and reality are never really separable once one is in a subjunctive mood. The viewer engages his concern for extremely serious matters—war, heroism, love, friendship, self-sacrifice, even survival—in a hypothetical world; everything the viewer knows about people, about society, about life's ambiguities is brought to bear on the speculating process of watching *Casablanca*. In that speculating process, the imaginary events in the film become all-important. The imagination, once activated, is a formidable foe of nice distinctions about the "reality status" of imaginary events.

Is speculative play with imaginary worlds merely an attribute of so-called escapist fiction? Not at all. Narratives always depend on invoking the speculative process. Ingmar Bergman's *Cries and Whispers*, for example, might be summarized thus: What if the woman in the center of the picture

1–2. *Cries and Whispers* (1973, Ingmar Bergman).

Museum of Modern Art, Film Stills Archive/New World Pictures

shown here were dying of cancer? What if the two women at the sides of the frame were her sisters, and the woman at the back were her companion and housekeeper? What if their family home were red-walled and red-carpeted, redolent with memories? What if the time were the beginning of this century, before the widespread use of painkilling drugs? How would the four women deal with the center figure's slow and painful death? How would the surviving three deal in their minds with the postdeath situation (1–2)?

Though the speculative involvement of the viewer of *Cries and Whispers* is hardly as festive as the involvement in *Casablanca*, the process by which the two films involve viewers is identical. Viewers of any film join the film maker in making assumptions, and then implicitly channel their anticipations according to the terms agreed on.

Once the viewer begins imaginative involvement in an "assumed" world, he can go along with astonishing and even outrageous extrapolations from initial assumptions. In Antonioni's *Zabriskie Point*, for example, the "what ifs" progress until a film that began as a study of a dissident student ends with a vision of refrigerators exploding—a poem on food flying through the air. Antonioni asks: What if a student were to buy a gun? shoot a policeman? escape? What if he were able to fly a plane? steal a plane? fly over the desert? encounter a young woman hippie? What if they fell in love? painted the airplane (1–3)? The "what ifs" continue until the young man is dead, and the

1–3. *Zabriskie Point* (1970, Michelangelo Antonioni).

young woman's imagination asks a final "what if": What if material culture itself exploded? The whole business is far-fetched, but in Europe at least, the film has been immensely popular, with long lines forming outside Paris theaters.

How far the speculating process can go depends in part on genre, in part on the skill of the storyteller. In documentaries, speculations are limited by a controlling supposition: that the film is a record of "real life." (That supposition is often as much a fiction as anything in fantasy.) In comedy, on the other hand, speculativeness can run wild, becoming itself a joke. In Keaton's *The Navigator*, for example, one sequence goes something like this: What if Buster's sweetheart were kidnaped by cannibals while Buster was underwater in a diving suit? What if he "saved" her by frightening away the cannibals, who took him for a monster? What if he were able to inflate his suit so that she could paddle him as if he were a small canoe (1–4)? By piling far-fetched suppositions on top of one another, Keaton achieves a cumulative comic effect. Similarly, René Clair's *Entr'acte*, the comic-Dada classic, makes a joke of disparate suppositions: yoking a funeral procession with a "Suppose the hearse were pulled by a camel?" Clair jolts his audience into the mood for a manic and absurd chase (1–5). To look at stills from Keaton's and Clair's films is to see just how much viewers will accept once the narrative process is well on its way.

1–4. *The Navigator* (1924, Buster Keaton).

Museum of Modern Art, Film Stills Archive

Just about anything can be plausible once the viewer or reader has accepted the requisite presuppositions. A shark with an obsessive taste for people in *Jaws,* a harpoon-tossing Pinkerton agent in love with his horse in *Missouri Breaks,* dental torture in *Marathon Man,* a giant ape in love with a blonde in *King Kong*—there are almost no limits to what the prepared imagination can go along with. And this is true of all narrative experience, regardless of the medium. The cinema has no monopoly on the subjunctive mood.

This is not to say that narrative speculation need be far-fetched. One can speculate about "real" conditions as easily as one can wander off into pipe dreams. John Cassavetes's films—*A Woman Under the Influence,* for example—engage the imagination (at least my imagination) as fully as do more fantasy-based films. One can ask, "What if a woman were to go insane in a working-class environment?" and continue the speculation with no less interest than one has in marveling over the latest gadgets available to international undercover agents. For me, the interest is greater in films where I have more knowledge to apply; my speculations are denser and more discerning. The process of narrativity applies in all time-based art forms: one can even speculate about abstractions and nonhuman content (as in the films of Peter Kubelka or Michael Snow). The process and not the content of speculation stands at the heart of the narrative arts.

1–5. *Entr'acte* (1924, René Clair).

Museum of Modern Art, Film Stills Archive

SOME CHARACTERISTICS OF NARRATIVE PLAY

The success of any narrative work is in direct proportion to the degree to which its audience can engage its imagination fully. For a viewer or reader to become fully involved, a work must guarantee a measure of safety, or the medium itself must guarantee safety. As Jean-Paul Sartre put it, narratives are willed and waking dreams. To confuse the subjunctive with the real would be to risk one's sanity, if not one's safety. The world of *Jaws* or even *Mean Streets,* to say nothing of *King Kong,* is a long way from ordinary life, at least the way I live it. Thus, in order to participate in narrative art, we must regard it as a form of play—as a "safe" activity, mentally, if not in fact, secluded from ordinary coping behavior.

In terms of how they are experienced, art and play can be described in similar terms. Johan Huizinga, in his classic *Homo Ludens,* describes play as:

an activity which proceeds within certain limits of time and space, in a visible order, according to rules freely accepted, and outside the sphere of necessity or material utility. The play-mood is one of rapture and enthusiasm, and is sacred or festive in accordance with the occasion. A feeling of exaltation and tension accompanies the action, mirth and relaxation follow.[1]

Except that relaxation often does not follow the viewing of a film, Huizinga's is a good short summary of most film experience. Further, art and play have structural similarities. Play involves a "stepping out of 'real' life into a temporary sphere of activity with a disposition all of its own. . . . It is 'played out' within certain limits of time and space. It contains its own course and meaning."[2] Again, the same is true of narrative art.

There are two possible approaches to the play aspect of narrative art. One can regard art as a subdivision of a larger, perhaps innate human capacity, the capacity for play. Or one can say that art must invoke the "spirit" of play in order to involve its audience imaginatively. Either approach is useful for understanding the appeal of narrative experience. I prefer the second, largely on semantic grounds. Narrative play is a mental, perceptual, and linguistic activity. It needs none of the safeguards and strict rules of physical play in order to function. In football or hockey, people might kill one another were it not for stringent rules about what sorts of violence are permissible and what are not. But in imaginative play, the only essential stricture is that activity must remain purely mental and perceptual. The essence of any hypothesis is that it wills its own limits and its own freedom; restrictions are not imposed from the outside. Therefore there are no rules in narrative play, except for conventions—informal agreements on how play should proceed, what symbolizes what, and so forth—and for the "rule" that hypotheses should build linearly on one another and interrelate so that the play can have internal coherence.

Because imaginative play has no fixed rules, except the rule of coherence, narrative art need stand in no single fixed relationship to "real" life. Whereas all games fix their metaphoric or symbolic "status" in relation to life through rules, narrative play does not. What a football game can "mean" symbolically can be expressed only in certain terms: competition, physical strength, teamwork, athletic prowess, tactical and reactive intelligence, and the like. All football games have pretty much the same potential meanings. But each work of narrative art can build around whatever terms the artist chooses, and thus each work must be "related back" to "real" life individually, through concrete analogies, if it is to be "related back" at all. Art "means" with more flexibility than do games or other kinds of play in which we participate more physically.

Narratives invoke the play spirit so that the restrictions of having a physically and culturally limited "self" break down. It is one thing to say that football is "just a game." It is another thing altogether to say, "It's just a movie." In narratives "just a" serves mainly to allow complete involvement in what may well be an experience with broad ethical, intellectual, and imaginative as well as aesthetic dimensions. The "just a" allows normally inhibited and cautious adults to become temporarily childlike, using the imagination to learn things that ordinary experience cannot teach safely or effectively. Children can say "Let's pretend" unabashedly. But adults seem to need to say "Let's *know* we're pretending" in order to become imaginative. Therefore, works of art tend to be playful—particularly in their uses of their media and conventions—in order to reaffirm the play spirit's presence. For the imagination to function, the viewer or reader has to postpone asking, "What has this got to do with *me?*" Once that postponement has occurred, the imagination can link the destinies of people, see all kinds of experience as interconnected, follow trains of thought and action wherever they go, and even observe with new eyes.

THE LIMITS OF NARRATIVE PLAY

The essential characteristic of the "what if?" ploy of narrative playfulness is imaginative freedom. Yet all narratives and all forms of narrative are not equally successful in invoking imaginative participation. In order to participate in a work, and to function well in the work's terms, the imagination must be properly prepared. First, the suppositions of the work must be of interest. Second, the viewer or reader must have the requisite preliminary experience for "living" in the terms of the work for a period of time. There must, in short, be a concordance between the viewer's interests and abilities and the "projects" the work undertakes. Here problems of taste, individual experience, and social background become crucial. The intelligence and literacy of the viewer are a priori tethers on the potentials for imaginative experience.

The willingness and ability of an individual to participate in a work of art can never be spoken of in ideal terms. In a homogeneous culture, perhaps all viewers or readers of a work can get equal pleasure from its terms and projects. But in contemporary culture, heterogeneity is the rule. Herbert Gans, in *Popular Culture and High Culture*, describes five different "taste aggregates" in contemporary American society alone: just as there are differences in life style, personal values, and imaginative background among different groups of people, so there are different preferences in art and entertainment.[3] Cross-culturally, tastes differ even more than they do in a single country: taste is, in part, a function of one's situation in life. Our lives give us the basis from which imagination proceeds. Our lives are not alike, so our expectations and desires for, as well as our abilities to handle, particular imaginative hypotheses are bound to be different, too. Clint Eastwood's *Dirty Harry* or *Magnum Force* and Alain Resnais's *Last Year at Marienbad* make quite different assumptions about what sort of imagining is fun. These assumptions are based on cultural background. Though there are structural similarities among all forms of narrative play, who is apt to enjoy and have the requisite skills for handling a particular work is a historical and sociological matter. How a narrative works can be described apart from the issue of cultural relativity. For whom and how well a narrative works is a question with only historical, cultural, and on occasion, "personal" answers. The apprehender of any work of art has one foot in the infinite possibilities of the imagination, the other foot—the one from which imaginative journeys start—firmly on the starting block of his own life situation. For a work of art to function well, it must create interaction between the two. How this interaction occurs, or even whether it occurs at all, depends on the individual work, the individual viewer, and the medium in which narrative play commences.

All narrative arts invoke the same mental processes. All narratives invoke the spirit of play. But what artworks play "with," how play proceeds, what the play is "about," and even, to some extent, for whom it is play, differs from medium to medium. Theatrical cinema differs from other narrative forms in each of these respects. Perhaps its most unique feature, as the next chapter shows, is that the theatrical situation itself is designed to reduce the viewer's self-consciousness, to minimize the effects of cultural differences, and thereby to enhance the viewer's perceptual and imaginative faculties.

NOTES: CHAPTER ONE

[1] Johan Huizinga, *Homo Ludens* (Boston: Beacon Press, 1955), p. 132.

[2] See Ibid., pp. 8–9. Though *Homo Ludens* gave me some ideas on which to build my theory, I have extrapolated from it, as from the works of other thinkers.

[3] Herbert J. Gans, *Popular Culture and High Culture* (New York: Basic Books, 1974).

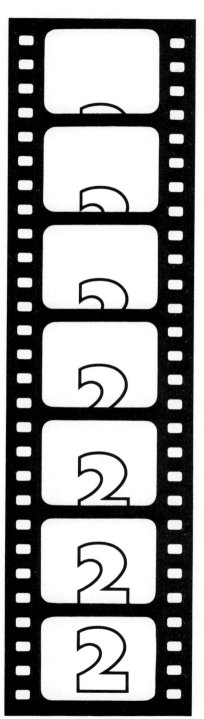

MEDIA AND AESTHETIC RESPONSE

THE THEATRICAL VIEWING SITUATION

Every situation in which we perceive art structures our response. Films, once made, end up in movie theaters, where our film experiences begin. However little the conditions under which films are made have to do with the situations in which we see them, films are intended for viewing in movie theaters. However little our conscious expectations about films take theatrical viewing into account, the structures through which we experience films are implicit in the ways in which movie theaters shape our responses.

Four things differentiate movie theaters from other media situations: relative uniformity, accessibility, insulation from distraction, and ritualized behavior. Uniformity, accessibility, and insulation require little analysis. Although theaters differ in size, comfort, location, and the like, all have essentially the same features: darkness, a fairly comfortable seating arrangement, and a large screen. Unlike museums, galleries, and "legitimate" theaters, movie houses exist virtually everywhere, even in towns too small for a bookstore. Though television is even more accessible than movies, it does not provide a uniform viewing situation; it is one thing to watch television in a bar, another to watch it at home. The movie theater more successfully insulates us from distraction than does any other medium; in the theater, we are safe from yowling children, the telephone, and friends and neighbors. Movie theaters protect us from the world and from ourselves. In the dark, clothes, social status, and race make little difference. Bum or bank president, wino or *Wunderkind,* it is all the same in the dark. Nobody watches us and we do not have to watch ourselves. Darkness provides anonymity and thus the freedom to participate fully in imaginary experience.

The rituals of moviegoing reinforce perceptual privacy. There are no publicly accepted rituals for reading or watching television; one creates each reading or television experience ad hoc. But there are rules for behavior in movie theaters. Attitudes that function almost as a social contract dictate that we do not bother other spectators or act on our reactions when the movie is over. We do not shoot each other when leaving gangster films or Westerns. Public pressure and private habit ensure that private responses remain private. Though discussion of a film often occurs after a viewing, it virtually never happens within the theater. Almost all discussions take place after the game is over, and merely serve to bridge the world of the film and the worlds of other films and the world outside. Buying a ticket to a film involves both renting a seat for approximately two hours and purchasing with that seat the promise of a measured, uninterrupted imaginative and perceptual spectacle. When the two hours are over we can leave the theater and the experience behind, except in memory. Because the familiarity of movie viewing turns conventions into habits, film is experienced as a kind of informal ritual, a game we play often enough to be good at.

Taken alone, each characteristic that makes a movie theater a special place is shared with one or more other art situations. But together they differentiate our experience of films from our experience with other art forms and media. For example, the novel, though it shares accessibility with cinema, only very rarely provides either a measured "dose" or a uniform and continuous experience in time. A novel ordinarily cannot be read in one sitting; the sittings are separated in time and often by place. One might begin a novel on a bus and finish it two days later at home. The experience of the novel—no matter how coherent the book is in itself—is apt to be fractured. Though live theater, like cinema, provides a continuous experience, it is hardly private or anonymous; live theater requires an open response to actors for a performance not to be "dead." Though art museums present pictorial material, art museums lack the uniformity of movie theaters. Further, in museums the perceiver is as well-lit as what he perceives: *he* is also on display. The museum-goer is usually confronted with a number of works in a room. He must not only choose what to look at and for how long; the multiplicity of works also dictates that he is not to become absorbed in a single work but to compare it with others. In contrast, a movie theater delivers its images through sequential processes and in doses commensurate with fully involved imaginative responses.

This is not to say that movie theaters are "better" than other art situations, but only that they work well for two-hour movies seen one at a time. It is impossible to compare artworks in a movie theater; for a live play, the poker-faced audience of films would be disastrous; for a long written narrative, sitting in one place from beginning to end would be torture. Further, movie theaters, like sports arenas before television, work strictly within the context of "public spectacles," catering only to those who find it easy to go to them. People with young children, or little money, or an aversion to going out are rarely to be found in cinemas. The theater system of distribution also limits choice, except for those who live in large cities. There are more book titles in the smallest bookstore than there are different movies running in the largest city; in smaller cities, movie choice is extremely limited. Sociologically, the movie theater is the cinema's curse. But for imaginative and perceptual participation, it is a very powerful instrument.

Why this is so requires, however, more than an analysis of the theater's uniqueness as an art medium. Theaters work because of what goes on in them. A film creates an imaginary world, structured as a narrative, in which the viewer participates perceptually. The theater allows perception to be enhanced; narrativity allows the perceptual process of anticipation and discrimination to work very efficiently. Narrativity and darkness combine to relax inhibitions that would limit both perceptiveness and response. The "playful" quality of the total film experience makes the imagination tenacious and hyperactive. To explain how all this works, it is helpful to review the basic processes of perception, relaxation, and playful concentration.

INVOLVEMENT AND THE EYE: THE STRUCTURES OF PERCEPTION

No matter the movie on the screen, how much and what we see when we look at it depends on what we bring *to* the theater. In any experience, what we expect to see largely determines what we *will* see; the mental sets we bring to experience restrain our observations. The perceptual processes at work when viewing a film are not exclusive to cinema but operate whenever we perceive. The processes always involve an interplay between preconceptions and the act of noticing what does not fit into preconceptions. Perception does not involve simply "learning to see." It involves learning to discriminate. In R. J. Beloff's terms, "perception may be regarded as primarily the modification of an anticipation."[1] Or, as E. H. Gombrich puts it:

> [Perception] is always an active process, conditioned by our expectations and adapted to situations. Instead of talking about seeing and knowing, we might

Courtesy of Christopher Kertesz

2–1. Photo by Christopher Kertesz.

do a little better to talk of seeing and noticing. We notice only when we look *for* something, and we look when our attention is aroused by some disequilibrium, a difference between our expectation and the incoming message. We cannot take in all we see in a room, but we notice if something is changed. We cannot register all the features of a head, and as long as they conform to our expectations they fall silently into the slot of our perceptive apparatus.[2]

Gombrich labels perceptual expectations "schema," and the process of discrimination "correction," terms that emphasize the fact that whatever we watch, we watch through a conceptual grid.

For example, most of us do not notice a great deal of our immediate environment simply because we have no reason to pay attention. How often do city dwellers see subway scenes like the one captured by Christopher Kertesz's photograph (2–1), not noticing them simply because such "scenes" have nothing to do with their immediate interests?

And yet, if something is out of place, we do notice it. For example, in the still from F. W. Murnau's *The Last Laugh* (2–2), everything fits except one thing: the dignified man saluting in the middle. In the entire photograph, that one figure catches attention, simply because it creates a disequilibrium within the scene, or rather, with what we expect to see in such a scene.

2–2. *The Last Laugh* (1924, F. W. Murnau).

The most striking images, in life or in movies, often occur when the difference between expectations and incoming messages is extreme, as in the following still from Luis Buñuel's *L'Age d'Or* (2–3). The bedroom, the man, and the objects in the room all fit. But the cow? It is precisely this kind of incongruity, written in smaller letters, that ordinary noticing is made of.

Film uses our ordinary perceptual processes as a base of operations. The most important fact about perception is that it is an intelligent process. Rudolf Arnheim makes this point definitively in his *Visual Thinking.* "Visual perception," Arnheim writes, "is not a passive recording of stimulus material but an active concern of the mind. The sense of sight operates selectively. The perception of shape consists in the application of form categories, which can be called visual concepts because of their simplicity and generality. Perception involves problem solving." Looking at an object involves "reaching out for it." To see is to recognize: "Noticed and attended to is all that matters." Arnheim notes: "When a frog starves in the presence of dead, immobile flies, which would make perfectly good food, he reminds us of a man whose mind is 'made up' and therefore incapable of responding to unforeseen opportunities." Perception is inseparable from intelligence: "To see an object is always to perform an abstraction because seeing consists in the grasping of struc-

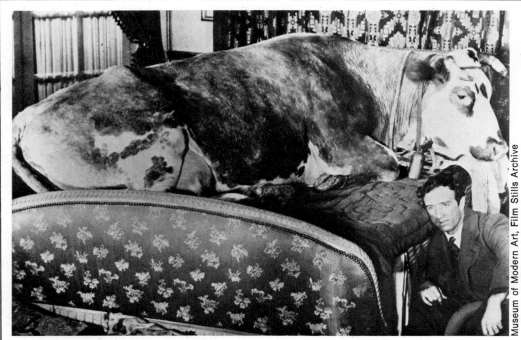

Museum of Modern Art, Film Stills Archive

2–3. *L'Age d'Or* (1930, Luis Buñuel).

tural features rather than in the indiscriminate recording of details. . . . In general, intelligence is often the ability to wrest a hidden feature or disguised relation from an adverse context." A good deal of thinking "takes place in the realm of the senses."[3] Thus film viewing involves a dialectic—one could even call it an intellectual dialectic—between what is on the screen and what is in the eye.

The structure of the eye itself helps determine the interplay between the brain, the eye, and the perceived world. Edward T. Hall summarizes the eye's physical structure:

> The retina [the light-sensitive part of the eye] is composed of at least three different parts or areas: the fovea, the macula, and the region where peripheral vision occurs. Each area performs different visual functions, enabling man to see in three very different ways. . . . The three different types of vision are simultaneous. . . . The fovea is a small circular pit in the center of the retina containing roughly 25,000 closely packed color-sensitive cones, each with its own nerve fiber. The fovea contains cells at the unbelievable concentration of 160,000 cells per square millimeter (an area the size of the head of a pin). The fovea enables the average person to see most sharply a small circle ranging in size from $\frac{1}{96}$ of an inch to $\frac{1}{4}$ of an inch (estimates vary) at the distance of twelve inches from the eye. . . . In man, needle-threading, removal of splin-

ters, and engraving are some of the many activities made possible by foveal vision. . . .

Surrounding the fovea is the macula, an oval, yellow body of color-sensitive cells. It covers a visual angle of three degrees in the vertical plane and 12 to 15 degrees in the horizontal plane. Macular vision is quite clear, but not as clear and sharp as foveal vision because the cells are not as closely packed as they are in the fovea. Among other things man uses the macula for reading.

The man who detects movement out of the corner of his eye is seeing peripherally. Moving away from the central portion of the retina, the character and quality of vision changes radically. The ability to see color diminishes as the color-sensitive cones become more scattered. Fine vision associated with closely packed receptor cells (cones), each with its own neuron, shifts to a very coarse vision in which perception of movement is enhanced. Connecting two hundred or more rods to a single neuron has the effect of amplifying the perception of motion while reducing detail. Peripheral vision is expressed in terms of an angle, approximately 90 degrees, on each side of a line extending through the middle of the skull.[4]

We usually use the less detailed parts of vision to "check out" a visual field and employ the foveal region to analyze closely and "correct" our original anticipations. The structure of the eye is adapted to—or, perhaps, is the cause of—the "anticipation-then-discrimination" process of perception.

In the accompanying still from Murnau's *The Last Laugh*, we can see how foveal and macular vision work in ordinary circumstances (2–4a). In the still as it is printed on the page, foveal vision allows us to see the expression on the old man's face—almost to count the wrinkles on his forehead. Macular vision reaches the entire upper torso of the man; to take in the entire photograph, one shifts the eyes, and uses all three kinds of vision at once. Macular and peripheral vision allow us to scan the photograph and to look at its general composition.

Were we to encounter a scene such as the one represented in Murnau's film, but in real life rather than on a page, we would see roughly the same areas of detail at a distance of twenty-five feet.

What movies do is make perception easier. The darkened theater cuts out the claims of peripheral vision. The large images on the screen open up the perceived world for analysis by the macula as well as the fovea, and allow the fovea to see details simply not available in ordinary experience. Because film makers can further assist perception by careful lighting, lens choice, and camera placement, and can guide expectations and discriminations in a thousand more subtle ways, they can radically enhance the efficiency of seeing. For example, Murnau, in *The Last Laugh*, brings us in close to his central figure, giving us details of skin texture and posture well beyond what we could see in everyday life (2–4b). Murnau brings the camera in low, letting us see the man's face and eyes; he lights the face to emphasize the wrinkles and destitute expression; he highlights posture so that the viewer gets the full message of dejection and fatigue projected in the image. Virtually every device in the repertory of cinematography is similarly designed to enhance perception, to

(a)

2–4. *The Last Laugh.*

(b)

help us see. And, in a sense, the film maker can make the viewer more intelligent perceptually, at least while the film is running. Movies use perception in ways that make being "perceptive" remarkably easy. That is one reason why they are so involving.

Everything I have said so far about theatrically enhanced perception would be true of even a brief viewing sequence; it would even be true, I think, if the materials on the screen were large slides rather than moving pictures. The anticipation-discrimination pattern works whether one looks at a still picture or a moving scene. But the fact that films are structured narratively, in a continuous "linear" sequence of images, allows both anticipations and discriminations to be channeled with radical effectiveness. Each image creates the conditions for intelligent viewing of the next image, and so on through the movie. This is true whether or not a film is obviously a narrative—a story. What happens when we watch a film is that our anticipatory and discriminatory faculties accelerate in efficiency until they reach a maximal state (which in my experience occurs within the first ten minutes); the efficiency is maintained, with slight oscillation, through the entire film. The process is akin to extreme perceptual concentration.

We could not, however, enter or stay in a state of highly efficient perception unless we were willing to "let it happen." The reasons we let it happen derive from the loosening of inhibitions and social responsibility implicit in both the theatrical situation and narrativity.

RELAXING INHIBITIONS

What Norman N. Holland says about literature in *The Dynamics of Literary Response* can be applied even more closely to movies. Literature, Holland argues, loosens boundaries that inhibit imagination. "One of literature's adaptive functions is that it allows us to loosen boundaries—between self and non-self, inner and outer, past, present, and future. In this loosening process we have emotions of a special tone and kind." In a narrative situation we are "free to range up and down the entire keyboard of our prior development," for "we take in the literary work, all literary works, in a very primitive oral way: what is 'out there' is felt as though it were neither 'out there' nor 'in here'—boundaries blur. Our awareness of ourselves becomes markedly less." Further, literature provides two kinds of safety. For one thing, it frees us from "internal" censorship of fantasy and imagination. Secondly, "we come to a literary work with [the] expectation . . . that it will not require us to act on the external world."[5] The movie theater situation makes explicit the "loosening" and "safety" implicit in all narratives; the darkness of the theater, the differences between the theater and the outside world, the rituals of viewing behavior—all reinforce the expectations and responses we bring to any narrative experience.

Perhaps the most important effect of theatrical narrative is on memory. All narratives free us to remember suppressed elements of mental experience. As

Ray L. Birdwhistell has shown, a good part of our consciousness is conditioned by the ways in which we have learned not to notice some things or, if we have noticed them, to "forget" we have noticed them.[6] Our memories are as censored as our mouths. But in a movie theater we can set aside niceties and liberate our memories, our intelligence, and our imagination, thereby bringing more to the viewing of a movie than we bring to everyday experience. I personally find that movies often resonate with experiences I could have had only in childhood. Moreover, I find that my responses to films are often the responses of a more complicated and intelligent person than I ever am in my everyday life. I doubt that my responses are eccentric; my students report a similar opening-up during films. We are the same people when watching movies as we were outside. But we have more of ourselves open than we do in ordinary life.

What makes openness and receptivity possible is simply that what happens in a movie theater is agreed to be "inconsequential" to normal behavior. Watching movies is not a serious activity, but a form of play. The viewer takes a role for himself. He puts it on when he begins watching and sheds it when the movie is over. As long as he treats it all as play, he is "safe." His role: that of a voyeur.

THE MECHANISM OF CONCENTRATION: VOYEURISM AS PLAY

The most basic appeal of any motion picture is to voyeurism—to the satisfaction of our curiosity through visual and auditory images. The movie theater, with its darkness and large screen, necessarily places the viewer in the role of voyeur. He sees efficiently without being seen or becoming explicitly involved in what he sees. Though voyeurism has been given a bad press by moralists, its appeal is central to the medium of film.

Film is essentially a speculative art form, a form based on asking "what if?" The film viewer asks with his eyes and ears and, of course, his imagination. His job is to "find out by seeing." People cannot be expected to pay several dollars and two hours to find out something they already know a lot about; thus the subject matter of narrative film is always to some extent the unknown—or, more simply put, "secrets." What the film viewer does, implicitly, is simple: he asks what he could find out if he had privileged information. Perhaps the most basic process of social organization is the management of information. The most basic requirement of the voyeur-viewer is information that will reveal what is below the surface of culturally structured appearances.

Voyeurism has traditionally been identified with an anticipation of sex or violence, but the case is far more complicated than that. Sex and violence are interesting to watch because, since they are taboo public activities, we lack good information about them. Psychoanalytical and cultural reasons aside, anxiety usually comes from inadequate information. Anxieties that cannot be allayed in normal life must be handled through either dreams or play.[7] The act of imaginatively playing out anxiety is hardly limited to the handling of sex and violence. So much of life gives rise to anxiety that narrative speculative play has as its territory an immensely large number of subjects. The cinema, like the other narrative arts, serves as a playground-classroom for dealing with virtually anything about which society provides inadequate information (or, what amounts to the same thing, inadequate resolutions). Often the voyeur is simply concerned with understanding "other people." He or she asks: What are other people *really* like? Are their love affairs like mine? What is it like to be beautiful? sexy? a gangster? a hero? What is it like to have two lovers? to be rich? poor? to be in a war? to be young now? The cinema exists to provide imaginary information, to speak to problems where they exist—below the level of conscious awareness.

Yet, at every level, the viewer plays voyeur in order to escape the restrictions of self-consciousness, and even the restrictions of having a self. Without the tether of self-consciousness, the viewer can allow aesthetic reactions full play, enjoying the beauty available to eyes and ears, and in ways that ordinary life does not permit. At a basic level, the accompanying still from D. W. Griffith's *The Birth of a Nation* gives voyeuristic pleasure of an aesthetic sort: the man, the woman, and the landscape are all so beautiful that to pause and watch them wholeheartedly gives pleasure (2–5).

2–5. *The Birth of a Nation* (1915, D. W. Griffith).

Museum of Modern Art, Film Stills Archive

It would be a mistake to say that voyeurism is ever separable from an apprehension of beauty, or that the cinema could exist apart from the hedonism of the eyes and ears. (Perhaps we are as anxious about beauty—our own and the beauty of the world—as we are about any other aspect of our existences.)

The voyeuristic role of the film viewer has everything to do with how movies mean. Therefore I will return to the subject after analyzing how movies work. But for now it is essential to emphasize the visual and auditory aspects of voyeurism. For it is precisely the visual and auditory aspects of anxiety that cinema speaks to—the world of sensory apprehension is a world about which none of us has adequate information; it is, except through art, uncharted—and this provides the sensory pleasure of moviegoing. The film viewer spends most of his time speculating about the world of the senses.

And yet speculative play always begins from what is known. The film maker and viewer begin in the same place. They construct speculative-narrative worlds using the everyday languages of perceived reality as a base. Therefore to analyze how, and why, movies work, it is necessary to step back from the viewer and ask questions about the world he brought to the theater with him in memory.

NOTES: CHAPTER TWO

[1] R. J. Beloff, quoted in E. H. Gombrich, *Art and Illusion* (Princeton, N.J.: Princeton University Press, Bollingen Series, 1969), p. 172.

[2] Gombrich, *Art and Illusion*, p. 172.

[3] Rudolf Arnheim, *Visual Thinking* (Berkeley and Los Angeles: University of California Press, 1971), pp. 37, 19, 20, 21, 68, 70, 233.

[4] Edward T. Hall, *The Hidden Dimension* (Garden City, N.Y.: Doubleday Anchor Books, 1969), pp. 70–71.

[5] Norman N. Holland, *The Dynamics of Literary Response* (New York: Oxford University Press, 1968), pp. 82–83, 79.

[6] Ray L. Birdwhistell, *Kinesics and Context: Essays in Body Motion Communication* (Philadelphia: University of Pennsylvania Press, 1970). See pp. 39–46. *Cineliteracy* owes more to Birdwhistell's thinking than to any other person's; I gratefully acknowledge my debt.

[7] Professor Edward Jayne of the University of Massachusetts, Amherst, has begun testing narrative response, using standard psychological profiles, sociometric profiles, and other measuring devices, to begin determining who responds to what kind of narrative in what way. The most curious thing about narrative response is that it *is* measurable, and that literature and film teachers have preferred to leave it unmeasured until now. Professor Jayne's work is remarkable; I only wish that full results had been available before *Cineliteracy* was published. Preliminary data indicate positive correlations between excitability on the part of the reader or viewer and strong narrative response. There seems to be a negative correlation between paranoia levels and narrative response. It may be that narratives please by displacing the viewer's ordinary anxiety, and that people with strong delusional tendencies of their own resent the competition of narrative. I suspect that ego strength and sociometrically measurable factors help determine the adventurousness of viewers and readers.

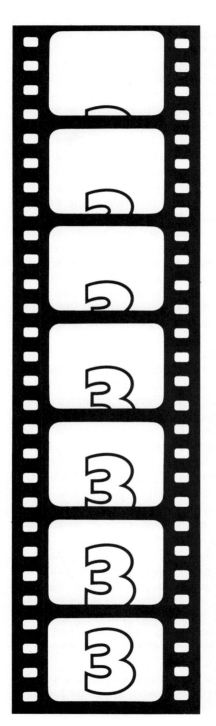

THE STRUCTURES OF EVERYDAY LIFE

THE CONTRIBUTIONS OF CULTURE

We bring to movies our experience of everyday perception. Movies would not be intelligible if ordinary life were not. The world used by film makers as they create—used as a resource, not as a direct model—is the same world we ordinarily walk about in. That world is not "innocent" of structures. It exists to be perceived.

T. S. Eliot was the first modern to realize the extent to which civilization monopolizes our experience. Eliot lamented that, unlike Wordsworth, he had never had the sense of having seen "nature." Man's mark is everywhere; nothing is uncontaminated by the history of man's uses for nature as he "makes sense of" his life. Civilization's thrust has been, from a perceptual point of view, an attempt to make meanings accessible to the eye and ear through manipulations of environment. Culturally rendered significations dominate our everyday visual fields. Without that fact the activities of our eyes, ears, and brains would be futile, or at least highly frustrating. If society's structures are not "natural," they function as if they were replacements for nature's way of organizing things.

To enable perception to proceed intelligently, cultures, through historical evolution, assign conventional values—what Gombrich would call "schema" —to virtually everything that can be seen or heard within them. These values are always relational, never absolute. A skyscraper, a split-level house, a top hat—these mean nothing inherently. But in terms of one's culture and in terms of the context or purpose for which one looks at a building, a hat, or anything else, meanings emerge. We expect that a house is to live in. We look at it and question it in those terms. How many people live there? How do they live? Who are they? The house gives clues, but only in terms of the culture. I once lived in a house in Germany that in local terms was large for the three families that occupied it. It was a status symbol. The same house, located in the prairie town where I grew up, would be regarded as a small, one-family, probably working-class dwelling. Arthur Koestler has written that, before tourism became an industry, the Alps were regarded by local people in terms of pastureland, timber, and useless territory; beauty did not enter into the equation. Meanings exist only in cultural terms, because culture determines what we anticipate when we look at something and how we have to correct our anticipations in order to arrive at "correct" appraisals.

As Edward T. Hall puts it in *The Silent Language* and *The Hidden Dimension,* nonverbal languages are often specific to societies, even to subcultures.[1] In the military, for example, a person's rank and status determine how late he or she can be for an appointment without giving offense. Time is a matter of cultural convention. In Italy being late for appointments is normal; in Germany or the United States it is an insult. Being late "means" in terms of who and where you are. Organization of things such as space and time (on both of which perception depends) is conventionalized by cultures. The French, Hall notes, organize space in star patterns rather than in grids as Americans do. In a French office, the most important person has the center desk. French highways radiate from cities in star patterns. The French reverse the American pattern: workers live in suburbs; better-off bourgeois live in the center of cities (though pollution is changing all that).

Objects too vary in their cultural meanings. Hall notes that Germans feel that doors are in their normal position when closed, while Americans like their doors open. To Germans open doors are untidy; to Americans a closed door means that a person wants privacy, is having sex, or is angry. Even rooms depend on culture for meaning: in Britain the bedroom is the husband's haven; in the United States it is the wife's. As with objects and rooms, so with clothing: British men often dress better than British women; in the United States the opposite is true.

Gestures? Germans expect a handshake when meeting or leaving you; the French prefer a hug if you are a friend; the British often are embarrassed by more than a nod. The British look one another in the eye when talking; to

Americans that often is overbearing. Americans avert their eyes; the British regard that as impolite. Southern Europeans talk at closer quarters than Northern Europeans. To smell and touch when talking is a convention in the south of France, but disorients Swedes. We bring our sense of social conventions to everything we see, including films. As Ray L. Birdwhistell has shown, even "gender display"—the gestures which signal our masculinity or femininity—are culturally relative.[2] Because we use culturally conventionalized patterns of gesture as the basis for anticipating and reacting to the behavior of others, what we bring to any visual encounter are always the assumptions of our own culture.

Sensory Envelopes

In Hall's terms, a person's communicative body extends beyond the skin. Furthermore, people carry with them a sense of what interpersonal distance means, since distance does communicate, especially about social relationships and feeling; people therefore use distance to regulate their social lives. Hall delineates four kinds of distance: intimate, personal, social, and public. He calls each kind of distance a "sensory envelope"—a sort of social skin or border. At intimate distance people can touch and smell one another; the voice is soft, vision is distorted (3–1). At personal distance (eighteen inches to four feet for Americans) two people are within arm's reach and tend to be close socially; both speak in moderate voices and retain eye contact (3–2). "Close" social distance goes from four to seven feet for Americans and is used for business. Communication is more formal. "Far" social distance simply extends the range to perhaps fourteen feet. Public distance goes beyond fourteen feet: subtle shades of communication are lost; the voice and body must become rhetorical, amplified. Each sensory envelope provides a schema against which we can judge the social relationships of people interacting. Correction involves noting oddities: two lovers identified *as* lovers because they talk quietly and use "intimate" postures and gestures even though they are across the room from one another; two businessmen speaking loudly at a distance of two feet—something is amiss! Our awareness of social conventions makes possible virtually instant assessment of social relationships.

As Birdwhistell points out, normal communication is astonishingly rapid, complex, and "multichannel." Verbal communication and kinesic communication operate as "subsystems" that work together to create a total communicative act; rarely is either verbal behavior or bodily behavior a complete communication system in itself. A person speaks, using a particular language, particular words, particular intonations, rhythms, and stress. But his stance counts too, as do large movements and small gestures. Gesture, like speech, involves "bound" forms (some forms always accompany certain others) and "degrees of stress." Gesture is organized like language. But it and language operate in counterpoint to one another, reinforcing, modifying, undercutting, producing "statements" describable only in terms of the whole. Further, the

3–1. *Hiroshima, Mon Amour* (1959, Alain Resnais).

absence of a communicative element can count as much as its presence, if the element is an anticipated part of a communicative act. Thousands of interconnected messages pass between two people in a few minutes. Amazingly, both people can understand what is going on, despite the fact that the face alone is capable of at least 250,000 separate expressions.[3] Ordinary communication relies on what Edward Sapir calls an " 'elaborate and secret code,' written down nowhere, but understood by all."[4] It is on the basis of our ability to use and apprehend complex webs of information that we can function in society. Without that ability, movies as well as ordinary life would be incomprehensible.

Yet perception works, in part, by categorizing objects and behavior. Social categories provide our largest stock of "grids" for perception. Clothes, cars, and furnishings mean in terms of social contexts and expectations. A man who smokes Marlboros is one man if he rides a horse on television ads, and another if he wears suspenders, affects a limp, and prefers absinthe to bourbon. Often detective and spy fiction provides clear, stereotyped treatments of what objects mean socially. The following example is from John Le Carré's *Call for the Dead.*

He opened the door and put out his left hand to guide Smiley through first. Maston's room contained not a single piece of government property. He had

3–2. *The Mother and the Whore* (1973, Jean Eustache).

New Yorker Films

once bought a collection of nineteenth century watercolors, and some of these were hanging on the walls. The rest was off the peg, Smiley decided. Maston was off the peg too, for that matter. His suit was just too light for respectability; the string on his monocle cut across the invariable cream shirt. He wore a light grey woolen tie. A German would call him *flott* thought Smiley; chic, that's what he is—a barmaid's dream of a real gentleman.[5]

What Smiley sees are differences between Maston's surroundings and what would be expected of a "real" gentleman. When we observe, whether in everyday life or in a movie theater, we take Smiley's "spy" role and, like him, judge what we see in terms of what we know about cultural categories. The arts of spying are not limited to spies: everyday perception is a matter of detection, of unraveling complex information so that it makes sense. Sociologist Erving Goffman uses "spying" as the basis for his study of face-to-face behavior in *Strategic Interaction*;[6] spying and deception are such normal parts of life that the study of real spies lends insight into how we behave ordinarily, and how we see.

Disguises

As if the problem of perceiving accurately were not involved enough because of cultural relativity and communication's inherent complexity, people complicate it further by role playing. The largest body of knowledge we bring to the theater is knowledge about people. People have to be watched: they are almost never innocent of guile. Acting and "authentic" action are ultimately inseparable. Erving Goffman puts the point succinctly when he writes in *The Presentation of Self in Everyday Life* that "the world may not be a stage, but it is impossible to state exactly the ways in which it is not."[7] We spend time managing our appearances and time trying to see through the ways in which others manage their appearances. Our eyes are as suspicious as Smiley's. Goffman finds an essential "asymmetry" between what people consciously express and what they express without realizing it: "The expressiveness of the individual (and therefore his capacity to give impressions) appears to involve two radically different kinds of sign activity: the expression he *gives*, and the expression he *gives off*."[8] We attempt to pay relatively little attention to the impressions people try to give; we pay much more attention to the expressions over which people have less control, those they give off. We heed not what a person says about a meal, but whether he or she eats with gusto. We believe what we see more than what we hear: verbal impressions are easier to manage than visual ones.[9]

Everyone, Goffman argues, has a personal "front" including "insignia of office or rank; clothing; sex, age and racial characteristics; size and looks; posture; speech patterns; facial expressions; bodily gestures; and the like."[10] We expect others' "fronts" to be reliable though our own fronts are determined by the roles we play. Goffman quotes William James on this point:

> We may practically say that [a person] has as many different social selves as there are distinct *groups* of persons about whose opinion he cares. He generally shows a different side of himself to these different groups. Many a youth who is demure enough before his parents and teachers, swears and swaggers like a pirate among his "tough" young friends. We do not show ourselves to our children as to our club companions, to our customers as to the laborers we employ, to our masters and employers as to our intimate friends.[11]

To know someone well is to know him in a variety of contexts. Yet socially, "a single note off key can disrupt the tone of an entire performance."[12] We test appearances by trying to observe others' behavior when they do not know we are watching. We expect that no one ever tells the whole truth about himself willingly:

> In our society, some unmeant gestures occur in such a wide variety of performances and convey impressions that are in general so incompatible with the ones being fostered that these inopportune events have acquired collective symbolic status. Three rough groupings of these events may be mentioned. First, a performer may accidentally convey incapacity, impropriety, or disrespect by momentarily losing muscular control of himself. He may trip, stumble, fall; he may belch, yawn, make a slip of the tongue, scratch himself, or be flatulent; he may accidentally impinge upon the body of another participant. Secondly, the

performer may act in such a way as to give the impression that he is too much or too little concerned with the interaction. He may stutter, forget his lines, appear nervous, or guilty, or self-conscious; he may give way to inappropriate outbursts of laughter, anger or other kinds of affect which momentarily incapacitate him as an interactant; he may show too much serious involvement and interest, or too little. Thirdly, the performer may allow his presentation to suffer from inadequate dramaturgical direction. The setting may not have been put in order, or may have become readied for the wrong performance, or may have become deranged during the performance; unforeseen contingencies may cause improper timing of the performer's arrival or departure or may cause embarrassing lulls to occur during the interaction.[13]

Though officially each of us pretends to be only the "role" we are playing, we know better, and so we are experts on the slip-ups through which other people reveal themselves.

Most of us are seasoned observers of the situations in which a person's management of impressions slips up. Again I quote Goffman:

One of the most interesting times to observe impression management is the moment when a performer leaves the back region [any area in which he can safely slip out of character] and enters the place where the audience is to be found, or when he returns therefrom, for at these moments one can detect a wonderful putting on and taking off of character. [In *Down and Out in Paris and London*] Orwell, speaking of waiters, and speaking from the backstage point of view of dishwashers, provides us with an example:

It is an instructive sight to see a waiter going into a hotel dining room. As he passes the door a sudden change comes over him. The set of his shoulders alter; all the dirt and hurry and irritation have dropped off in an instant. He glides over the carpet, with a solemn priest-like air. I remember our assistant *maître d'hôtel*, a fiery Italian, pausing at the dining-room door to address his apprentice who had broken a bottle of wine. Shaking his fist above his head he yelled (luckily the door was more or less soundproof).

"*Tu me fais*—Do you call yourself a waiter, you young bastard? You a waiter! You're not fit to scrub floors in the brothel your mother came from. *Maquereau!*"

Words failing him, he turned to the door; and as he opened it he delivered a final insult in the same manner as Squire Western in *Tom Jones*.

Then he entered the dining-room and sailed across it dish in hand, graceful as a swan. Ten seconds later he was bowing reverently to a customer. And you could not help thinking, as you saw him bow and smile, with that benign smile of the trained waiter, that the customer was put to shame by having such an aristocrat to serve him.[14]

The whole business of impression management becomes further complicated for two reasons. First, we act even for ourselves. The mind is the ultimate backstage, and the thing that, as perceivers, we search for hardest when observing others—despite or because of the fact that most of us have little idea of what is going on in the back reaches of our own minds. Secondly, a person rarely performs alone: people conspire to help one another maintain their "fronts." Business partners, friends, or family members often operate as teams in public situations. And while they operate as teams, supporting one anothers' impression managements, "internal" communication is also going on, often in "codes" that only team members know. Thus the odd sense, when eating with someone else's family, that one is being left out of the conversation even though there is no overt evidence to support the feeling. Thus the almost astonishing complexity of communication at something as simple as a barbecue to which one has invited four different families, each of which has a different role in the total group, a special relationship (and a different one) to each other family, and a private language known only to family members.

Even if a movie theater did nothing other than protect a spectator by darkness and by the knowledge that what is happening on the screen will not change its appearance in relation to his reactions, movies would be a pleasantly relaxing experience, a break from the fantastic complexity of managing one's own behavior while observing that of other people. But movies do more than that. They simplify interplay between people, give the viewer privileged perspectives on "backstage" behavior and, because of narrativity, allow the viewer a sense of how behavior might turn out if social life were not so complicated as to seem almost directionless. Above all, movies distill the essences from behavior, making what is communicated less "noisy"—less full

3–3. *Aguirre, Wrath of God* (1972, Werner Herzog). Movies distill the essences from behavior.

of data the viewer is in no position to understand—than it is in everyday life (3–3). Just as writing is a radical simplification of aural language, so movies are a radical simplification of ordinary "multichannel" communicative behavior.

THE PROBLEM OF INTERCULTURAL COMMUNICATION

Everyday visual languages serve as the basis for understanding films. Those languages are culturally variable and remarkably localized; we communicate, and understand communication, in terms of our own everyday cultures. How is it then that we can understand films from other cultures, and that often they are even "popular"? To answer this question, we must analyze not merely the kinds of information we are trying to understand, but also the process by which we grasp it.

Socially structured units of time, space, object-relationships, and behavior (including verbal language) do not in themselves constitute a communication system; they provide only half of what goes on when communication happens. The other half happens during perception. I have described the basic processes involved—anticipation and discrimination—in the previous chapter. What happens during perception is that we *create* meanings for ourselves out of the signals confronting us. We make what we see meaningful. The meaning thus made differs from viewer to viewer as well as from subculture to subculture. This holds true for both everyday life and movies. There is no such thing as the "real" meaning of any communicative act apart from the meaning-making process inherent in the act of perception.

Our ability to make sense of things is extraordinary. A foreigner can stammer out a compliment: "You daughter. He is handsome." My mind translates instantly: he is saying my daughter is cute, not that she is a cause of gender-confusion. We have the uncanny knack of making sense of virtually any articulation if we have an idea of what might have been meant.[15] Sometimes of course this results in a comedy of miscommunication. But quite often, even if we misunderstand what was "meant," a failure of communication at one level—again to use Birdwhistell's terms—is a success at another. To cite an example from film criticism: it took the French *Cahiers du Cinéma* critics to show us that American "genre directors," such as John Ford and Howard Hawks, were important film artists. The critics, who did not understand English well enough to be put off by dialogue clichés, therefore saw the larger structures and beauties of American films. Their ability to discount dialogue—to escape the mental censoring that occurs when one senses something is a cliché—allowed them privileged insights. Form, structure, and myth came together without alarms going off. Often "misunderstanding" is essential to "real understanding." The most extreme example I know of the value of understanding "wrongly" is that of Faraday. In good part because he had a faulty understanding of what was thought to be correct mathematics, physics, and mechanics, he managed to invent the dynamo and outline the principles of the electric motor. Misunderstanding—that is, the creating of a new meaning rather than the grasping of an old one—is probably an essential of both perception and creative thought. Without misunderstanding, I doubt that either everyday life or movies would "make sense."

Yet we do understand far better than we have a right to. Our misunderstandings are often remarkably close to what seems to have been "intended." There are two reasons for this. All forms of communication have what linguists call a "generative" aspect. And second, we can understand complex patterns of communication far better than we can simpler utterances.

No communication system is closed. One of the characteristics of human speech is that it is "generative." Any speaker can utter and understand an indefinitely larger number of expressions than he has ever encountered before. Similarly, any person can devise new sequences of nonverbal behavior, which both that person and a viewer will be able to understand despite previous unfamiliarity with them.[16] Not only can a person say and express ever new things, a perceiver can understand in ever new ways. Thus when we watch an everyday scene or a film, we do not merely apply "old" anticipations and categories to what we see, but continually invent new ones.

Further, we understand complex patterns of communication better than simple utterances because they *are* patterns, and it is easier to grasp patterns than it is to decipher discrete expressions. All elements in communication "mean" in terms of their relationship to the larger act of communicating: they function as elements in a cluster. When we watch, we watch for what is "out of place"—what will allow us to modify our anticipation-discrimination process in order to understand an act or event. It is quite difficult for an amateur to tell when a single note played alone on a musical instrument is out of tune. But a note out of tune with the other notes in a chord is easy to hear. Similarly, as students of foreign languages quickly learn, one does not need to understand each word exactly in order to grasp a sentence or utterance. One grasps the cluster, hears it as a kind of "meaning-chord" and fills in what the words would have to mean for the utterance to make sense. This is precisely the kind of thing that takes place when we watch things that make sense relationally but would baffle us if we encountered them alone. It is no accident that children can usually jabber whole "sentences" in gibberish, with perfectly adult rhythm, stress, and intonation, long before they can speak actual words. Our ability to grasp patterns is, perhaps innately, far better than our ability to manipulate the cultural units that comprise parts of larger chordal communicative structures.

To encounter a new communication system in everyday life is frustrating. Trying to travel or order a meal in a culture in which one knows neither the verbal nor the nonverbal languages produces considerable anxiety. But the reason for this anxiety is that one's acts have consequences, if only for oneself. Take away the consequences and the whole business becomes play, fun, even adventure. Children learning to talk really seem to enjoy playing with language patterns, until they understand that language is consequential —that it makes a difference to their lives. From then on, it is traumatic; patterns become simplified, utterances painfully repeated until they get results. The film viewer can "learn" cultural languages inconsequentially, with the pleasure of a one-year-old. The movie theater is a tour bus, the images on the screen a magic carpet of patterns, and the act of learning is all pleasure, a playful encounter with the new. This is not strictly escapism. Rather, it is a return to the naïve state when mommy could be relied on to hold your hand, when the world was not so dangerous, and when learning was the most enjoyable thing in the day. If films did nothing more than put the fun back into learning cultural languages, their existence would be justified.

MIMESIS AND PLEASURE

Everyday cultural languages provide the information viewers use to make sense of films. While viewing films, viewers not only get to "use" their skill with perceptual languages, but also get to learn new ones—all without paying the consequences of real-life learning. Yet films are fun for the viewer not only because of the pleasures of using or learning perceptual languages in a playful context. They also provide an opportunity for the viewer to conspire with the film maker to take the perceived world lightly. Films imitate a good chunk of the behavioral and perceptual world. And imitation itself—whether as subtle mimesis or broad mimicry—gives pleasure.

Even at an early age, children enjoy mimicry. To turn the world of "authentic"—that is, consequential—behavior into a game is an act that liberates one from anxiety. What can be mimicked might not, after all, be totally "serious." As we get older, our ability to mimic and to get pleasure from watching mimicry becomes more subtle and takes new forms, but the basic pleasure remains. Essentially it is a comic enjoyment. Comedy makes light of very serious things: the more serious the butt of laughter, the better the comedy. To be enmeshed in the complexities of perception and behavior in everyday life is pretty serious business. To many people, it is even sacred business. Whatever is sacred in a culture is prime material for comedy, or that subdivision of it called mimicry. Religion, sex, social stature—whatever is taken too seriously is likely to be the butt of comedy. Our culture is undeniably oriented toward the visual and the aural; it is a world we have to take seriously with our senses. And because of that we have to take our senses of sight and hearing seriously, too. The cinema mimics both the perceived world and, to a lesser extent, the act of perception. Thus the cinema, viewed as a mimetic medium, is always to some degree a comic phenomenon; it turns the world into something with no real consequences. For the viewer who conspires in this act, both the world and the act of perceiving are lightened.

But there is a second, opposing element to mimicry and mimesis: celebration. This is what I think Siegfried Kracauer, in *Theory of Film*[17] and especially in his German-language essays, was trying to get at when he called film a "redemption" of physical reality. The business of dealing with the world of cultural relativism, role-playing "deceits," and perception is a remarkable thing in itself; the artist celebrates man's ability to survive all the complexity and uncertainty of living in a sensory world by turning the elements of that world into the materials for a play universe. Recent experiments have shown that people who are paranoid about life—who find it too much for them, and are threatened by it rather than merely anxious—have almost no inclination to spend time on narrative art, and get little pleasure from what they do deal with. But those who can handle cultural reality can also enjoy approaching it as entertainment.[18] It is not our weakness but our resilience and strength that playfulness celebrates. There is always a heroic element in playfulness.

Yet movies are more than a re-creation of the world outside the theater. Outside the theater, imagination must serve life. Inside the theater, life serves imagination. As the next chapter shows, that distinction is essential to understanding art.

NOTES: CHAPTER THREE

[1] Edward T. Hall, *The Silent Language* (New York: Fawcett World Library, 1964). See Chapter 10. Hall, *The Hidden Dimension* (Garden City, N.Y.: Doubleday Anchor Books, 1969).

[2] Ray L. Birdwhistell, *Kinesics and Context* (Philadelphia: University of Pennsylvania Press, 1970)

[3] Ibid., p. 8.

[4] Ibid., p. 182.

[5] John Le Carré, *Call for the Dead* (New York: New American Library, Signet Books, 1962), p. 18.

[6] Erving Goffman, *Strategic Interaction* (Philadelphia: University of Pennsylvania Press, 1969). See also Goffman's *Interaction Ritual* (Garden City, N.Y.: Doubleday Anchor Books, 1967).

[7] Erving Goffman, *The Presentation of Self in Everyday Life* (Garden City, N.Y.: Doubleday Anchor Books, 1959), p. 2.

[8] Ibid., p. 2.

[9] Ibid. See especially pp. 10–24.

[10] Ibid., p. 24.

[11] Ibid., pp. 48–49.

[12] Ibid., p. 52.

[13] Ibid., pp. 52–53.

[14] Ibid., pp. 122–123.

[15] Edmund Leach, "The Influence of Cultural Context on Non-Verbal Communication in Man," in *Non-Verbal Communication*, ed. Robert A. Hinde (Cambridge, Eng.: Cambridge University Press, 1972), pp. 315–344.

[16] Ibid., p. 317.

[17] Siegfried Kracauer, *Theory of Film* (New York: Oxford University Press, 1960).

[18] See footnote 7, Chapter 2.

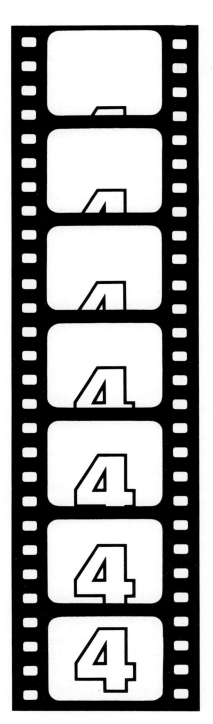

ART AS
ARTIFICE

CONSTRUCTION VERSUS DOCUMENTATION

Thus far we have been concerned with the structures of the movie theater, the special kinds of attention and memory the viewer brings to the theater, and the most basic appeals of film itself. The common theme at each level has been playfulness. The film maker manipulates the screen world in order to focus and direct the anticipations of the viewer, so that the viewer will participate imaginatively in a radically "subjunctive" experience. At every stage the common denominator is artifice, and heavily conventionalized artifice at that. For though the viewer may ultimately wish to see things on the screen that can provide imaginative models for "real life," the mimetic photographic means at the heart of the film making process do not make film realities instantly transferable back to the everyday world. Though movies are photographic at base, they are products of artifice imposed on their materials. The heart of the film image is not its documentary quality but rather its suggestiveness.

The cinema is a temporal medium. In film a single image does not stand by itself or stand *for* a moment of perceived reality; rather, it stands as *one* moment in a larger narrative gesture. One can speak of a still photo as being "of" a real-life situation. Henri Cartier-Bresson and Walker Evans could capture significant moments when bits of perceived reality make statements. With their cameras they could witness moments when life coalesced into profundity. But unlike still photographers, film makers do not "witness" real moments; rather they are condemned to "tell" them, framing them in time and rhythm and story. Still photographers can use a silent, unobtrusive Leica; they can work alone, blending into social scenes. They can do this because they need no continuity between shots; they need not satisfy a demanding viewer for two hours. But movie cameras and recorders inevitably disrupt what they film. More important, film makers must deal with the viewer, whose enhanced perceptual and imaginative demands cry out for more than an eight-by-ten-inch document. The essential structural situation of film makers has little to do with their ability to capture moments on movie film: they are *makers* of experiences more than recorders of them.

Thus the entire arsenal of techniques and equipment used by film makers —the cameras, lights, lenses, reprinting, re-recording and editing equipment of the film industry—have evolved for a single reason: so that film makers can keep viewers coming to theaters to get ever new experiences. If film makers could get away with it, I doubt they would spend millions of dollars to make films, since spending so much means that they have to work for studios. If the studios could find a way of doing it cheaper and still success-fully, I doubt they would be willing to lay out so much cash. Capitalists are, after all, capitalists. Even documentary film makers would never need $8,000 editing benches except for the fact that these benches make "finding the story" in documentary footage easier, cheaper, and faster. But more impor-tant, all the techniques of film making are story*telling* techniques. Images are arranged into shots of effective length; shots are arranged so that their continually changing angles allow the editor to fit them smoothly into scenes; scenes are arranged to meet the needs of being part of a story. The stories themselves are molded to fit into two hours. Films must be effective enough to match the viewer's perceptual and speculative power. For, as Oscar Wilde once wrote, "it is the spectator, and not life, that art really mirrors." The viewer demands tightly paced anticipations and revelations. Everything else in cinema proceeds from that fact.

Can a film maker provide such an experience simply by "replacing real life with images of real life"? Hardly. E. H. Gombrich puts the point correctly when he argues that artistic images do not replace experiential ones; rather, they become them. Just as in child's play a few blocks "become" a train, elements in art "become" lifelike. For my children, a piece of wood can become a horse not because it looks anything like a horse but because they can straddle and ride it. My children have ridden real horses, but given a choice, they prefer the wood piece. The wood does not resemble a horse; it becomes a horse's essential features, the most essential of which is ridability. A real horse would be a poor playmate, especially in the kitchen. In art, too, the made image often works better than the original could.

Why? The history of art indicates that real life is a Medusa's head that can be looked at only through "mirrors" provided by expressive images. Our habit of seeing the world as a picture, that is, with built-in grids that provide meaning, functions only as long as our own intentionality is active—as long as there is a purpose for seeing the world that way. Pictures do not smile back at us when we smile; in art there is no positive reinforcement, no sense that the work responds to our responses. The act of looking must itself provide enough challenge (if only the challenge of "seeing reality" in the image) to be an active enterprise, something that fully engages the mind. The more the mind works on an image, resonating with it—literally playing with it—the more the image seems "alive." That is why E. H. Gombrich can write:

> All artistic discoveries are discoveries not of likenesses but of equivalences which enable us to see reality in terms of an image and an image in terms of reality. And this equivalence never rests on the likeness of elements so much as on the identity of responses to certain relationships. We respond to a white blob on a black silhouette of a jug as if it were a highlight; we respond to a pear . . . as if it were Louis Philippe's head.
>
> It is precisely because these identities do not depend on the imitation of individual features so much as on configurations of clues that they are so difficult to find by mere looking. What we experience as a good likeness in a caricature, or even a portrait, is not necessarily a replica of anything seen [in the original subject].[1]

The key word is "clues," the configurations of which can be played with by the detective-viewer. If a picture cannot be "completed" by the viewer, it cannot hold attention. The speculative process functions even at the most immediate moments of looking at images (4–1).

What can happen when reality is taken as a substitute for something more "image-involving" was aptly described, in an interview, by François Truffaut:

> I'll give you an . . . example of our lack of expertise. It concerns a film made by a director who had previously done only four or five movies. In them, he had never shot a love scene and was distraught at the prospect of having to shoot one in his next film. He was so frightened, in fact, that when he came to the scene all he could do was tell the actors actually to make love. And do you know how the audience reacted to the fornication? "Not bad," they said, "but the scene is nothing special."[2]

Old studio hands would never have made the scene that way. The first movie to "show" orgasm, *Ecstasy*, did not even bother with sex. The cameraman

4–1. *Seven Beauties* (1976, Lina Wertmüller). The viewer looks for clues in the image and, from those clues, speculates on the image's meanings.

4–2. *Cries and Whispers* (1973, Bergman).

focused on Hedy Lamarr's face while the director pricked the soles of her feet with a needle. I recently looked at the shot on a viewer; to tell the truth, it does look as if Lamarr were having her feet pricked with a needle. But in the context of the film, the viewer sees her expressions as facial expressions during orgasm; the viewer completes the picture. And though one cannot help but speculate on the deleterious effects of getting one's education about sex from the cinema, there is a beauty in the whole sham. Film is a poetic medium because the viewer views poetically.

If film makers were restricted to re-creating rather than suggesting the real, their range of expression and subjects would be severely limited. In *Cries and Whispers,* for example, Ingmar Bergman suggests the pensive agony of a dying woman through carefully composed elements taken not from an actual event but from his imagining of it. Bergman's vision includes flowers, a posture, a facial expression, fingertips savoring the touch of a flower petal (4–2). Together these elements suggest the essence of death—and of life—far better than if he had simply photographed a person dying.

The film maker's job, then, is not to re-create but to suggest. What Tennessee Williams wrote about theater is true of film as well: ". . . truth, life, or reality is an organic thing which the poetic imagination can represent or suggest, in essence, only through transformation, through changing into other forms than those which were merely present in appearance."[3] This process of transformation is essential to the "art" of film.

THE LEGACY OF THE LARGER ART MILIEU

It is a truism in art criticism that an artist learns as much or more from other artists as from "nature." The principle extends itself to the viewer-artwork relationship as well. Anthropologists have long noted that people of simpler cultures have difficulty learning how to see films. Our ready acceptance of film's "fly's eye" camera perspectives, framing, story viewpoints, and musical counterpoint are all dependent on familiarity. Familiarity allows the viewer to identify mood, genre, style, and tone quickly, and so to see a film in terms that are appropriate to it. A film "makes sense" largely as a conceptual scheme with clues and conventions signaling the viewer how to react. All forms of communication are idiomatic, and film is no exception.

Idioms in art vary with locale and change with time, as do idioms in speech. Coming off the street, we are never quite ready for the speech of Shakespeare or the sensibilities of Tintoretto or Sophocles. But we adapt by dredging up from our experience ways of dealing with such artists. We grasp conventions remarkably quickly, and change categories from film to film with remarkable ease, largely because the game of playing "what if" can start anywhere. Though categories and attitudes appropriate to, say, *The Cabinet of Dr. Caligari* do not work for even a film on a similar subject such as *One Flew Over the Cuckoo's Nest,* viewers ordinarily have little trouble shifting from one set of conventions to another. The only group of people who have trouble making such shifts are film critics: identifying themselves with a set of criteria, a stance toward films, they often can handle only a limited cinematic range, largely because they have difficulty playing the "what if" game essential to adaptability. Most viewers, I think, have few such problems. But problems do arise when experiences other than looking at films are necessary to grasp the conventions of a particular film.

The conventions of popular cinema are shared in part with other forms of popular narrative. (Part Two of this book discusses the subject at length.) But certain imaginative conventions may not be universally understood. An intelligent viewing of *Last Year at Marienbad* depends more on experience with the French "New Novel" than on experience with film. To appreciate Peter Kubelka's or Michael Snow's films one has to know how to "play the game" of contemporary "structural" art. For the uninitiated, it is a hard game to play. Films tend to reach large audiences only when they share conventions either with the mainstream of films or with other popular forms. An example is *Love Story*. Essentially *Love Story* is a soap opera; it is the perfect film for audiences who rarely go to movies but watch a lot of afternoon television. When Ingmar Bergman wanted to appeal to a larger audience, he took up the soap-opera format for *Scenes from a Marriage*. Conventions never determine the quality of a film. And a film maker can reach audiences by appealing to a remarkably wide variety of conventionalized expectations. In one sense a convention is merely a point of reference, and in a cultural milieu as broad as ours, what viewers are willing to accept as points of reference is remarkably liberal. A film can "pretend" to be a documentary (*Battle of Algiers*), a book (*The Sting*, organized playfully by "chapters"), even a movie (*Persona*, *Number Two*). Hybrid forms are probably the norm rather than the exception in the contemporary cinema.

The game of "what if?" played by both film maker and viewer is remarkably flexible in part because of narrativity. The film maker leads, the viewer follows. The film maker teases the audience, implicitly saying, like the Pied Piper or a child playing tag, "follow me, if you can or dare." Once the viewer is seduced into following, the directions in which the narrative game can go are almost infinite. A cinematographer can—as Gunnar Fischer did in Bergman's *The Seventh Seal*—make images that look like still photos of sculptural, Vermeer-like paintings; the viewer can see the world that way. Or a cinematographer can play with Manet-like, or Matisse-like, or Walker Evans-like images. That *The Last Picture Show* looked like a film of Walker Evans's documentary images did not hurt its appeal, either for those who know Evans's photographs or for those who do not. A story can work like a novel by Dickens (as Griffith's did) or a story by Hemingway. The legacy available to the film maker is eclectic because our culture is eclectic. And the more the arts steal from one another, the easier our apprehension of any art becomes.

There are no absolutes about what a film can or should be. The cinema is more flexible than that. The legacy of the arts to which a film can appeal is so rich that nothing is an absolute except the basic "what if?" premise. One artifice or another—as long as the viewer can "suppose," what does it matter?

It is the involvement of the viewer's imagination that counts. Involvement is created by participation—by perceptual participation in completing "pictures," by imaginative participation at every level. For invoking involvement, almost any set of suppositions will do.

Still the cinema has, throughout its own history, developed a set of fairly standard suppositions or conventions. Though none are really absolute, we do expect them when watching movies. Thus an examination of film's conventions, of its special artifices, must come next in our analysis.

NOTES: CHAPTER FOUR

[1] Ernest Gombrich, *Art and Illusion* (Princeton, N.J.: Princeton University Press, 1969), p. 345.

[2] Charles Thomas Samuels, *Encountering Directors* (New York: Capricorn Books, 1972), p. 55.

[3] Tennessee Williams, Production Notes to *The Glass Menagerie* (New York: Random House, 1945), p. iii.

FILM'S PRIMARY ARTIFICES

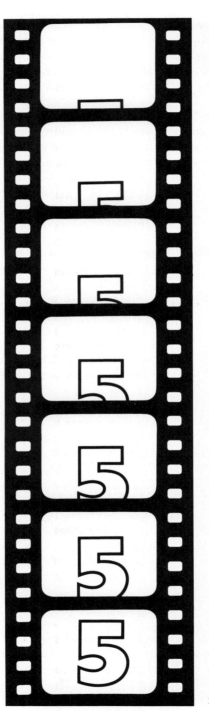

Every art form and every medium has basic rules of the game which allow viewers to feel that its world is special, and which provide guides for apprehension. For cinema, the rules of the game function at three levels: at the primary level, to provide standard anticipations about the theatrical film experience; at the story level; and at what, for want of a better term, I would call the human level—the level of characterization and meaning. At each level, the cinema is conventional.

This chapter deals with what viewers expect of all films at a primary level—that they watch a screen; that the world seen there becomes animated and alive; that the images be narrative; that images and scenes be "readable"; and that the experience be limited in time. In subsequent chapters I will take up story and acting. At each level the cinema relies on conventions to assure the viewer that the game of movie viewing will make sense.

SCREEN SHAPE

Unlike paintings, which come in all shapes and sizes, from miniature oval portraits to murals, the picture in a movie house is fixed, and fixed as a rectangle. The screen image is a picture the shape of which is not determined by the picture's content but which, to some extent, determines what we will see in a picture. A movie screen picture is supposed to be "effective" whether watched from the back or from the front rows of a theater; there is no ideal distance from which movies should be watched (even though distance from the screen and the size of the screen do in fact affect response).

There are roughly four kinds of rectangles available to film makers—all wider than they are high. Every movie is designed to function pictorially within one or another of them. Old movies are usually 1.3 times as wide as they are high. "Ordinary" movies are 1.66 times as wide as they are high in Europe, and 1.85 times as wide as they are high in the United States. Cinemascope, Panavision, and similar ultra-widescreen processes currently in use have a width 2.3 times the image height. Once a movie starts with a screen ratio, it sticks with it; unlike a theatrical stage, a movie screen cannot mechanically expand or contract our perceptual fields. It frames the areas in which the viewer's eyes move in an extraordinarily rigid way. The screen ratio used affects every one of the viewer's perceptual acts. Movie perception is reliable: one knows where to look, and what the limits of looking will be. The movie will not come off the screen, nor will it startle the viewer by appearing in unexpected places, as actors in experimental plays often do.

In everyday life, we must continually shift our attention so that our eyes can probe certain things and temporarily ignore others. If we were to borrow terms from art criticism, we could call what we momentarily look at closely "figure" and simply call the rest "context." What is figure and what is context are continually in flux; our attention is likely to shift hundreds of times in a few seconds. Where it shifts depends on what is going on and what we are doing. A movie screen limits the range of our eye movements. But it also places loose boundaries on what we can expect to be figure and context. Essentially what screen shape does is to limit the overall relationships between figure and context. In any movie, because it is a designed structure, there is likely to be a lot of figure and very little context in a given composition. But screen shape and ratio determine the expected ratios of figure to context, too.

Take the following still from *Zabriskie Point*, for example (5–1). Though the movie was shot in a 2.3 ratio, the still I had available is in "standard" screen format: 1.85 to 1 (5–1a). The "figure" at which one would ordinarily look is the young woman. She is small, standing in a pattern of large geometric shapes. What would she look like in relation to the rest of the picture if we were to "make" a fresh 2.3-to-1 composition? The second version of the still (5–1b) tells the story: she becomes smaller in relationship

(a) 1.85:1
(standard
American
widescreen)

(b) 2.3:1
(ultra-
widescreen)

(c) 1.3:1
(television or
silent movie screen)

5–1. *Zabriskie Point* (1970, Antonioni). Screen shape: Three common aspect ratios.

to the width surrounding her—in a sense, more "alienated" from it, despite her relatively larger size in relation to the "cropped" picture. What would she look like on television, which uses the movies' old 1.3-to-1 ratio? The vertically cropped still (5–1c) gives a pretty fair idea. How we use our eyes, and the connotations implicit in what we see, are determined by the way the figure fits into its context.

As the screen gets narrower in our cropping exercise, the image of the woman seems less lonely because the ratio of the woman's height to the picture's width changes; simultaneously, the image seems to have more depth, to be less flat, even though the picture is from the same negative. Connotation depends on relationships, which we've seen are determined by screen shape. Screen shape limits perceptual parameters. And it affects how we take the relationships within the image.

THE DYNAMIC QUALITY OF THE IMAGE

We expect moving pictures to move. A film image is always dynamic, with figure and context in a continually changing relationship. The cameraman can dolly, zoom, pan, tilt, and change focus; people can move within the composition. Within single shots, the whole image can shift in content, internal graphic composition, and meaning. The entire composition is alive, not just the people or animals within it.

Because the image is dynamic, even objects become animated—and often seem animistically, mythically "alive." This is important in two ways. First, it is a different state than ordinary life provides; usually our bodies do not allow our eyes to function quite like cameras. The camera world separates the screen image from the world of normal perception. And secondly, it turns the objects of the screen world into "animistic" elements. When my children turn a piece of wood into a horse, part of the pleasure, I imagine, comes from this act of animation. So much of play involves either personification or animation of objects that one suspects animation is integral to playfulness. Certainly the act of seeing things "come alive" is part of the pleasure in perceptual behavior. Moving pictures provide more than moving pictures: they provide a totally alive world.

An animistic world is pagan in both its intensity and in its linking of the physical with the human. In the following two stills from *Citizen Kane*, the statues seem almost to be commenting on the characters—mocking Kane's pomposity, counterpointing his second wife's despair (5–2 a, b). Both the characters and the statues, of course, are fictions; that is partly why they operate on the same level. But there is something else happening, too: the act of perceptual completion that makes the characters seem alive makes the statues come alive, too. The result: the statues seem almost to exist on the same level as the characters.

(a)

5–2. *Citizen Kane*
(1941, Orson Welles).

(b)

Film critics often write of the locations and objects in films as if they were "characters." Objects and locations in films are not only functional; their animistic quality allows the viewer to "personify" them. John Ford's Westerns—I am thinking especially of those made in Monument Valley—depend heavily on the spirit of place, the personality of their tragically beautiful, fully alive locations. City-based films partake of the same quality. Neither *Scarface* nor *The French Connection*, Part I, would be effective without the personalities of the cities—Chicago and New York—which make them work. Martin Scorsese's *Mean Streets* and *Taxi Driver* depend to an even greater extent on the ways objects within New York become part of a larger, driving, alive city personality. In some degree, to animate is to mythologize, to mythologize is to make alive by personifying. If film's photographic processes make people objects to be photographed, they also can make objects resonate in the imagination as if they were people. Poets have always made it their business to personify locations, anthropomorphizing them through phrases such as "majestic" mountains, and the like. But this poetic process in verbal language is achieved through metaphor; in cinema it exists as a function of the moving picture's animating potential.

THE NARRATIVITY OF THE IMAGE

What we see in an image or series of images depends on our anticipations about what is important in that image. Anticipation and discrimination are processes involving time. Movie images "mean," and are "seen," differently when put on a page out of context than they do as sequential parts of a movie. Thus a dynamic movie image can make an utterly "dead" still in a book when excerpted. The anticipation and discrimination processes of watching a film are guided by sequence. Each image "works" in terms given by the images that precede it. Even the opening images in a film, those that guide the anticipation structures for what follows, are hardly "pure"—exempt from previous anticipations—because the anticipations that brought the viewer to the theater will in part determine the ways *those* images are taken.

All film images are parts of a larger narrative gesture. Simultaneously, they are only parts of a larger narrative gesture. Though an image may be an image *of* the world—an image very much like a still photo in every visual way—it is always an image *in* a narrative sequence, which takes its meaning from its location at a specific moment in a larger imaginary event. It would be possible, as experimental "collage" films have shown, to make movies without moving images; a sequence of stills can tell a story. But it would be impossible even to think of movies without sequentiality. Movies are sequences. One could, in the same spirit that caused moving pictures to be called "movies," call them "sequencies."

MAKING SCENES "READABLE": ANGLE, FOCUS, AND SHOT LENGTH

By convention, the movie viewer has the "right" to see what he needs in order for his perceptual processes to proceed efficiently. But he must not see too much all at once; he must be seduced by each image so that it serves as foreplay for the next, and so on. Thus how film makers handle angle, focus, and shot length is not derived from the nature of the material filmed but rather from the double function of each shot: to show and to tease. The film maker puts the viewer wherever he has to be to grasp what is significant. It is perfectly all right for a film maker to use perspectives utterly unavailable to any unwinged human, to limit focus and depth of field, to show the viewer what is important in a shot, and to change shots in whatever way he feels will help the viewer see how an event really works. But at the same time, the film maker has a second objective: to give the sense of momentary "revelation" while leaving the revelation incomplete—something that demands completion by the next image, and the next. The film maker gives information the viewer could not get except by transcending his body's physical limits. But the viewer never gets enough to be satisfied. Films must withhold information as well as give it in order to sustain interest. Again, what is given and what is withheld are determined by narrativity.

The Edited Image: Imaginary Continuity

In an imaginary world, the viewer needs ground rules about which images will be taken as parts of a single sequence and which are meant to be separate. By convention, the film maker uses locations in standardized ways in order to provide such rules. The physical location of a sequence and the style of visuals within a single location serve as guides about what can be seen as a single sequence and what will be taken as separate. As long as visual style remains constant within a location scene, it will be taken as a unit, a chunk of time as well as of space. Location coherence is the basic unit; the continuity of visual style signals that the film maker accepts the coherence of a location as the basic unit by which the film's sequences are organized.

Unless told otherwise, the viewer will accept whatever happens in a location as a continuous action. But visual style changes are a way of signaling other patterns—breaks in the continuity of imaginary space-time. Thus within a single space-time chunk, visual style must be relatively continuous. Film makers go to extraordinary lengths to match color tones, lighting ratios, and action continuities within materials meant to be viewed as single actions. (This is, in practice, rather difficult because of continually changing shot angles.) Though the camera can be placed anywhere, and shots arranged for maximum effectiveness, everything within a sequence must have a similar look. If either the look or the location changes, the viewer will apply a new imaginative "set" to what he sees.

Settings function in several ways. They fix images within a scene, provide dramatic contexts for action, serve as sources of visual and aural motifs, and act as stages for the progression of imaginary actions. Thus, in *Casablanca*, Rick's café is the main setting. Bustling with people, it provides contrapuntal background for shots. The café's location in Casablanca during World War II suggests that the people there—French, Germans, North Africans, and émigrés on the run—are apt to be in conflict. Arguments can build that throw the larger themes of the film into a coherent direction. And though the progression of locations in a film—as, for example, in *Citizen Kane*'s move from the open West to the gothic Xanadu—can in itself make a statement, the main function of setting is to locate the viewer's imagination in one place at a time.

A location is always a *mental* place within a narrative. The relationship between mental places can be signaled in a variety of ways. Usually locations change according to story needs: the film maker goes to wherever the characters would be likely to go next. But because the imagination has no physical restraints, relationships between scenes are a matter of convention. Straight cuts between locations usually signal narrative continuity. A fade-out, fade-in now signals a large jump in space, time, or mental state; it once was used more freely than it is now. A dissolve between shots—with the fade-out and fade-in superimposed—signals an even larger break. Very great jumps are signaled by changes in photographic style. Thus, in *Hiroshima, Mon Amour*, Alain Resnais used two totally different photographic styles for the Hiroshima scenes (5–3a) and for the Nevers scenes (5–3b). The Nevers shots, more documentary and less sculpted, are a different imaginary world than the Hiroshima ones. Similarly, to mark a difference between the ordinary narrative world in which *Persona* moves and the utterly ambiguous half-dream realities it explores in certain sequences, Ingmar Bergman switched from a clearly delineated style to a foggier one (5–4 a, b). The grainy, softly lit second image lets the viewer know that the actions are out of the ordinary.

Thus a sequence of shots that either looks the same or looks as if it were in one continuous setting will be taken as a unit; a cue that something else is going on can be signaled either visually or through setting.

The Functions of Sound

To reinforce location and visual continuity within a scene, film makers impose a "location sound": a particular timbre similar to what we find in any single place in ordinary life. It is easier to describe how this is done than how it actually sounds: acoustics are virtually untranslatable into verbal language. Film makers often mix a *location loop* of sound with a scene's recorded sounds to give a location a specific feel. And recordists attempt to achieve continuity within a scene's sound tapes, so that a room will have a specific liveliness or a location a specific range of "openness" within a sequence. Sound style reinforces the continuity given by visual style. Like visual

(a)

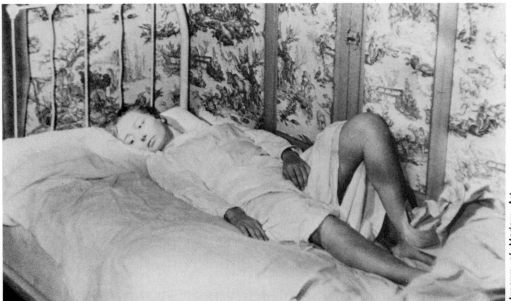

5–3. *Hiroshima, Mon Amour* (1959, Resnais).

(b)

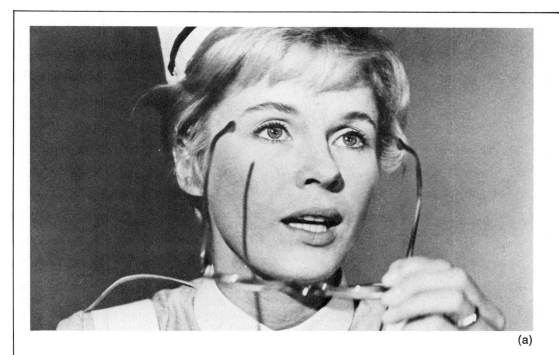

(a)

5-4. *Persona* (1965, Ingmar Bergman).

(b)

continuity, it requires a great deal of craft to achieve, because shots present different sound-recording problems, and different microphones give sound a slightly different feel, and actors move about within shots. Since sound continuity is difficult to achieve—if it is lacking, we are aware of it, but if it works, we don't notice it at all—it is rarely used by film makers to signal breaks in continuity. It could be used this way, however.

Sound also functions in terms of conventions that are more obvious. Dialogue ordinarily "goes with" a scene, not with a shot. One expects dialogue to overlap between shots. Rarely does dialogue overlap between scenes; when it does, it reinforces the visual breaks by making them stand out. Film music is, in contrast, unlocalized. Traditionally, film makers use music to reinforce mood and continuity between scenes. Music usually functions as a way of modulating storytelling tone or attitude, taking the place of the voice of a narrator in written fiction or the place of a chorus in Greek tragedy. Music often establishes anticipations: it directs the eye as well as the mood, helping the viewer see how to react to the images on the screen. In old-fashioned narratives, music often "hyped" the action, building melodramatic overtones. Recently music has come to be used more sparingly, but is still available for directing attitudes. For example, in *Cries and Whispers*, Karin and Maria begin to touch one another's faces and shoulders, virtually carried away by their attempt to reach some kind of human contact with one another. Without any sound the scene would look ludicrous; if dialogue were added, it would only cheapen the scene. Bergman made the scene profound rather than funny by putting a cello solo on the sound track. Emotional connotations seem especially controllable through use of music. Thus the importance of theme songs and scores in films.

Sound can make a film seem magical, animated. Because music is added to narrative as sheer artifice, it reinforces the playfulness of the film's world. And because objects can be made to sound acoustically very alive, films often raise the physical world to an anthropomorphic level by auditory as well as visual means. In everyday life, our ears and minds filter out most of the sounds of our surroundings as we concentrate on what is important. In films, what is important and what is not are different: the auditory world can come alive in ways similar to the visual world.

The Illuminated World

What we see on the screen and hear on the sound track are irreducibly different from anything we will ever see outside the movie theater. Though a film can sound like a tape recording, it will always sound reproduced, mediated. And though a film image can be made from the same negative as a photographic print, the effect will be different. A print on a page, or an ordinary photographic print, has light reflecting from it, just as objects have light reflecting from them in ordinary vision. But a movie image, like a slide, looks iridescent, luminescent, because it is the product of light sent *through* a picture and reflected off a bright screen. The luminosity of the screen rein-forces the special kind of attention we pay it; it also enhances the animated quality of what is photographed.

Further, the luminosity of the screen can be modulated by such factors as lighting, exposure, and the ratio of what is significant to what provides location continuity. The brightness or darkness of images on the screen determines in part the kind of anticipations we have about individual images, and perhaps also the kind of anticipations we have about movies in general.

We expect revelations when we go to films. Another word for revelation is illumination. And the screen gives us both a physical and metaphoric version of an illumination.

THEATER TIME

Movies are special in duration. The standard length of one and a half to two and a half hours provides the viewer with an anticipation structure within which he can adjust his own time sense, knowing the film's tensions are going to build and end within a set period. Though this time-set limits film makers in what they can accomplish in a single film, it does help make movies a playable, enjoyable viewing experience. Less than an hour and a half and a film would not be "big" enough to bother going out for; more than three hours and it would infringe on the viewer's strength and ability to concentrate, as well as on his personal life. Within the standard length, the viewer can comfortably adjust himself to what is expected of him.

The viewer expects movies to be fun to see, to hear, and to sit through. A good many of the cinema's conventions and techniques, especially the con-vention of the two-hour format, are specific guarantees of that expectation's being honored. A film offers the viewer more perceptual and imaginative intensity than is normal outside the theater. The two-hour format makes sure that "more" does not become "too much."

There are three physiological phenomena that coincide to make the two-hour format an ideal viewing time. First, of course, is the problem of sitting still for too long at a time: one's posterior is not indefatigable. Second, short-term memory is used to integrate the experiences of a film into a coherent whole.[1] Short-term memory becomes inefficient if pushed too far: one re-members everything that happened a few minutes ago, but one begins to forget quickly. If a film maker wants more than a vague recall of a film's beginning to be available for the film's end, his picture cannot run too long. Third, brain researchers have long known that the brain operates cyclically. About every ninety minutes, around the clock, one slips into a period of high alpha-wave activity. During this time, which lasts from a few moments to several minutes, one daydreams or slides into reverie, often without realizing it. Apparently this activity allows us to integrate experience with our deep unconscious life, or, alternately, allows the subconscious to talk back to conscious experience. In times of stress or concentration—including, I think, the time spent watching a feature film—the alpha cycle is postponed. But it cannot be postponed indefinitely unless survival is at stake. In going too long beyond ninety minutes, a film maker would risk losing the viewer's attention during a daydream—especially since viewers are, on the average, already into their ninety-minute cycles when a film begins. If a viewer daydreams during a film, the break in attention will harm the film's imaginative coherence. The two-hour convention allows the viewer to hold off on daydreaming until the film is over. If the daydream pattern occurs right after the film, it can help integrate the film with the viewer's own deep mental life. I personally almost invariably catch myself daydreaming at some point soon after seeing a film. When I have watched audiences coming out of theaters, many—if not most—seem less than fully attentive to the world around them. The concordance between physiological realities and the two-hour convention of cinema allows a viewer to adjust himself to the demands of the screen.

Yet it is important, I think, that the two-hour format be anything but precisely fixed. Since films can fall short of or go beyond two hours, viewers have a certain amount of anxiety toward a film's close about exactly when it will end. Unlike television programs, films need not be resolved by the demands of the clock, with virtue triumphant at five minutes before the hour. The advantage of unpredictable length is that anticipations do not lose their momentum.

What we hear and see in movie theaters is highly special. Images are fixed in shape, the relationships of the human to the inanimate world are changed by film's ability to animate the latter; images obey the laws of narrativity, and tease us into looking at the next images in special ways while they give us revelations. The images are edited so that scenes can be read in special ways and continuity and discontinuity can be comprehended by reference to conventions. Sound has its own special place, its conventionalized relationships to visuals. The screen and everything we see on it are illuminated. The whole process is designed to give the viewer an intense and absorbing two hours, two hours with their own conventions, their own "realities," their own kind of logic. For many viewers, two hours in the world of movies are a physiological maximum, at one sitting, anyway. The backside and the brain cannot take much more than movies give.

NOTE: CHAPTER FIVE

[1] Memory is stored in two ways in the brain. Short-term memories apparently self-erase quickly. A second information-storage system—less efficient but virtually permanent—retains information patterns over long stretches of time. Researchers have found that a rat that has just learned a maze, if cooled to five degrees centigrade immediately—brain waves almost stop at this point, though the rat, once thawed out, is unharmed—will have to relearn the maze from scratch because he will have no memory of it. If the rat, however, has been allowed an interval of time before the cooling and thawing, he will remember the

maze, though he will be a little slow in negotiating it. No one yet knows how the transfer from short- to long-term memory occurs. It is reasonable to suppose that films individually rely on short-term memory for coherence, while generic expectations and resonances are provided by the long-term branch. See Colin Blackmore, "The Unsolved Marvel of Memory," *New York Times Magazine*, Feb. 7, 1977, pp. 42–54, for a short summary. Blackmore's full analysis is in his *The Mechanics of the Mind* (Cambridge, Eng.: Cambridge University Press, 1977).

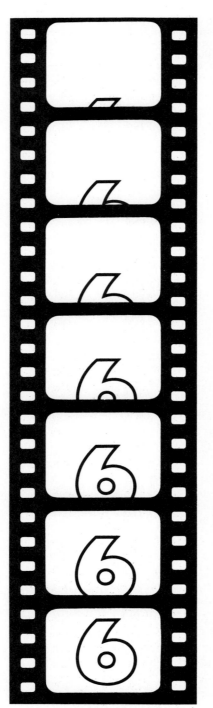

STORY CONVENTIONS

From its beginnings, film has been used as a medium for telling stories. Though inherently a narrative medium, by convention it lacks a narrator. The viewer expects a story, and moreover expects guidance about what kind of story is being told. The film maker's job is not only to give the viewer what he expects from stories, but also to give cues about the kind of story it is and how it is to be interpreted. In the cinema, a variety of conventions give such information. Primary among them are genre and visual stylization, though the concept of a story itself is conventionalized and artificial.

THE STORIED WORLD

Jean Mitry has called the cinema "a world made into a story." I have returned again and again to the narrativity of film at every level. Just how much narrativity itself is a convention, an agreed-on artifice, must be emphasized. Stories differ from ordinary experience. Just as all visual arts stem from the convention that the world's meanings are available through pictures, the narrative arts stem from the convention that experience can be distilled into stories. Both conventions are artificial: there are always differences between the meanings available to perception and those available through pictures; there are differences between experiences and stories. The cinema developed as a means not for conveying experience but for telling stories. The cinema borrowed and adapted storytelling traditions as old as history, and thus from its beginnings had embedded in it conventions determining what a story is, how it works, and how it means. Except in pictorial aspects, those conventions are remarkably similar to the storytelling conventions of the novelette and of theatrical drama.

What is a story? Reduced to its most basic terms, a story is simply a meaningful sequence of events that produces some kind of aesthetic response. What separates a story from ordinary experience is the story's playfulness, suggestiveness, compactness, and strong structure. Virtually any experience has within it elements of an indefinite number of stories, all tripping over one another, all interwoven, all beginning and ending someplace else. A storyteller, no matter what the medium, sorts experience through a value-structuring grid. Though every storyteller has a different sense of what "right" would mean in the phrases that follow, most would agree that a story's characters are the right people to confront the right conflicts in the right experiences in the right places at the right times. Unlike ordinary experience, which mixes the meaningful with the amorphous and random, a story's ingredients are selected for appropriateness to the story's intended effects, meanings, and structures. A story can therefore be almost free from redundancy, meaninglessness, and, especially, inexpressiveness. Stories have what electronics technicians call a high signal-to-noise ratio. Thus a story promises comprehensibility in a way that ordinary experience does not. Its sounds, to use a musical metaphor, are all elements in chords, and the melody and accompaniment are sorted out. It has strong rhythm patterns, a "key," a careful arrangement, and selected "instruments." And above all, a story has a premise—what I call a "what-if?" structure—that places its events in imaginative rather than strictly experiential modes.

Stories are, almost by definition, of manageable size. Lives must begin with birth and end with death. The meaning of any act is dependent on everything that has gone before it, on its momentary contexts, and on projections toward an indefinite future. But stories need not begin with birth nor end with death: as imaginary worlds, they can be limited by conventions. Most film stories follow literary and dramatic conventions. Characters are introduced. They encounter conflicts. As the characters act to overcome the problems they face, the problems in turn change. Conflicts and characters are of somewhat appropriate sizes: a character who overwhelms his problems, or problems that overwhelm characters—all in the first reel—are not the stuff of two-hour stories. Tensions build toward a final image, which puts characters in a "final" or "resolving" position in relation to their conflicts. And the story is over.

The whole thing sounds simple, and is. Simplicity is part of beauty. And though plots and conflicts can appear complicated on paper, compared to experience, the basic movement of a story is easy to chart. Take, for example, Chaplin's *Modern Times*. The film's early images introduce Charlie (though most viewers, of course, know him already) and his conflict: he lives in an age to which he is utterly unsuited. He is freedom loving, human, flexible; the assembly line at which he works forces him to try to behave as if he were a machine (6–1).

The images reveal the tension. When Charlie goes berserk, his problems are compounded. When he behaves humanly—befriending a waif, for instance—his problems multiply. But his capacities for rebellion and ad-hoc solutions are also revealed; he remains roughly equal to what should, at first glance, have destroyed him. By the film's end, Charlie has discovered that he and his gamine cannot continue in the city. So they leave. The final images, with him and his friend strutting off defiantly into a large landscape, show the distance he and the film have gone (6–2). How the assembly-line victim went on the road—that, and everything that happens in between, is the story structure or frame.

Because the intellectual, emotional, visual, and formal movement in a story is "made to measure," it produces aesthetic satisfaction. And to the extent that stories are made to measure, they are all pretty much alike structurally. It is what is within the basic story structure that varies infinitely from story to story.

GENRE: THE GUIDING OF ANTICIPATIONS

The first thing a film maker must establish is "what kind of film is this?" In *Modern Times*, the sight of Chaplin is enough to establish this, even for viewers who go to a sneak preview without knowing what they will watch. Insofar as films do establish their "kind" unambiguously, all films are generic. Genre provides categories for structuring anticipations. Often genre is established by a film's title and advertisements. *Jaws* announced its genre with its title and ads picturing a toothy shark. Given the ads and the title, the opening scenes of people frolicking on a beach were enough to immediately raise tension and channel anticipations. *Missouri Breaks* promised Marlon Brando and Jack Nicholson—two "gritty" and brilliant "anti-hero" actors—in a Western. *The Exorcist* and *The Omen* suggested their spook-show genre in their titles. Usually viewers know what kind of film they will be seeing when they enter the theater; if they do not, the titles and opening sequences announce it fairly plainly. Some actors and directors are like brand names: to see a Bergman or a Fellini is to have certain anticipations. Anticipations, once established, serve as a built-in reference system, allowing film makers to work, and viewers to see, in terms of relatively formulaic "shorthand" cues that aid communication.

6–1. *Modern Times* (1936, Charles Chaplin).

6–2. *Modern Times*.

In literature and drama, genre is often treated by the theorists as if it were a highly abstract entity. In *The Anatomy of Criticism*, for example, Northrop Frye talks of only four genres—tragedy, comedy, irony, and romance, each corresponding to the mythos of a single season. But in film, genre is a way of making experience less amorphous: it functions to make anticipations relatively specific. Detective films, gangster films, war stories, newspaper films, intercultural romances—the list could go on and on—are each kinds of films that serve as reference points for any particular film. A film's genre can be "pure"—as, for example, *Little Caesar* is a pure gangster film, containing everything we expect in a cops-and-robbers movie with a gangster as a protagonist. Rarely, however, is genre unmixed: the conflicting expectations inherent in hybrid genres help raise interest levels. Thus *Jaws* is both a man-against-beast thriller and a study of a small society's tensions. *The Sting* is both gangster film and comedy. *The Godfather*, Part One, is a gangster film and a study of a family. *The Godfather*, Part Two, is a gangster film and two biographical studies. *Citizen Kane* is a newspaper film, a biography, a detective story, and so on. The possibilities for producing conflicting expectations at the generic level are rather broad. There is nothing inherently uninteresting about a film that is a war story, a love story (actually two love stories), a story of friendship, and several other kinds of stories, too, provided that expectations compete with but do not confuse one another, and provided that the film is as well made as *Casablanca*. Genre simply lets a viewer know what to expect, and which mental sets are appropriate to an imaginary experience. If there is conflict about which genre to expect—as long as the choices are limited—so much the better. Curiosity functions best when uncertainties are under control but extant: when there is some room for the imagination to play in.

One can, of course, speak of genres with either a capital or a small "G." The genre of the Western rates a big "G" simply because it has proved so perennial that anticipations are strongly gridded. But a genre is no more than a narrative tradition, a frame for expectations. Genres are not invented as genres, but rather evolve. Stories beget similar stories. Once enough stories of a kind have become familiar, their conventions become so formulaic as to serve as reference points for further storytelling. Perception is probably always an analogy-making process; thus it is easier to apprehend a story if one has encountered one something like it. In a two-hour dramatic medium, the generic makes quickly apprehended stories easier to tell.

Genre can function simply on the level of subject matter. Usually, however, it involves structural and formal considerations as well. Westerns are classified by locale—the American West—and frequently by historical period—the nineteenth century. Gangster films are, however, about a class of people, whether they are urban gangsters (*Scarface*; *The Sting*) or rural ones (*Bonnie and Clyde*). Spy stories are about a kind of activity—spying—and a class of people who make a living doing it. Love stories are about love, a kind of emotion rather than a kind of activity. The affinities that link genre films to one another can be of virtually any kind. But usually certain kinds of stories are told in certain ways and with certain attitudes. Thus one comes to expect a lot of shooting in gangster films, a certain amount of kissing in love stories, and some complicated subterfuges in spy films. In genres such as that of the "traveling protagonist" one expects changed locations and a serial plot structure to affect the story; one does not expect only a traveling protagonist or set of protagonists. Moreover, one expects the mythos of a time to make a difference: one could no more make *Scarface* now than one could have made *The French Connection* in the early 1930s. Rumrunning is of little importance now; heroin traffic was not a social concern in 1930. Our anticipations take history into account. In a contemporary film, one expects contemporary versions of generic materials.

Generic anticipations are extraordinarily adaptable. Watching old movies, we easily adjust our imaginative responses. *White Heat* invokes the generic expectations current in the late 1940s, and we adapt to them. In a contemporary film, we would howl with laughter if a Cagney character stood atop an explosive tank and delivered a monologue to his dead mother. But when watching *White Heat* I find the scene rather affecting, as I never would in a modern film that attempted similar theatrics. Likewise, after a few minutes of watching a German Expressionist film, such as *The Cabinet of Dr. Caligari* or *M*, the outdated conventions become quite normal, a stylization quickly accepted as part of the game. Though films date rapidly because they use cultural materials that change with time and fashion (cars, clothes, even gestures), films are always a play world, so the viewer can adjust simply by playing at being a viewer in another time.

Often the nationality of a film functions generically, too. As Birdwhistell has pointed out, American dramatic traditions place emphasis on a few main characters; in American dramas Americans notice, and are expected to notice, mainly the main characters.[1] The French have different traditions: secondary characters are more important than in the United States. Watching French films, one adjusts to the Frenchness. In François Truffaut's *Small Change*, for example, one quickly gets used to the idea that almost all of the people are important. And although in Renoir's *The Rules of the Game*, attention must be divided among almost a dozen "main" characters, the viewer quickly adapts to the tradition and sees the film in its own, very French, terms, without asking who the "main" characters really are. Films ask "what if?" Viewers respond by watching "as if" they were the appropriate viewers for a film. Those viewers who cannot play the required roles either stop going to movies or go to only certain kinds of movies.

STYLE AS GENRE

Genre provides a kind of world view within which anticipations can be funneled. But genre is often achieved in effect as much by style as by subject matter or by storytelling structure. A particular kind of stylization imposed on the perceptual world functions as a world view, as a signal of "kind." John Ford, for example, developed an eye-level camera style which I can only describe as a visual equivalent to "deadpan" storytelling. What would be described in music as "key" and in literature as "tone" is dominated in Ford's films by his distinctive camera style, which tells us both how his world *is* and how it is to be interpreted. No film maker ever completely invents his own style. Style resonates with the memory and imagination to help the viewer tell which set of expectations to apply when viewing a film.

For example, the so-called expressionist style creates certain perceptual expectations. Attitudes will be reinforced by very graphic lighting, by severe camera angles, and by strongly sculpted gestures. Films as different in period as Dreyer's *Joan of Arc* and Bergman's *The Seventh Seal* are linked by a similar "way of seeing," as the following stills illustrate (6–3 and 6–4).

But stylization of perception works subtly, too, to direct the eye in specific

6–3. *The Passion of Joan of Arc* (1928, Carl Dreyer).

Museum of Modern Art, Film Stills Archive

ways, or rather in specific kinds of ways. Fairly early in *Citizen Kane*, style directs the viewer to pay attention to certain sorts of signals—for example, postures, physical distances, and furniture—and thus to distinguish easily between the kinds of "statements" made by the accompanying stills. The way of seeing required for *Kane* is not new, of course. One uses it for a whole class of paintings, from Rembrandt onward, in which the visual "project" is to look into suggested depths, often murky and ill defined, on which the imagination can play.

The most curious thing about generic anticipations at the level of style is that they can appeal to our whole memory of art. Thus Bergman's "Pietà" shot in *Cries and Whispers* evokes more than a single Pietà on canvas; it evokes them all (6–5).

In some kinds of films, architecture directs the eye; a room is taken to be an extension of its occupants' personalities. The first of the two shots on p. 69 reinforces the estrangement between Kane and his first wife by drawing a line

6–4. *The Seventh Seal* (1956, Ingmar Bergman).

Museum of Modern Art, Film Stills Archive/Courtesy of Janus Films

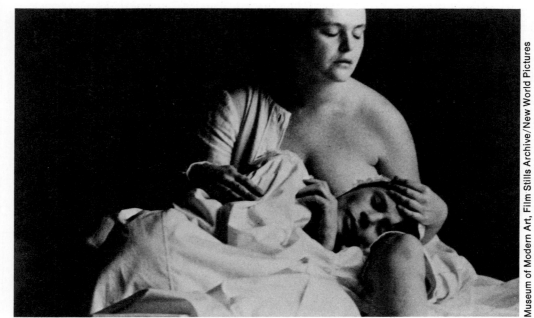

6–5. *Cries and Whispers* (1973, Bergman).

between them with ceiling beams (6–6). In the second shot the camera is at eye level: Kane's posture is patronizing, above the bric-a-brac and cheap furnishings of the room (6–7). Lighting shows us what to look at: the people, the teddy bear, the cheap wallpaper. The visual style is "baroque"—that is, one expects the important things to be well back in the shot, with the foreground serving as context. This generic expectation leads the viewer to expect "reactions" in the foreground, the real action in the depths of the shot: as in the two stills on p. 70, in which architecture and camera placement act in collusion to drive the eye into a suggested depth (6–8 and 6–9).

Often when a "new" style appears in the cinema, it is new only in the sense that the style has not appeared prominently before in movies. A close examination usually reveals that the style is a synthesis of a well-worked genre in the visual arts with the possibilities of cinematography. Though very few viewers say, "ah—Vermeer!" when they see softly sculpted visuals such as the Bergman Pietà, ways and traditions of seeing have so infused Western culture that pictorial stylization is as genre-based as is choice of subject, and as effective in making us see efficiently.

Visual stylization is heavily influenced by the technical processes current in cinema.[2] At present, the subtle shadings possible with Eastman 5454 and 5247 film stocks have created a 1970s "generic expectation," or norm against which individual films are seen. The new soft lights popular in the industry

6–6. *Citizen Kane* (1941, Welles).

6–7. *Citizen Kane.*

6–8. *Citizen Kane.*

6–9. *Citizen Kane.*

make for a different lighting texture than the hard, spotlit lighting popular in the 1950s. In the late 1960s and early 1970s softened colors were popular among film makers—for example, in *Butch Cassidy and the Sundance Kid*. In the 1930s through the 1950s, bright, "technicolor-looking" colors were the norm, and were often achieved with the dye-based Technicolor process. *Gone With the Wind* relied heavily on its rich coloration, and so did 1950s Biblical epics. Perceptually, period style has much the same effect as genre does. Though most films are made in contemporary period styles, a film maker has older styles at his disposal. And no matter the style used, it will evoke memories and associations in ways that guide the eyes and the moods of the viewer.

The function of style, as with the function of content, structure, and other generic elements in film, is to name the terms so that the viewer can participate perceptually and imaginatively as fully as possible. A style, like any other generic element, is a reference system. And though it may serve as a metaphor in terms of the film's relationship to everyday experience, often its function is simply to make viewing easier.

There is no such thing as a good or a bad style. It all depends on how the film maker would have us see his narrative. For Eisenstein, a montage-based style was appropriate for *Potemkin;* an expressionistic style was better for *Ivan the Terrible. Potemkin* is concerned with the idea of revolt—the factors that make a society turn on its masters. For that purpose, because it shows contrasts and juxtapositions clearly, montage works well. But for the study of a paranoiac personality, an expressionist style is more appropriate—hence the severe camera angles, long-held shots, and deep shadows of *Ivan.* Hitchcock's coy, clever, and slick style works beautifully for thrillers but would not do much for neorealist explorations of social realities. Nor would a neorealist style do much for a Hitchcock thriller such as *Frenzy* or *Family Plot*, which depend on slickness for effect. *Citizen Kane*'s deep-focus baroque expressionism is right for *Citizen Kane,* but would spoil *Casablanca* as badly as *Casablanca*'s style would spoil *Citizen Kane.* Chaplin's eye-level camera works for Chaplin; it would have destroyed *Hiroshima, Mon Amour* as certainly as it would *Jaws.* If a style invokes appropriate generic expectations and helps the viewer *see* a film, it is a good style for that film. To go beyond that would be to engage in idiosyncratic and purely personal preferences, to engage in the aesthetics of private taste.

IRONY AND ALLUSION

In its simplest formulation, genre tells the viewer what kind of story a film is, whereas style lets the viewer know how to react to it. But in practice, especially in contemporary American films, the case is more complicated than that. Films are often made against their genres, or even against the conventional uses for their styles. When this occurs, genre and style serve as allusion systems that counterpoint what a film is actually doing; the viewer is asked not to accept, but to be conscious of generic and stylistic conventions *as* conventions, as mythlike systems that have lost their ability to engage the imagination fully.

In its most obvious form, this often takes the form of a spoof, burlesque, or satire of a genre. Woody Allen's *Take the Money and Run* treats the conventions of the gangster film as a joke; his *Play It Again, Sam* spoofs the Bogart "hard-boiled" genre; his *Sleeper* takes on science fiction; *Love and Death*, the epic-romantic genre of historical spectacle. Similarly, Mel Brooks's *The Producers* does in the musical, while Brooks's *Blazing Saddles* upends the Western, and *Young Frankenstein* parodies the conventions of both its "original" and the horror film genre as a whole. *Young Frankenstein* looks more like a horror film than most horror films do; the artifice of style becomes as much a butt of irreverence as the material of the horror genre. There is, of course, nothing new in this parody of genres and styles: Mack Sennett made it a stock in trade; Chaplin took on genre after genre; Keaton made hay of the conventions of romantic travel and melodrama. Genres are, functionally, allusion systems, and any allusion system familiar enough to be known well can be the subject of comic ridicule.

A genre in itself is a specialization of the story; attitudes toward its elements are not necessarily implied in the genre's identifying elements. In recent cinema, there has been a great deal of genre-mixing. But there has been even more activity in the redefining of attitudes toward genres themselves. From the *film noir* of the 1950s (in which the darker sides of life are a primary subject) to the present, film makers have gone to extraordinary lengths to debunk popular formats. *Chinatown* and *The Long Goodbye* dealt with the gritty, brutal realities beneath the myth structures of the old detective film. *McCabe and Mrs. Miller* and *Missouri Breaks* were but two recent films attempting to debunk the myths underlying the Western. *Thieves Like Us* and *The Friends of Eddie Coyle* undercut the romanticism at the heart of the gangster film genre. Essentially such films work by substituting an ironic-realistic-pessimistic "mode" or attitude for the romantic attitudes traditionally associated with action-adventure genres; only rarely do they attack the structural conventions of the genre itself. Often they try to have it both ways— with thrilling bank robberies *and* an exploration of the plight of the gangster (as in *Thieves Like Us* and *Eddie Coyle*).

Moreover, the genres undercut in recent films are often those most alive and most popular, especially on television. When a genre or style appeals to a large, unsophisticated audience, an additional play element often enters film making and film viewing: an elitist ironizing of the popular myth. Because films now appeal to a young, relatively sophisticated audience, snob appeal— the appeal of "knowing better"—is itself a strong aesthetic factor. The film maker and film viewer act in collusion to congratulate themselves by ridiculing the more naïve myths underlying forms that film makers and viewers still enjoy but feel they have outgrown. One must not, however, place a negative connotation on the double attitude of being "above" a genre while participating in its conventions. To stand above a structure while using it to organize experience is probably an essential process in growing up. The double appeal—to belief and to intelligence—enhances rather than detracts from speculative involvement. Like the self-conscious and myth-conscious forms of modernist literature, the debunking modes of contemporary film often salvage the pleasure of play by injecting a note of self-consciousness into the play activity. One plays *with* rather than plays *in* the world of a genre, and in playing with, opens up new areas for speculative participation.

In any kind of playful activity, whether poker or football or movies, it is knowledge of, rather than belief in, conventions that counts. As long as the "player" and "spectator" share an attitude toward the play, no one feels cheated. Though it would infuriate spectators to learn in the fourth quarter that the players of a basketball game were "putting them on," that the game was a joke, groups such as the Harlem Globetrotters can delight crowds by signaling their attitudes at the beginning of play—or, better yet, prior to play. Similarly, film makers can take any attitude whatever to their materials as long as the spectator is included. Because attitudes toward conventions are unfixed and open to variation, conventions themselves have no fixed meanings, and the playing out of formulaic anticipations can satisfy in an indefinite number of ways. And the ironic mode can, by injecting a layer of unpredictability into the anticipatory process, make a film's internal contradictions a source of plot tension.

PLOT AND STORY ARCHITECTURE: LANGUAGES VERSUS ARTICULATIONS

Strictly speaking, plot is a function of character rather than of story architecture, because it is the personal concerns and conflicts of characters which most directly involve the viewer's imagination. But plot is also a function of story architecture. A plot can always be phrased as a question. Will the bank robber get away? Will the man-eating shark be killed? How will it be done? How long will it take? Although the characters in a story are usually the focus of attention, story architecture helps in phrasing the questions and in projecting the directions they take. Thus the structures implicit in genres and styles, in conjunction with the inferred tone of a film, are essential elements in raising expectations as well as in guiding the processes of anticipation and discrimination.

Figuratively speaking, a story provides a generalized program or "grammar" for action, a set of rules about what will happen, to whom, when, and where. A genre functions almost as a verbal dialect does: within a general language or grammar, it provides specialized phrasings and inflections suited to particular ranges of experience. And style functions as idiom, a way of treating "linguistic" problems and usages in an individualized and "familiar" way. For example, one can take the case of Hitchcock's *Frenzy*. The film follows the generalized pattern of most film narratives. Characters are introduced, conflicts are set up, complications follow, and finally those complications are resolved: the killer is caught, the hero absolved of blame. *Frenzy* works within the genre of the horror story, too: the action occurs in such a way that tension is maintained until the end, and the expectation of gruesome events is continually aroused. Yet *Frenzy* also reveals the idiom of its maker, Alfred Hitchcock. Hitchcock's peculiarly sly way of constructing stories and making them darkly comic identifies *Frenzy* as more than just a story, more than just a sensationalistic tale of horror.

Yet there are always potential conflicts among the generalized grammars of storytelling, the dialects implicit in genre, and the idiomatic expressions of a particular film. The tension in film viewing is in part a response to the structural tension between the overall "rules of the game" of storytelling, the more specialized grammars implicit in genre, and the idiomatic articulations on the screen and sound track. The viewer has generalized expectations about horror movies. But what will be on the screen at the next moment in *Carrie*, a sophisticated take-off on the genre, depends on the particular logic of moment-by-moment articulations, which the viewer must follow with nearly total attention, even while he keeps general story-grammars and generic expectations at the back of his mind.

Story, genre, and style determine the *range* of speculative viewing activity; articulations are comprehensible as long as they stay within this range. But grammars and ranges are general; articulations always speak to the moment. Thus in storytelling there is always a conflict between what semiologists such as Christan Metz call *langage*—total linguistic structure—and *langue*—the "spoken" or "used" language. This conflict keeps even the most formulaic stories interesting. Hitchcock's *Frenzy*, for example, sets up its cinematic *langage* explicitly in the first twenty minutes. But the film continues to fascinate because Hitchcock is a master of surprising articulations—of bodies that will not bend enough to "hand over" the evidence of who killed them, of henpecked detectives, of unexpected murders. Similarly, Stephen Spielberg's films follow the grammars and dialects of suspense-genre storytelling without a great deal of invention at the story or genre levels. But Spielberg's uncanny inventiveness makes films such as *The Sugarland Express* and *Jaws* almost totally spellbinding. Knowing what, in general, will happen, our attention is consumed by fascination with "how?" "when?" and "with what new twist?" Done well, a formulaic film can make a viewer watch with almost obsessed attention.

But the conflict between articulation and generalized expectation can work in the opposite direction, too. Given any articulation in ordinary life or in a theater, the viewer automatically attempts to find contexts or categories within which to place it. As I have argued in my analysis of perception, when we look we both *apply* form categories and *make* them. Perception is both a deductive and an "inductive" or inferential process, in which the basic process is always a leap between the seen and the known. A film maker can show us a scene and then show us what we should watch in it, perhaps with an establishing shot and then a close-up, or he can do it the other way around, showing first the detail and then the context. At the story level, a film maker can excite interest by teasing the viewer with articulations that never quite fit ready-made contexts.

Antonioni's films, for example, are precise and totally clear at the articulatory level, showing us *this* man in *this* activity at *this* time in *this* place. The problem is to figure out what is going on, to find appropriate categories within which to see the film. A film that does not stick within given categories forces the viewer to create them. This categorizing process can, for some viewers, be as interesting as mental processes that work in the opposite direction. Once one accustoms oneself, shots that make no sense at all in ordinary terms become exciting. One example is a shot from *The Passenger* (6–10).

After more than two hours of watching *The Passenger*, the articulation is perfectly clear. The man whose legs we see is the protagonist, now dead. The

6–10. *The Passenger* (1975, Michelangelo Antonioni).

four standing people have come to see what has happened to him. We know their surface social identities—the woman on the left was the man's mistress, standing next to her is the man's wife, and so on. But who those people "really" are and what each had to do with the man's death is a mystery solvable only by inferences from the subtle clues provided by the film.

Thus a film can be generative in two directions: (1) a generalized grammar can "create" articulations never before encountered; and (2) concrete articulations can force the viewer to create previously unimagined categories to handle the experience. In practice, films often alternate between the two kinds of activities or move from one to the other. *Chinatown,* for example, starts as a straight detective film with most viewer interest at the articulation level. By the film's ending, however, the viewer is searching for mental constructs to handle the action almost as if he were watching an Antonioni film. In most contemporary American and European "serious" films, grammars generate interesting articulations that do not quite fit the grammars. The viewer reaches for new categories to force the articulations to make sense, then watches new and "disconcerting" articulations, then comes up with a new grammar, and so on until the final image. Though films such as Robert Altman's can appear plotless in overview, at any moment they "thrill" because they force intense perceptual and mental activity to resolve the alternating directions of the current between grammar and articulation.

While the film viewer watches, he is ordinarily unaware of "thought." But the process of unraveling stories is inherently intellectual as well as perceptual and emotional because it is a category-making as well as category-applying process. Films activate the mind as well as the eyes and the imagination. The story structure, with its tension between the concrete and the general, is essential to the kind of excited concentration on which the cinema depends.

NOTES: CHAPTER SIX

[1] Ray L. Birdwhistell, *Kinesics and Context* (Philadelphia: University of Pennsylvania Press, 1970), pp. 54–55.

[2] See James F. Scott, *Film: The Medium and the Maker* (New York: Holt, Rinehart & Winston, 1975), for a compact, reliable treatment of the relationships between technology and film style.

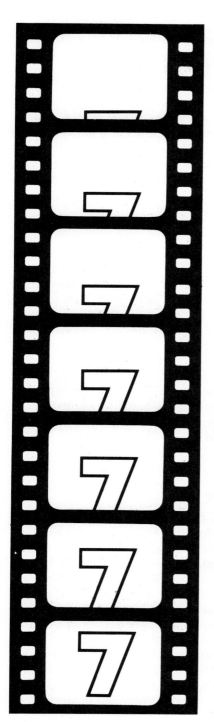

THE HUMAN DIMENSION

CHARACTERS VERSUS PEOPLE

In any story, characters are the most important ingredients. It is the people in a story that interest us most, and whose actions stimulate our anticipations. Yet characterization—the creation of fictional people—is probably the least understood element in filmic storytelling. A good character is often quite unlike a real person. Rather, a character is a construct, a fiction, a complex "idea of a person" that fits into stories as a substitute for a real person, a substitute that works better than the real thing. Most characters could not "survive" in real life, though they get along perfectly well in stories; most people would make poor characters because their personalities are too loosely structured and pragmatic.

What does characterization involve? In individual film characters, an actor often personifies conflicts balanced against one another so that we will be interested in their resolution; these conflicts often reflect stereotypical ideas in our culture. Actors lend their voices and bodies to characters, thus making the conflicts and even the stereotypes real. Often, actors so embody social ideals that the characters they portray become charismatic. One key to characterization is that it is suggestive, even caricaturelike in its basic simplicity; yet in motion the simplest ideas can become profound and involving. The actor's main job is to make us believe in him and thus in the world his character lives in. In ensemble acting, whole societies based on fictive premises can suddenly become real, paralleling our own while serving as imaginative alternatives to it. Characterization is probably the most important and least understood aspect of cinema. Without good characterization, no film is interesting; without interesting characters, no film really has much to say.

Conflict

The essential ingredient in characterization is conflict. Though I have known many people without deep conflicts, I have never known a good character without them. Real people tend to try to resolve conflicts by adapting to heavy outside pressures while trying to dominate petty problems. Only at special moments are problems and the power to resolve them in relatively equal proportion. Only at very special moments are desires, problems, and conflict structures of a kind that observers could readily identify, seeing the situation as a competition between relatively matched forces. But for story characters, conflict is a matter of balanced forces, of "competition," usually between only two opposites at a time. Characters are balanced against forces of the right size. Furthermore, internal conflicts are matched against nearly equal (and thus competitive) forces within a character's personality. Playfully imaginative involvement is enhanced when conflict can be seen as competition.

Social Stereotypes in Characterization

Often characters are created by merging contradictory social stereotypes. Pretty-but-smart; poor-but-honest; small-but-tough; tough-but-sensitive— such phrases are no more than clichés composed of matched social stereotypes. But embody such clichés in performance, with "real people" acting them out, with the clichés unspoken except in the viewer's subconscious, and they become articulated, living characters. Bogart, in *Casablanca*, *To Have and Have Not*, *The Big Sleep*, and half a dozen other films, plays a man who is small-but-tough, hard-boiled-but-sentimental, and (not despite but because of the clichés involved) fascinating to generations of viewers. So also Chaplin's poor-but-smart, small-but-resilient, pragmatic-but-idealistic tramp appeals to generations of viewers. Thus *Hiroshima, Mon Amour*'s happily married adulterers also appeal—as do Hitchcock's charming murderers. The closer the ingredients of a character are to social cliché, the longer they are likely to interest viewers; social stereotypes have a long, long life. The viewer delights in recognizing familiar categories and types as long as he recognizes the types in an individuated person; delight comes from recognition, never from being told. Therefore characterization depends on articulation of social clues in ways that allow viewers to make connections without noticing that what they are doing is interpreting in terms of clichés.

In the accompanying still from the "Babylon Sequence" in D. W. Griffith's *Intolerance*, we see a woman in rags (7–1). She is the "Mountain Girl" who will save the kingdom. Her clothes are the stereotypical rags of poverty. Her face and body, however, are those of a movie heroine. Not for her the buck teeth, malformed and muscular body, and fatigued expressions one might expect to go with the clothes. This woman should wear a queen's robes. An even more blatant example is the second still, from Bergman's *Cries and*

7–1. *Intolerance* (1961, D. W. Griffith).

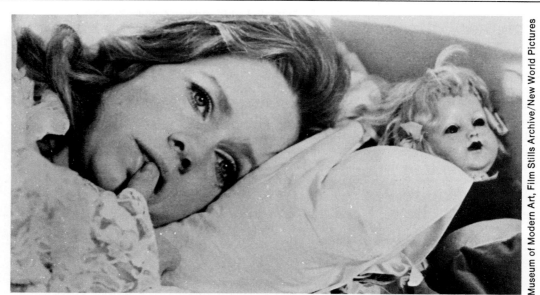

7–2. *Cries and Whispers* (1973, Bergman).

Museum of Modern Art, Film Stills Archive/New World Pictures

Whispers (7–2). Liv Ullmann plays a woman who is a bit childish, who has never grown up. Bergman—perhaps pushing the child-woman paradox a little far—early in his film shows us Ullmann with thumb in mouth, a doll on her pillow. Oddly, neither picture looks too obvious in its film; it is only out of context that they look blatant.

Social categories and expectations provide a good part of the "grammar" of acting; the actor provides the articulation that both implies the "deeper" structure and keeps it from becoming offensively simple-minded. The faces of the two actresses here generate such "real" emotions that the structural simple-mindedness of the stills goes quite unnoticed, becoming the context for very humanly individuated expression, the content of which is extraordinarily mysterious. The actual expressiveness of an actor or actress is often beside the point, however. What counts is that the viewer must read in depth. An actress such as Greta Garbo teased millions of viewers by being beautiful visually, suggesting an unknown past with her slight Swedish accent, and then presenting an absolutely bland surface; she is best when she does nothing at all. Marlene Dietrich suggests a similar mystery, again with an accent, but evokes, in addition, conflicting stereotypes of femininity and masculinity that allow her to be expressive but still ambiguous, and therefore fascinating. (She often wears men's clothing and looks at young women in an interested fashion; yet she is ultra-"feminine.") Lauren Bacall, in *To Have and Have Not* and *The Big Sleep,* plays her youth, girlish face and build, and frilly clothes against her bass-clarinet voice, creating a tomboy-grown-up version of the "fascinating woman" image. Brigitte Bardot's appeal comes in part from the contrast between her little-girl face and her adult woman's body; she also plays on an animal-human paradox by suggesting felinity. Jeanne Moreau's body and face are bland but her voice, eyes, lips, and hands usually suggest tragic depths. In acting, it is the paradox that counts; no two really good actresses achieve it in quite the same way.

Male actors equally embody structural conflicts. I have mentioned Chaplin and Bogart, and might in addition stress Bogart's lisp playing against his gritty voice and wolflike smile, and these in turn playing against his spaniel-like eyes. Orson Welles plays his organlike voice against a very ordinary visual appearance in *Kane* (a prince inside a frog, as in the classic fairy tale). Marlon Brando plays a soft, drawling voice against a leonine, powerful body. Jack Nicholson's New Jersey accent is apparent even under the Southern accent he assumed for *Easy Rider* and the Western drawl he used in *Five Easy Pieces*. Brando and Nicholson alike suggest both lower-class roughness and sophistication; whatever their roles, they seem to be rednecks with master's degrees. Whatever parts of their personalities are revealed in a role, the other parts remain suggestive and provide mystery. Even a "classic" actor such as Max von Sydow embodies paradox: his body and face are those of an ascetic; his voice is that of a seasoned and expressive actor, full, humorous, and rich. In every case, a good actor makes us expect something beyond the surface level and read into him a depth that will make him charismatic.

Charisma

Yet good characterization in film is more than a matter of embodied conflicts or implied social stereotypes. A third quality, difficult to describe, might be called charisma or grace. To put it bluntly, some people, in both real life and fiction, are more interesting to watch and listen to than others. The reason? They somehow embody some of a culture's values, and embody them in such a way that the effect seems almost chordal, musical. Thus Jean-Paul Belmondo, like Jean Gabin, is endlessly fascinating to the French as a figure of masculinity, just as Sophia Loren is a symbol of womanliness to Italians. No description of obvious features gets at what Belmondo, Gabin, or Loren symbolize; their appeal can be explained only in terms of the psychology of their cultures. Often such actors are not classically handsome or pretty so much as "striking." Their grace resides in our automatically seeing them as enormously attractive, even though, by any describable standards, they are not.[1] I strongly suspect (though I have no way of knowing) that many actors are strongly charismatic only when responding to a camera, that their attractiveness is in part a behavioral response that "matches" the special kind of attention paid while watching in the state of being a viewer-voyeur. Thus two factors may be involved: charisma and "camera grace"—the ability to be photogenic when in motion, an ability not parceled out equally to equally pretty people, or even to equally photogenic people.

Film characterization involves an additional paradoxical factor. People who are interesting in still pictures often are not interesting on film; film actors rely on kinesic behavior to achieve the suggestiveness on which fascination depends. Nevertheless, suggestiveness in still pictures has a lot in common with suggestiveness in motion, and a great deal can be learned about pictorial suggestiveness from analysis of nonmotion traditions in visual art. Before returning to the problem of movie acting, it is useful to review the basics of visual suggestion without motion.

THE LESSON OF CARICATURE

Caricature is probably the most suggestive of all visual forms; it uses the fewest means in order to suggest extraordinarily powerful and complex senses of character. Caricature is of course far more than a matter of comic strips, though comics are the form of caricature with which we are most familiar. Caricature is a sophisticated and complex genre which boasts such masters as Hogarth and Daumier as well as such popular cartoonists as Al Capp and Walt Disney. The study of caricature reveals, in sharp outline, the processes involved in visual suggestiveness and the processes by which a viewer "makes a picture come alive."

E. H. Gombrich, who has written better on caricature than any other art critic, argues that the basic appeal of caricature is to our sense of relationships.[2] A caricature produces instant recognition and instant response. It is a radically economical art form: by minimizing pen strokes, the caricaturist keeps contradictions from spoiling illusions. In a "realistic" painting, any gap is disturbing, but in a caricature, the gaps are read as part of the narrative: the viewer projects humanity into what is no more than an outline.[3] Caricature does not necessarily refer to nature but rather appeals to a purely conventional symbolism. The key to caricature is that it does not involve representation so much as suggestion. What makes caricature work is a matter of a society's visual languages.

As the following examples show, caricatures can be suggestive and therefore expressive without being mimetic in any strict sense. I have taken the examples from Gombrich; Gombrich borrowed them from the nineteenth-century Swiss caricaturist Rodolphe Töpffer (7–3).[4]

Each little drawing affects us differently: some look smug and stupid, others look glum, and several seem to have a sense of humor. All are simplifications of symbol structures embodied in heads. Essential to the process of caricature is the equation between physiognomy and personality, an equation which, however "unfair," we all seem to make.

Gombrich cites the French caricaturist Philipon's illustration of how a caricature is achieved. Working progressively from King Louis-Philippe's head, Philipon evolved it into a caricature that suggests both a person and a pear (7–4).[5] All one has to do is recognize a relationship between the con-

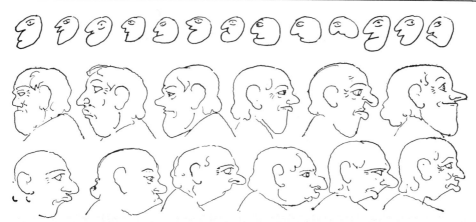

7–3. Sketches from the *Essay du physiognomie* by Rodolphe Töpffer.

LES POIRES,

Faites à la cour d'assises de Paris par le directeur de la CARICATURE.

Vendues pour payer les 6,000 fr. d'amende du journal le *Charivari*.

(CHEZ AUBERT, GALERIE VERO-DODAT)

Si, pour reconnaître le monarque dans une caricature, vous n'attendez pas qu'il soit designé autrement que par la ressemblance, vous tomberez dans l'absurde. Voyez ces croquis informes, auxquels j'aurais peut-être dû borner ma défense :

Ce croquis ressemble à Louis-Philippe, vous condamnerez donc ?

Alors il faudra condamner celui-ci, qui ressemble au premier.

Puis condamner cet autre, qui ressemble au second.

Et enfin, si vous êtes conséquens, vous ne sauriez absoudre cette poire, qui ressemble aux croquis précédens.

Ainsi, pour une poire, pour une brioche, et pour toutes les têtes grotesques dans lesquelles le hasard ou la malice aura placé cette triste ressemblance, vous pourrez infliger à l'auteur cinq ans de prison et cinq mille francs d'amende!! Avouez, Messieurs, que c'est là une singulière liberté de la presse!

7–4. From person to pear: Charles Philipon's caricaturing of Louis-Philippe.

Reprinted, by permission, from E. H. Gombrich, *Art and Illusion*, Princeton University Press.

figuration and the original person to connect the idea with the living articulation, and the caricature sticks as an embodiment of Louis-Philippe, and by extension, of a social type—kings. Social typology becomes conventionalized so that within a culture one recognizes instantly what is meant.

In works by artists such as Hogarth, caricatures allow us to see whole societies in compressed format.[6] The accompanying illustration by Hogarth shows the difference between "characters" and "caricatures" as ways of treating people: at left they are individuals; the ones at right are types (7–5).

Caricatures, portraits of people as human types, are a standard device of the cinema just as they are in drawing. During the silent film era, of course, obvious caricaturing was a central device for characterization. Witness, for example, the two following stills from E. A. Dupont's *Variety*. The first still (7–6) is a group scene, Hogarthian in its effect; the two workmen at center, though obviously watching the same event, portray absolutely different attitudes, and in their expressions and physiques enact distinct human types. In the second still from *Variety* (7–7), a traditional love triangle is caricatured: at left is the eye-averting, conniving lover; at right, the jealous husband; between them is the preening, vain wife. Of the three, the wife is most clearly a caricature. But is she more of a caricature than Giancarlo Giannini is in the still from Lina Wertmüller's recent *Seven Beauties* (7–8)? Giannini plays the vain, suave Latin lover *par excellence*, complete with cigarette holder. Caricature is still with us in the cinema, still a source of pleasure.

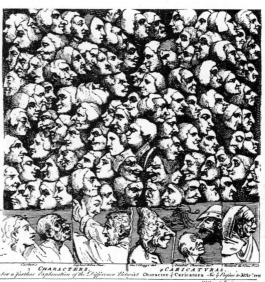

7–5. William Hogarth: (left) *The Laughing Audience*, 1733, etching (right) *Characters and Caricaturas*, 1743, etching.

Reprinted, by permission, from E. H. Gombrich, *Art and Illusion*, Princeton University Press.

7–6. *Variety* (1925, E. A. Dupont).

7–7. *Variety*.

7–8. *Seven Beauties* (1976, Wertmüller).

Cinema 5

There are three lessons to be learned from caricature. First, that suggestiveness depends not on discrete features but on configurations and relationships. Second, that social types and ideas can be as "alive" as—or even more alive than—individuated people, who "articulate" only themselves. And third, and most important, the suggestive is essentially a "match" for the leap between the seen and the conceptual that is inherent in every act of perception. The eye and the mind leap between articulations and ideas, and it is the leap that makes a few lines on a page—or, by extension, a gesture by an actor—come alive and be endowed with meaning.

MIME: CARICATURE IN MOTION

Actors of course lack the freedom of line of pen-and-ink artists. They make up for it, however, through motion and through dramatic means. Visually, acting is the art of mime; an actor evokes the same perceptual and mental "acts of completion" in viewers as a caricaturist does, but by slightly different means. Thus, in *Casablanca*, the crowds are a collage of human types whose identities are exaggerated for easy recognition. Even the main actors play caricatured people. Claude Rains, for example, plays a corrupt police official who embodies every American cliché about sophisticated Frenchmen current in American films in the 1940s. Rains's "drawing" is so exaggeratedly suggestive that it achieves a caricature effect. The headwaiter is so waiterly and so Dutch that no real Dutch waiter could possibly mimic the effect; the bartender is such a Russian Cossack that, again, no real Russian Cossack could parody himself with the same effect. Sidney Greenstreet plays the caricature type he made famous, using his fatness along with a single gesture—swatting flies—to evoke an almost Hogarthian persona. Some film makers (most notably Federico Fellini and Lina Wertmüller) have made mimed caricature their trademark, populating their films with people we recognize immediately as the perfect embodiments of social types. But all film actors, to one degree or another, work through caricatures when they create characters. In so doing, they use the oldest tradition in cinema, the art of the actor in silent film, to lend power to their creations.

In either sound or silent film, mime is the heart of acting. Mime has little to do with duplicating ordinary behavior; rather, it is an art of suggestion. Pure mime, such as the art practiced by Marcel Marceau, is rare in cinema because it involves a solo performance rather than interactions among characters. But the study of mime, like the study of caricature, has a great deal to teach the student of film acting, because the mime artist creates belief purely through suggestive gesture. The mime artist can thread a needle with neither thread nor needle, and can juggle balls without balls; we believe in the thread, needle, and balls—and in the pain when the mime performer jabs his thumb or drops an imaginary ball on his toe. In film, mime is understated since the actor need not project from a stage. But mime's basic formula—the turning of trivial details into "telling gestures" that are both "human" and ideationally profound—is also the means by which film actors make fictional characters come alive. The logic of mime, like the logic of children's play, is based on the psychology of the imagination, in which the suggestion of something takes that thing's place and a system of interrelated symbols functions as a parallel to ordinary experience.

The process is easiest to see in comedy, the most overtly playful of film genres. There is relatively little distance between what my children do when playing and what Chaplin does in two sequences in *The Gold Rush*. In one, Chaplin and his comrade are starving; Chaplin cooks up and serves his boots for supper (7–9). The situation is tragic enough. It comes alive, and becomes comic, when Chaplin treats his share of the meal as if it were pasta, handling his shoelaces like noodles. In the second sequence, Chaplin has been stood up by his invited dinner guests. He lapses into the world of imagination, and constructs a bun dance so poignant that it distills dance to its essence (7–10). The intentness of Chaplin's shoe eating and the wistfulness of the dance trigger the imagination. Chaplin's ability to do this through mime is what makes him the cinema's greatest actor.

Chaplin's actions are "trivial," but their effects are profound. In the imagination, and thus in imaginary worlds, there is no strict separation between the

7–9. *The Gold Rush* (1925, Charles Chaplin).

7–10. *The Gold Rush*.

7–11. *The Gold Rush.*

trivial and the profound; rather, the trivial and the profound are yoked. Caricatures such as Töppfer's and Hogarth's "work" because trivial aspects of physiognomy embody profound characteristics of human types. The needle-and-thread mime act works because it connects the trivial act of threading a needle with a sense of humankind's promethean struggles for achievement. Chaplin's silly walk would be only a superficial gesture if it did not suggest our eternal struggle to get somewhere with inadequate means. Chaplin's clothes (which are fully part of his gestures) are trivial embodiments of our attempts to see ourselves as dignified in a world in which there is a radical disparity between what we are—and would be—and what we must be to survive. In strongest visual form, Chaplin is a man in a city hat, carrying a cane, facing the arctic. The concept is silly and funny, but also evokes our largest dilemmas (7–11). The imagination finds life in such gestures and situations. The suggestive is the magical stuff from which imaginary worlds get their punch.

THE VALIDATING FUNCTION OF ACTORS

Structurally, the actor not only suggests a character's conflicts and problems, but also embodies the human projects that drive the plot and provide most of a film's anticipation structures. Further, the credibility of the story world of films is provided by the fact that characters can "live" in the imaginary worlds on the screen. If we cannot take characters "seriously" we cannot fully participate imaginatively in a film's other artifices. Thus the actor must be not only suggestive, but also convincing. I am continually amazed by just how convincing great actors can be. In *The Passion of Joan of Arc*, for example, Dreyer's lead actress, Falconetti, embodies the conflict between idealistic

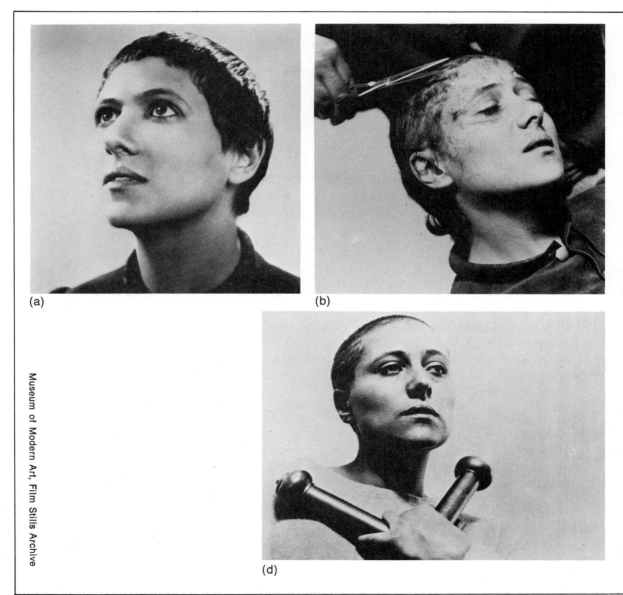

(a)

(b)

(d)

Christianity and having a body that suffers—an essential Christian conflict. And she makes her suffering as she is humiliated by her captors seem absolutely real. The first still from the following series shows Falconetti in "repose." The others are in themselves an essay on acting (7–12).

The crux of good acting is that actors not only make us believe in their personas; they also convince us of the "validity" of the stories they are in. If characters can "live" in a story—however blatantly artificial—it comes alive

(c)

7–12. *The Passion of Joan of Arc* (1928, Dreyer).

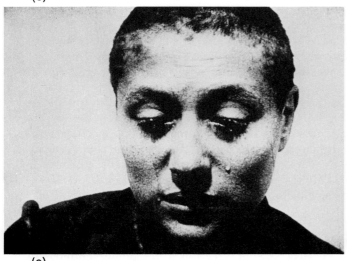

(e)

(f)

in the imagination. If we cannot take the people in a film seriously—if their performances scream "fake!" through false intonations, bad timing, or other signs of phoniness—our imagination refuses to lend credence to the whole film. For example, *Zabriskie Point*, an otherwise brilliant film, is wrecked for American audiences by the flat delivery of the lead actors, who speak as if they were in a high school play. Because we cannot take the lead actors seriously, the film fails utterly. A second example, also by a master director, is Bergman's *The Touch*. Elliot Gould's dialogue is so unidiomatic and flat that he is not convincing. The result is that an extraordinarily intelligent film, a sort of diary of a bored housewife, becomes hard to watch.

If unconvincing acting can ruin otherwise brilliant films, completely convincing acting can save almost any film. If characters can live convincingly in a film's generic and stylized world, they trigger our imaginations to take the film as a valid endeavor.

Here I will cite two examples. Personally I am not very interested in the almost hysterical agonies at the heart of Dreyer's *Joan*; in ordinary life I find this aspect of Christianity rather unmoving. But because Falconetti convinces, the whole myth structure of the film takes on life whenever I watch *Joan of Arc*. Similarly, as a liberal humanist, I find the world view of *Gone With the Wind* racist, sexist, and childishly romantic. Conceptually the film is inane. But the performances, especially Vivien Leigh's, are so wholehearted that I forgive everything and become entranced every time I watch the film. Certainly *Joan of Arc* and *Gone With the Wind* have beauties and attractions other than their acting, but they work only on condition that the performances "validate" them for the imagination.

Some actors (many of them stars) are capable of playing only one character again and again, no matter what the film. Though certain actors are so fascinating that one can see them repeatedly, revisiting them as if they were old friends, the stories they play in must be tailored to them, not vice versa. Bogart and Gable and Mae West were like that; Orson Welles is not. Thus Bogart plays one role again and again, while Welles plays several versions of Charles Foster Kane in the same film. Welles works within the tradition of theater which dictates that a good actor be able to play dozens of roles with virtuoso adaptability. It is therefore a matter of course for Welles to validate different characters and different worlds in every film he appears in. We expect "character acting" from him; he is a chameleon. But in cinema the Bogarts also have their function. Nobody does Bogart better than Bogart. Familiarity with an actor's persona and mannerisms—Bogart's cigarette in mouth, nasal poker-faced delivery, spaniel eyes, and amused eyebrow lifts—can create anticipations on which whole stories and genres are built. The convention of appropriateness dictates that if the characters do not fit the story, the story must be made to fit them.

More than in any other medium, the vitality of the cinema depends on convincing acting. This is because cinematography and the big screen move us so close to the actors. A director can work from a weak script, film sloppily, create unconvincing locations, and have a muddy sound track, inappropriate music, and a weak rhythmic structure. But if the characters seem alive, so will the film. And if characterization fails, no amount of expertise in other areas will save the film. Admittedly, an actor's job is far easier if the architecture of the film is good. And it is true that good acting is in part a question of "appropriateness." The wrong characterization for the story and genre can wreck a film as surely as simple bad acting can. In genres such as the spy story, the Western, and the gangster film, characters must be convincing in terms of their worlds in order to validate those worlds. A Cagney, Bogart, or Edward G. Robinson can validate a crime story through good acting; they are convincing in certain terms, just as they make certain story terms convincing. And some film makers—notably Alfred Hitchcock—have learned to make do with reasonably flat performances, though Hitchcock's best work (for example, *Psycho, Vertigo, Rear Window,* and *Frenzy*) does have very good acting. But even in genres that do not require really good acting, vitality is dependent on the absence of really bad acting; no film is immune to the crucial function of performance.

ENSEMBLE ACTING: CHARACTERS AS AN IMAGINARY SOCIETY

A single actor can sometimes make a film believable. But actors fortunately seldom have to work alone. Ordinarily the validity of a film's world results from a group effort. The actors conspire to live together in a story as if it were real. They thereby reinforce one another's ability to convince and reinforce the viewer's willingness to take their play world as an imaginative entity. Often, even the power of a single image depends on group work. An example is the still from *The Seventh Seal* on the following page (7–13). Each actor is a human type: Jof's clowning, Raval's greed, and Plog's loutishness are signaled by the sharply etched postures of the actors. But looking at the still as a whole, the eye compares and contrasts the postures, attitudes, and smaller signals so that we see the characters in terms of a momentary reality that all the actors reinforce. Jof's two-handed clutch on his chicken contrasts with Raval's grip on the bracelet; Jof's playful glance at the bracelet contrasts with Raval's intent stare; Plog seems to be taking Jof's meat seriously indeed. The characters come alive for the viewer because they are alive for each other. And by extension, the whole scene comes alive, perhaps the more so because Bergman lights and composes so that our eyes fall on precisely those gestures, postures, and expressions that give the shot its impact.

For Bergman's story, his actors provide the right sub-society, the right social milieu. But those same actors and gestures work because they are appropriate for *The Seventh Seal.* The difficulty in casting and acting is a matter of putting the right characters into a story.

Museum of Modern Art, Film Stills Archive/Courtesy of Janus Films

7–13. *The Seventh Seal* (1956, Bergman).

SOCIAL SETTINGS

Unlike printed fiction, films rarely let us get into the consciousness of single characters; whatever we see, we see in terms of interpersonal and "interspatial" relationships. It is from the interpersonal aspect of film performances that we learn about society's "secrets" and principles of organization, and even about what makes people tick. Good film directors arrange the contacts among characters precisely to reveal the social structures of their filmic worlds. To grasp just how much is revealed by single glances at character ensembles, compare the following three stills. The first is from John Ford's *Stagecoach*; the second, from Truffaut's *Jules and Jim*; the third, from Bergman's *The Seventh Seal*.

In each of the three stills, the story world within which the group fits, the dynamics of the group, and the position of individuals within the group are all immediately apparent, even if we do not know the specific films. Still 7–14 is obviously from a Western, circa 1940. The style of the cowboys' and women's clothing, the clean soldier uniforms, the character types of late 1930s and early 1940s Westerns are all evident. John Wayne is the most easily recognizable star. Most of the other actors played picturesque types in Western after Western. There are only two women: this will cause tension in the film, especially since the one at left is dressed in the manner of a woman of ill

7–14. *Stagecoach (1939, John Ford).*

repute, too gaudy to be anybody's wife in this sort of milieu. The younger
woman at back right is an innocent, a sweet young thing. The table, table-
cloth, chairs, and walls designate the location as some sort of frontier way
station. The presence of soldiers indicates there will be Indians: if there were
soldiers in a Hollywood Western of this period, there were Indians; no
soldiers, no Indians. Each of the characters is differentiated from the others
not only by costume (and thus, social role), but by their different reactions to
the man speaking. The still is obviously about a group of disparate people
forced together; there are no signs of camaraderie in the characters' gestures.

Still 7–15 (p. 96) is also from a period film. Clothing, posters, and the newspaper headline signal the time as the early 1900s, the place as France, and the
location as a café. Instead of a single large table, there are small round tables,
closely spaced. All the people in the shot are in a homogeneous milieu, where
one can be comfortable in close social proximity. The film is a romantic
comedy: witness the expressions of the couples, the disparity between the
journal *Guerre Sociale* and the well-to-do clothing, and the self-absorbed
behavior of all the people, despite the romance implied by the posters and
turn-of-the-century setting. The figure at front center is alone, while everyone
else is in intimate twosomes. Obviously he is the protagonist, probably
waiting for someone. The film's flat lighting and tone structure indicate that it
was probably shot in double-X negative—the preferred black-and-white stock

in the early 1960s. And of course the film is French: the minor characters are working harder than they do in American films to stay in role; the newspaper is in French; the scene represents a French, rather than an American, romanticizing of the café milieu (in American films the table would be made to fit the main actor, not French-sized people).

In still 7–16 we see another period film, this time signaled as the Middle Ages by the costumes and social types—a knight, a more roughly dressed squire, a troubadour. The lighting and film stock indicate a European film of the 1950s; American cinematographers liked to fill shadows and etch outlines more clearly and avoid washed-out faces. The picnic is primitive (two bowls for all). Despite differences in social class, the group is engaging in communal, egalitarian behavior. The postures indicate camaraderie. The squire at left (Gunnar Bjornstrand) is the center of attention. The young woman with blonde hair (Bibi Andersson) is amused by him, but the knight (played by Max von Sydow) is not. The musician is in his own world. The position of the other woman is ambiguous, but her grimness suggests that she is not an entertainer, but rather part of the knight's and squire's world. Everyone feels comfortable, seated not by group-affinity, but relaxing together.

7–15. *Jules and Jim* (1962, François Truffaut).

Ensemble images often reveal the tone of stories as well as the kinds of societies portrayed and the genre of a film. Again, I will contrast three stills, but more briefly: two (p. 98) are from *Citizen Kane*; the third (p. 99) is from *The Birth of a Nation*. Though the stills do not capture all of the meaning they take on in their respective films, they roughly suggest the tone, societies, and genre of their moving counterparts.

In the first *Kane* still, the only person taking the stage situation seriously is Kane's second wife, sitting in the foreground (7–17). The others stare with indifference, distaste, or disbelief. The scene would be comic, a parody of spectacle, if all the characters played it that way; because the "lead" does not, the tone is one of pathos verging on the grotesque. The second *Kane* still shows the ambivalence (or, more correctly, multivalence) of attitude toward the characters (7–18). The young Kane has no liking for the man reaching toward him; he looks to his mother as a guide. The man in back, Kane's father, watches the situation with trepidation. Something is happening of an ambiguous nature: the "meaning" of the scene can be interpreted in several ways. The Griffith still is straight melodrama (7–19). Papa has caused the family grief. He is apart from the others and doing the talking. Mama is

7–16. *The Seventh Seal.*

Museum of Modern Art, Film Stills Archive/Courtesy of Janus Films

7–17. *Citizen Kane* (1941, Welles).

7–18. *Citizen Kane.*

7–19. *The Birth of a Nation* (1915, Griffith).

Museum of Modern Art, Film Stills Archive

agonized. The girls cling to her legs: one is despondent, the other looks hopeful. The family is a value for all; mama is the moral center of the family—and so forth.

The information implicit in any single ensemble shot is enormously rich, and validates and informs characters, groups, genres, tones, and stories. In motion, such images reveal far more information than they do as stills. The average film has perhaps 400 shots, usually at least a third of which show two or more characters interacting. The reinforcing, information-giving, and vitalizing power of ensemble acting is therefore potent indeed.

MOVIES AS SOCIAL MODELS

The characters in a film are more than elements that determine how the plot unfolds. The actors who portray them do more than validate the premises of the film. Every film presents, through its human dimension, a version of how society would work if it were built on different premises than it is. Every film shows us a fictional culture as well as fictional people and events within it. Each complex story structure generates a fictional society in which premises can be followed to their consequences. Each fictional society has its own mores and standards, and fictional people especially adapted to it who play out what life in it would be like. A motive behind moviegoing and moviemaking may well be a dissatisfaction with the limits of everyday social structures; our pleasure in films may well be a consequence of our attempts, through narrative play, to create more plausible social worlds than those we live in.

The societies created by film characters are to a great extent extrapolated from real cultures. The cultural languages used by films are directly informed by those of the parent culture. There are two differences, however, between the cultures from which fictions spring and the fictional cultures themselves. The first and primary difference is in playfulness: film's fictional societies have both a freedom and a set of limits that are artificially imposed. They are free from what philosophers would call "facticity" and "historicity." The consequences of actions are not binding on the viewer in the way real social experience is; the events in a film need not follow the complex, and inevitably compromising, determinism of real social actions. Films, like all narratives, give viewers what Jean-Paul Sartre has called a "freedom which wills its *own* limits." The second difference between historical and fictional cultures is that the fictional is almost inevitably a rebellion against the real, particularly a rebellion against the everyday. The societies one sees portrayed in films are therefore often exotic: inordinate numbers of films are set in a fictional past; inordinate numbers deal with the heroic, the primitive, the very rich, the very poor, the outlaw, the cop, the super-sexy. In films it is easy to be in love, strong, or an outlaw, because fictional cultures are designed so that such qualities can be celebrated as play. Such societies need not be exotic in the full sense of the word: they need only be somewhat different from what the viewer is stuck with everyday. Though films can, through the privileges granted by cinematography, transform even the ordinary into the exotic, most stories give a voyeuristic view of cultures or subcultures different from those of their primary audiences. For example, Murnau's *The Last Laugh* (7–20a) brings us into streets and scenes of quiet poverty beyond the ordinary experience of middle-class audiences, while Howard Hawks's *Scarface* (7–20b) takes us into the world of machine-gun wielding gangsters. Both are as far from the everyday lives of viewers as is the Civil War in Griffith's *The Birth of a Nation* (7–20c) or the high society of Abel Gance's *Napoleon* (7–20d) (see pp. 102–103). Our encounters with the societies in such films are touristic if not escapist. What viewers rarely see is a reflection of their own societies.

Watching films therefore involves the viewer in a very special kind of social thinking. He asks: what would life be like if *this* were not true, but *that* were? What would society be like? How would it work? What kind of people would live there? What would a person have to be like to succeed in such a world? What would love, hate, greed, or ambition be like in such a world? And to focus such questions, the film maker provides test cases: what would happen if character "X" did such-and-such within this value structure? One watches a film's fictional society, and by speculating within its terms, indirectly reflects on the virtues and limitations of one's own social world.

One of a film maker's jobs is therefore to present us with a sense of the society within which a story functions. *The Seventh Seal* may be a story about a knight and his squire journeying home from a failed fourteenth-century crusade. The knight wants knowledge of God; the squire wants to live as well as possible. But *The Seventh Seal* is also a study of trying to achieve such goals in a society where the still on p. 104 represents the norm (7–21). The people are plain, careworn, and exhausted, and live in primitive circumstances, obsessed by superstition and fear of the plague. They are huddled in what is, metaphorically, darkness. *The Seventh Seal* asks not what "finding God" and "living well" mean, but what they mean in these social terms, at this time, in this place. It is only by a process of comparison and contrast between the film's fictional society and the viewer's own that a viewer can arrive at the film's meaning. The portrayal of society in a film impregnates all its other meanings.

The Seventh Seal, of course, represents an extreme case: the society Bergman invents is, in some ways, far removed from the everyday world of the viewer. But it is an interesting case nonetheless because it reveals the essential ambivalence of play toward everyday reality. In the world of *The Seventh Seal*, the knight's religious quest makes more obvious sense than it would in our secular society; in a film with a medieval setting, it is even plausible for the knight actually to see death personified. But the medieval world, as Bergman presents it, is also worse than ours, especially on the cultural level. Most films have a similar ambivalence. In some ways, their societies are wish-fulfillment visions; in other ways, they are nightmares. This ambivalence characterizes the societies portrayed by almost all films: a purely wish-fulfilling or purely nightmarish society seems to be uninteresting. A viewer gets pleasure from asking what would happen if satisfactions were removed from cultural reality, as well as from asking what would happen if certain wishes were to come true.

Two examples may be cited. Vittorio De Sica's *Bicycle Thief* tells the story of a man in postwar Italy who, without a bicycle, cannot support his family. The film is a neorealist classic, and gives a moving portrait of life in its "realistic" dimensions. But the film's basic premise—that a lower-class man could not get a bicycle—is, at least according to a number of Italian socialists with whom I have talked, pure invention. Given the extended family structure and mores of the postwar Italian slums, someone would have come up with a bicycle so that the man could support his family. The film asks, for Italians, not what the plight of the slums is, but what would life be like if the element of extended family and neighborhood unity were missing. Only in terms of an unstated, assumed question does the film really make sense. A second example is Martin Scorsese's *Taxi Driver*. *Taxi Driver* is a study of a psychotic ex-marine who attempts to right his deluded moral universe by personal and highly violent action. The man looks fairly normal, and holds an ordinary job. By chance, the man happens to kill several hoodlums rather than a politician, and thus becomes a sort of hero. But either kind of victim would have served his purpose. The film's setting is New York City; the behavior of most of the people in the film's society looks "real." But the film's assumed social premise

(a)

7–20. (a) *The Last Laugh*
(1924, Murnau)
(b) *Scarface*
(1932, Howard Hawks)
(c) *The Birth of a Nation*
(d) *Napoleon*
(1927, Abel Gance)

(b)

(c)

(d)

Museum of Modern Art, Film Stills Archive/Courtesy of Janus Films

7–21. *The Seventh Seal.*

is nearly as paranoid as its protagonist: what if more of the anonymous people we meet everyday—the taxi drivers, for example—were crazy? The premise on which social actions are based is that most people are sane. It is taken for granted that the veterans who come back from wars adjust adequately, and that most behavior will fall within our social norms. In the world of *Taxi Driver*, that simple assumption is removed. The world of films need not be far removed from the everyday. *Bicycle Thief* is, in most respects, an accurate portrait of postwar Italy. *Taxi Driver* is, in most respects, an accurate treatment of one social milieu in New York. But to hold viewer attention, the societies within the films are, and must be, different in at least one respect from what we ordinarily experience. How they are different varies totally from film to film.

Films such as *The Seventh Seal, Bicycle Thief,* and *Taxi Driver* are not necessarily fun to watch; the pleasures they give are conceptual. They make sense in their own terms, and, because the societies represented by the films are fictions, the border between play and reality becomes extremely important as a source of pleasure. In wish-fulfilling fictional cultures, the separation between the viewer and the world of the film is an unlikely source of pleasure, but in grim fictional worlds, the more obvious the artifice, the more direct the pleasure. The viewer is reassured by his own privileged and safe vantage point.

At the point where the fictional societies of films are juxtaposed with those of viewers, it is necessary to begin to face the full implications of culture and history. Herbert Gans, in *Popular Culture and High Culture*, demonstrates convincingly that no subculture enjoys seeing itself on film: lower-middle-class audiences enjoy soap-opera's treatment of the rich; upper-middle-class audiences get enjoyment from neorealistic portrayals of the working class. Fictional cultures are interesting and "convincing" to the degree that an audience lacks the experience to be able to judge veracity fully. For a fictional culture to engage the imagination, it must be plausible. The job of actors is to make fictional cultures plausible. But it is the job of every other aspect of cinema to make sure that there is a difference between the plausible and the real.

NOTES: CHAPTER SEVEN

[1] Sex symbolism is obviously a factor in screen appeal, but easy conclusions or stereo-typed assumptions are dangerous. Animal researchers have long been puzzled by the unpredictable (to people) sexual preferences of animals such as dogs. Some animals are more attractive to the opposite sex than others; no factors have been identified so far to predict which animal will be more attractive than others of its kind. Sex appeal seems unequally parceled out in all species. In humans, prettiness alone is seldom the same as sexiness; the suggestive has more impact than the obvious.

[2] Ernest Gombrich, *Art and Illusion* (Princeton, N.J.: Princeton University Press, 1969), p. 331.

[3] Ibid., p. 339.

[4] Ibid., pp. 340–341.

[5] Ibid., p. 345.

[6] See Herbert J. Gans, *Popular Culture and High Culture* (New York: Basic Books, 1974), chap. 1.

PART TWO

The
Cinema in
Cultural
Perspective

All narrative films function in pretty much the same way. But all films do not work equally well for all viewers, nor does one film evoke the same response from everyone who sees it. This is due partly to the differences in potency among films, to the differences in film makers' abilities to get viewers to imagine along with their films. But it is also because a person watching a film must extrapolate from his own memories, experiences, and anticipations in order to follow the film's hypotheses, conventions, and narrative development. Only a viewer who is prepared for and skilled at handling a film's "terms" can become fully engaged in the imaginative experience it invites; only a viewer with appropriate expectations can, on leaving the theater, articulate his experience in terms appropriate to the film's. Inappropriate expectations can dilute or destroy imaginative involvement; inappropriate categories and terms make for skewed and distorted judgments and criticism.

The conventions and experiences drawn on by films are not all alike, because films are made for particular kinds of audiences at particular historical times. A film made to please assembly-line workers with aching bodies and bored minds must appeal to different anticipations and experiences than a film made for film buffs or college professors. A film made for 1935 will invoke different anticipations and experiences than a film made for 1975. A film made for French audiences will differ from a film made for American distribution. Even within one country, films are made to suit their audiences; in the United States, as Herbert Gans points out in *Popular Culture and High Culture,** there are five different "taste aggregates"—the aesthetic equivalent of social class, though it is not determined by economic factors alone. An art that appeals to the cultural elite will not appeal to those who, in sports, prefer roller derbies to soccer. An art that appeals to those who like Proust is unlikely to appeal to those who prefer Jacqueline Susann. Though

* Gans, *Popular Culture and High Culture.* See pp. 65–118.

audiences are often able to "straddle" taste structures—going to James Bond movies for entertainment while reading T. S. Eliot for intellectual stimulation—generally speaking, works of art are made to appeal to the needs, experiences, and expectations of particular taste aggregates. And thus terms used to explicate *Last Year at Marienbad* must necessarily differ from those used to explicate *Jaws,* which was aimed not at an elite but at lower- and upper-middle-class audiences, seeking diversion on Saturday night.

Our culture is no more monolithic aesthetically than it is economically. Every taste aggregate functions as a kind of "aesthetic institution" that serves the tastes of its public. Like other institutions —churches, schools, businesses—they compete with one another for dominance and for survival. There is more difference between popular art and "highbrow" art than there is between popular films and popular novels. Although media function, and are economically organized, as competing aesthetic institutions, what appeals to, say, a cultural elite in one medium will have close cousins in other media as well: the novel and the film of *Jaws* appeal to pretty much the same audience for pretty much the same reasons. The expectations we bring to films depend on the kinds of books we read, the kinds of plays we go to (if any), the kinds of visual art we like, and on film experience; even film experience differs among social groups. Understanding the cultural assumptions on which particular films are based requires an approach to more than just films: it must be cognizant of multiple-media applications. Further, it requires a knowledge of how artists have developed conventions in particular media that take advantage of the experiences and assumptions of their chosen audience. To grasp how a film works one must, in short, have a sympathetic feel for what it is trying to do, for whom, when, and in what terms.

As Gans points out, the upper-middle and upper classes have reviewers to help sort out the plethora of art experiences available to their publics.* Popular arts are reviewed and criticized by the same people, and according to the same standards, as are works aimed at better educated audiences and audiences with more "modernist"—that is, self-consciously sophisticated—tastes. The result: misunderstanding, and a condemnation of the popular. Lower-middle-class publics have no reviewers at all; their judgments of films are formed by word-of-mouth discussions. Critics value

* Ibid., pp. 116–118.

most highly the works they understand best, those that appeal to their assumptions about what art should do. Critics, like university professors, value most highly of all works that make the existence of critics and professors necessary. (Everyone likes to feel his life is useful.) That is fine for some kinds of art, for some kinds of film. But the cinema is, historically, an art aimed mainly at popular audiences; until recently only a few avant-garde artists made films to appeal to those who expect the values common in modernist art. Unless one adjusts expectations to the conventions, experiences, and taste levels to which particular films appeal, one cannot help but misunderstand individual films. Unless one adjusts anticipations to take into account that the history of the cinema is mainly a history of a popular art form, one cannot help but misunderstand film history.

To be sure, some few films seem to have almost universal appeal. Charlie Chaplin's films and Welles's *Citizen Kane* straddle expectations so well that no matter where one is "coming from" one will get a solid, invigorating experience from them. At the level of the popular, Chaplin's films appeal to working-class experience and expectations because they use vaudeville traditions, employ slapstick humor, and deal in the struggles of a man without social advantages. Simultaneously, Chaplin's films win critical respect because they are brilliant satires of social structure and exemplary and sophisticated statements of the human condition. We can enter a Chaplin film from virtually any taste perspective, social level, and degree of sophistication; no matter what we bring to the theater, we will come out with something of value.

Citizen Kane has universal appeal for quite different reasons. *Kane* is a different film to almost every kind of viewer. It appeals to the popular film audience on several counts. The feel of its sound track is that of radio drama; though it sounds a bit strident to us today, the style was totally familiar to the film's original audience in 1941. *Kane* appeals to the expectations of several popular-film genres. It is a biography and a detective story. It is a newspaper film in the vein of *The Front Page* and *His Girl Friday;* the newspaperman-in-search-of-a-story genre was popular throughout the 1930s, and thus familiar to audiences. *Kane* is also a gothic thriller, appealing to audience experience with everything from *King Kong* to *Frankenstein;* the "misunderstood monster" was a strong 1930s genre. *Kane* is also an exposé of the rich and powerful. Like the Harold Robbins *roman à clef, The Carpetbaggers,* it partook of an old, old genre in popular art; it is the story of a poor little rich boy, or what happens when a nice kid has too much money. And above all, *Kane* moves and feels like an old-fashioned melodrama: it is full of sound and fury, quick reversals, cockatoo shrieks, and the *Sturm und Drang* of popular art. *Kane* appeals to intellectuals for several reasons that have little to do with the film's popular appeal. It is structured so that viewpoints shift. Like Virginia Woolf's *To the Lighthouse,* it deals with experiences through multiple consciousnesses and multiple perspectives. Like Henry James's *What Maisie Knew,* narration is unreliable: a narrator mirrors himself more than his subject. Like Joseph Conrad's *The Heart of Darkness* and *Lord Jim, Kane* is a study of the corrupt effects of absolute power, and of what happens when people expect a great deal from a man just because he happens to be powerful. Like Proust's *Remembrance of Things Past, Kane* is an exploration of time and memory, of the search for the past. Like Shakespeare, *Kane* studies both a family and the fall of a great man. Like all modernist art, *Kane* is self-consciously a study of media, particularly the medium of film: it extends the explorations of Picasso, of Joyce, of Dziga Vertov's *Man With a Movie Camera.* And, for those familiar with myth, *Kane* echoes the Narcissus story, telling about a man so in love with himself that he could not love others, and finally was destroyed from within. Whatever one knows of, or expects from, sophisticated art, one can find in *Kane,* though it is the rare viewer who can articulate how he came by his expectations.

Kane made film history because Welles had the wit to provide his own plot-summary or Cliff's Notes before the jigsaw puzzle of the film begins its shifting perspective: his newsreel introduces the whole film, telling viewers what to expect and how to make discriminations. The job of any film maker is to define and develop the terms through which his work can be understood. Welles did that for a popular audience in the film's first ten minutes. But few—astonishingly few—films provide a viewer's guide at the beginning. Instead, they signal viewers to watch for particular clues; they appeal implicitly to what viewers know about how movies work. Only those who respond to a film's clues and unstated assumptions respond to, or can appreciate, the film's particular beauties and meanings.

The job of film criticism is, in part, to make the unstated stated, to make the implicit explicit, so that the viewer, by stretching his mind and imagination, can become a connoisseur of tastes and experiences beyond those he would come by through experience alone. To make explicit the ways in which films function for their times and audiences, one must go back to the beginnings of the split between popular and modernist art, and follow conventions as they evolved toward their present forms. This is the job of Part Two.

Chapter 8 traces the history of the popular arts, including the cinema. It begins where it must begin—with the prehistory of cinema, with the social and aesthetic development of popular art from the time of the French Revolution and the rise of urban industrialism. Chapter 9, "The Antipopular Arts," traces the minority rebellion against the bourgeoisie that accompanied the growth of popular art; the results of this rebellion have dominated what is normally called modern (or as I term it, modern*ist*) art.   Chapter 10 contrasts popular film aesthetics with modernist literary aesthetics: I show that the divergence in social functions is accompanied by a parallel development of structures and forms. I follow this with a comparative treatment of film, theater, and the visual arts, again stressing differences in social function and parallel developments of structure and form. The last chapter in this part is on the recent fusions between popular art and "high" art. It looks at film makers' attempts to incorporate all aesthetic tendencies and expectations into their medium.

My analysis begins, once more, with the perspective of the viewer. It proceeds toward those who have made art. Again, it is concerned with the exchange that makes the art of cinema come alive.

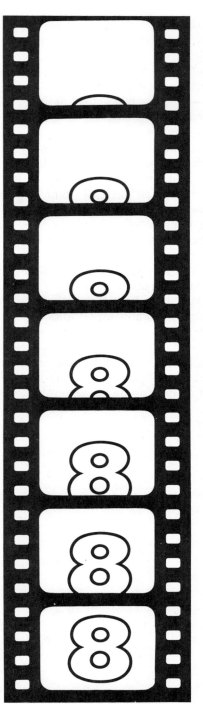

THE POPULAR ARTS
A Brief Prehistory of the Cinema

Northampton, Massachusetts, has a theater called the Academy of Music in which Sarah Bernhardt once acted. The Academy is like a thousand other movie houses: ornate, plushly upholstered, decorated in maroon and gold, originally intended for popular theater. Only movies show there now. The Academy would not work too well for modern plays anyway. Though its acoustics are good, its ornateness and proscenium stage would be a handicap to the informal actor-audience interaction on which the best modern theater depends. The Academy is a nineteenth-century theater, which means that movies are the best things to put into it. The cinema, like the Academy, was born to serve the aesthetic of spectacular romantic realism that dominated the popular arts of the nineteenth century. In the movies that aesthetic has survived. But only in the movies. Sitting in the Academy, watching two lovers kiss before they die, it dawns on you: the movies are not a new art at all. Technologically, psychologically, aesthetically, the cinema is archaic. And that is part of its beauty.

Unlike the older arts of writing, the theater, and painting, the cinema has never been forced out of joint with its past. Virtually every idea on which movies are based was thought through in the nineteenth century and has survived unchanged in principle, being merely refined over the years. The technology of movies, if compared with the technology of radio or television, is half a century old. Open up a movie camera and you find a more sophisticated version of the lever mechanics that characterizes all machines invented eighty years ago. Aesthetically, and in terms of how they appeal, movies are equally old-fashioned. They have a lot more to do with the art of Sarah Bernhardt than modern theater does. It is far more difficult to put on new plays in old theaters than to show movies in them. Movies also have more to do with the art of Dickens than do modern novelists such as Alain Robbe-Grillet. The picture on a movie screen resembles a nineteenth-century painting far more than either resembles the paintings on the walls of virtually any museum of modern art. Every other art has had to undergo a revolution in the last century. Movies, on the whole, are doing pretty much what they have always done. Which is to say, they are doing what the other arts used to do, too.

Film histories teach that the cinema is a modern art, an autonomous form of, by, and for our century. The standard view is that the great film pioneers —Edwin S. Porter, D. W. Griffith, and so on—created an art of the cinema by moving film away from the novel and painting and especially theater. It simply is not so. Men like Porter and especially Griffith made the movies what they are by teaching film makers not how to borrow from the older arts but rather how to steal their identities and functions whole. Their identities and social functions taken, the older arts, left with little but their proud names and their media, had little choice but to move on, to find new ways of living. The movies *became* the older arts by embodying their ideals. And the older arts responded by finding identities so new, so different from their old ones, that they now resemble their own pasts less than films do.

MELODRAMA AND THE GENESIS OF POPULAR THEATER

In the arts as in life, genealogy is a science that teaches that the past was no nobler than the present. Film historians like to attribute the birth of the cinema to the elegant and gentlemanly Lumière brothers, who first showed projected movies in a café. The technological breakthroughs that made theatrical cinema possible are attributed to Edison and his helper, Dickson. Such historicizing is accurate enough as far as it goes. But the world of nineteenth-century technological inventions, with its cast of charlatans, geniuses, and hustlers—sometimes embodied in a single man such as Edison, who was all three—provided only the material impetus behind cinema. The other and more important half of the marriage that produced cinema came from melodrama, probably the most banal form in theatrical history. Melodrama, born during the French Revolution, was a theatrical form aimed at the lower classes; its essential approach was pictorial. Melodrama and the mass-produced, usually serialized, popular novel were the first popular art forms. Though melodrama was the forebear of all modern mass media, it is little studied in theater histories. All histories are biased in favor of high-quality writing and the nobility of the past; melodrama had little of either. Melodrama, by and large, was not meant to be read; most melodramas read more like scenarios than like plays. And by standards of literate theater, melodrama —I know of no more accurate or honest way of saying it—stinks. Melodrama was to the nineteenth century what popular thriller films are to ours—cheap titillations for Saturday night.

Melodrama was invented by René Pixérécourt.[1] Pixérécourt's personality has formed the art of two centuries. Born an aristocrat, reared to idealize heroism, virtue, and chastity, Pixérécourt fought for and deserted *both* sides in the French Revolution. The materials of his life and imagination became compelling dramatic conventions. During the Revolution, he spent a good deal of his time being pursued; he turned that experience into the most basic of melodrama's forms, the chase. He hid in Paris during the Reign of Terror, with his name on the death lists. He lived in a room overlooking a street through which cartfuls of the condemned rode to their beheadings. To keep sane, Pixérécourt read the weepily romantic "graveyard" poets, Hervey and Young, and wrote plays. Thrilling enough to keep his mind off his troubles, the plays proved enormously popular when produced. They spawned hundreds of imitations and dominated the popular theater section of Paris, the "Boulevard of Crime." Pixérécourt's blood-and-thunder spectacles won him a governmental pardon; as a man who wrote for the people, he became a kind of public hero. And though he kept a mishmash of aristocratic views, he was proud of writing "for those who cannot read." No deep thinker, Pixérécourt turned the contradictions and paradoxes of his mentality into theater by adding energy and great quantities of noise.

Melodrama was anything but an intellectual theater. Frank Rahill has described its trademarks as "staunch fidelity to orthodox morality and an optimism which can only be described as incorrigible."[2] David Grimstead puts the morality in more specific terms: "The loss of 'maiden innocence'— the constant threat of this catastrophe was the emotional core of the melodramatic structure."[3] Heroines were always in danger because of the baseness of some men. "Because woman was 'the source of every earthly bliss' and her home 'the abode of universal felicity,' seduction became 'the unpardonable sin.' To suggest that any forgiveness for this was possible was 'obscene and impious morality.'" The formula of villain, heroine, and hero became immensely popular, catching on in England and America as well as in France: melodramatic conventions became international.

In large, uncarpeted theaters, words could seldom be understood very far back from the stage. Melodrama got along without many words. Rahill writes:

The popular melodramatic theatre had a tolerance for the spoken word, but it was scarcely more than a tolerance, especially in England and America. Basically this theatre worked with building blocks other than verbal ones . . . [including] almost continual movement contrived to mesh at climaxes with an elaborate and frequently gimmicky *mise-en-scène*. . . . talk was accessory to the central business of hubbub and spectacle.[4]

Writing did not count for much; frequently over a fifth of the script was stage directions. Rahill points out the structural similarity between melodrama and motion-picture production methods: "The man in control—whether he was called manager, house manager, stage manager, 'contriver,' or whatever—foreshadowed the motion picture director in diversity of activity and might be described as ringmaster."[5] And as in cinema, audiences seemed not to be bothered by trite plots as long as the productions were sensational enough, as D. W. Griffith well understood; in the accompanying still, lightning is used to add sensation to an already sensation-filled *The Birth of a Nation* (8–1).

And yet, aesthetically, there was method to melodrama. As A. Nicholas Vardac points out in *Stage to Screen*, "the nineteenth century witnessed a union of romanticism and realism in the arts of the drama and of staging." Pictorial realism served romantic ends: "The more romantic the subject matter, the more realistic must be the staging."[6] If it could be seen and heard in detail, the sensational became convincing.

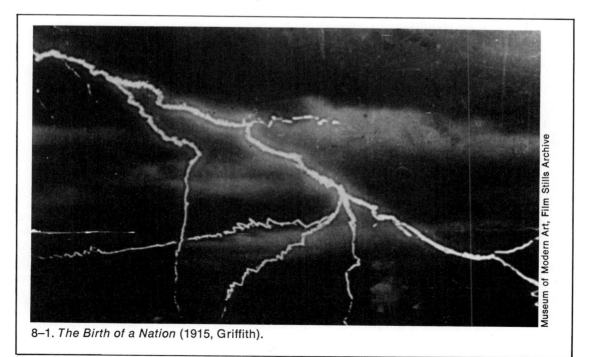

8–1. *The Birth of a Nation* (1915, Griffith).

Museum of Modern Art, Film Stills Archive

THE PIVOTAL ROLE OF LOUIS DAGUERRE

Louis Daguerre, the inventor of photography, was a central figure in the development of melodrama. Daguerre was trained as a painter, but, lacking talent, he could never have made much of a living as one, so he became a stage designer for melodramatic productions. As a stage designer he became famous. In the words of Helmut and Alison Gernsheim:

> His striving for extreme naturalism led him more and more beyond the bounds of art into the field of showmanship. Critics declared he had in "La Forêt de Senart" introduced a real stream on the stage, with real trees and grass. . . . It was the poetry that counted in classical tragedy and the comedy of manners, and not visual effects. But now the new kind of theatre-going public—the petite bourgeoisie—had a new kind of play to suit their tastes—the melodrama —and together with the novel decors of Daguerre and his imitators, it revolutionized the theatre.[7]

After a number of years working as a stage designer, Daguerre invented the diorama, a spectacle theater with no actors. He painted large-scale scenes on translucent canvas in such a way that one scene would show if the light were reflected from the canvas and a second scene would show when light was transmitted through the canvas from behind. An illustration shows the effect; the first scene shows the reflected image, the second shows the image with light transmitted through it by back lighting (see 8–2 a, b).[8] One of Daguerre's diorama shows, "A Midnight Mass at Saint-Étienne-du-Mont," set up in 1834, ran continuously for three years. This is a contemporary journalist's account:

> At first it was daylight, the nave full of [empty] chairs; little by little the light waned; at the same time, candles were lit at the back of the choir; then the entire church was illuminated, and the chairs were occupied by the congregation who had arrived, not suddenly as if by scene-shifting, but gradually— quickly enough to surprise one, yet slowly enough for one not to be too astonished. The midnight mass started, and in the midst of a devotion impossible to describe, organ music was heard echoing from the vaulted roof. Slowly dawn broke, the congregation dispersed, the candles were extinguished, the church and the empty chairs appeared as at the beginning. This was magic.[9]

Painting and promoting dioramas occupied only part of Daguerre's time. Obsessed with the problem of making realistic pictures, he began experiments aimed at creating photography. With the aid of Joseph Niepce's developments, Daguerre eventually succeeded in inventing the daguerreotype, the first real photograph. A good deal of Daguerre's success has to be attributed to luck. His approach to invention was more that of an alchemist than that of a scientist; he spent as much time publicizing early breakthroughs as he did breaking through. But even showmen and charlatans get lucky sometimes, and history respects luck as much as genius, so Louis Daguerre, an

(a)

(b)

Reprinted, by permission, from Helmut and Alison Gernsheim, *L. J. M. Daguerre: The History of the Diorama and the Daguerreotype*, 2nd revised edition, Dover Publications. Copyright © 1968.

8–2. (a) Dioramic lithograph of an Alpine village: daylight scene; (b) the same picture as a night scene.

entrepreneur who had already invented a kind of painted cinema in the diorama, and who seems to have sensed that to make a more sensational dioramic show—a real movie—he would need first to invent photography, became the most influential figure in the entire histories of painting and theater and writing.

Nothing has been the same since Daguerre—or rather, since Daguerre's invention. The effect of photography was twofold. First, it made available to a wide public the images that previously only painting could deliver. In so doing, it not only increased the taste for pictures, but made visual images something people expected in the arts. The traditional, verbal theater could never be reborn after Daguerre; words had strong competition. Visual artists had to compete with photographers as purveyors of spectacle. Although the appetite for images predated the photograph's invention, the photograph's existence turned what had been appetite into demand; and what had been a privilege became a kind of right. This meant that the visual bias of the arts was radically accelerated.

The second effect of photography was to make artists media-conscious. For Shakespeare, the play had been the thing. But for Henry Irving, the foremost purveyor of Shakespeare in the nineteenth century, not only had the words of Shakespeare "lost their necessity"; plays were "made for the theater and not theater for plays."[10] From the time of Daguerre on, it became evident to painters that what they did was paint, not reproduce reality, and it became evident to writers that their medium was not ideas, but words. Marshall McLuhan's shrilly overstated cry, "the medium is the message," is merely the end product of media-awareness fostered by Daguerre's invention.

Of the two effects of the photograph, the increased demand for visual spectacle had the first, and probably the most important, manifestations. Photography made pictures available to almost everyone. People who began to see themselves in terms of their portraits, and to see the world in terms of photographs, became more aware of, and demanded more of, the pictorial aspects of the arts and entertainment.

In the theater, as Vardac shows, producers virtually made movies without film. For example, when David Belasco did *Passion Play* in 1879, he used 400 people for the crowd scene; his cast also included 200 singers and a flock of real sheep. When Belasco did *The Octoroon* in 1881, he used a panoramic painting on several hundred yards of canvas as a backdrop for the chase scenes. With the aid of gas lighting, Belasco was able to cross-cut "shots" of the pursuer and the pursued as they stood on a treadmill in front of a moving painting. By the time movies were invented, the melodramatic theater was fully mature as a visual art form and could serve as a model for the cinema's development.[11]

Vardac sees a straight line of development from theatricians such as David Garrick to film makers such as D. W. Griffith. The combination of realism and romance and the emphasis on spectacle provided a popular formula on which the cinema could be built. The great film pioneers—in particular Porter and Griffith—borrowed the aesthetic, and many of the techniques, of the visually oriented stage, adapting them to the technical possibilities of moving pictures. Porter found ways of adapting melodramatic structure to the one-reel film format; the formula he created was the foundation for film's first large, stable audience. Griffith advanced the techniques, partly by invention, partly by borrowing heavily from melodramatic literature and from the stage (in which he was trained). He lengthened films, virtually a reel at a time, until they reached their present conventional length. Porter and Griffith were extraordinarily gifted at adapting techniques from other media. Porter's seminal *The Great Train Robbery* was an unacknowledged adaptation of a play popular at the time and proved to be a brilliant piece of structural thievery. Griffith, who knew more about theater and literature than virtually any other early film maker, carried novels by Dickens about with him on the set. One of his real talents was that he could turn everything from Browning to the Bible into melodrama, blending his literacy with what he learned from the popular stage.

The cinema owes to the melodramatic stage the practice of adaptation. Hampered by new copyright laws from stealing written works directly, theatricians swiped the plots, turned the stories into visuals, put on new titles, and mounted the results for popular audiences. The formula of plundering old (or new) works, leaving out the words, and switching the medium was so entrenched by the time movies began that it was as common as hubcap stealing in a modern city. The stage taught film how to steal, how to build on the past; without adaptation, the cinema could never have grown from infancy to maturity in the space of two decades. Had the cinema been hampered with highbrow literature's ethos of originality we simply would not have movies. Daguerre found the means by which theft could proceed smoothly. As a stage designer, he showed that theater could work as a mainly visual medium; as developer of the diorama, he showed the possibilities of theater as visual spectacle. When he also invented the technical means on which the cinema was founded, and increased the hunger for visuals in the populace, he ensured his central place in art history: he made the cinema possible. But he also doomed the popular theater, because it could never use his greatest invention as a primary tool. Daguerre transformed the theater. And by inventing photography, he doomed the theater as a popular form.

WHAT PRICE ART?

Actually, of course, the stage was never popular in the modern sense of the word. It was too expensive for the lower classes, at least in its full spectacle form. Melodrama required large, complicated stages. And while men like Belasco could do as much with spectacle melodrama as men like Griffith, Belasco's theater cost more. It required dozens of stagehands, hundreds of actors, expensive sets, and all the paraphernalia of live performance every night the play was performed. Only the large theaters of fairly major cities could do full-scale spectacle melodrama; smaller theaters had to compromise. Sets and actors had to be transported from place to place for road shows. That cost money. Although in the large cities stage melodrama thrived well into the twentieth century, economic and demographic factors made its demise inevitable.

The popular melodramatic theater came into being to service a new audience for entertainment: the newly affluent middle classes. In historical terms, this was a "popular" audience. The forces that created this audience—mainly industrialization and urbanization—created a still larger audience in time: the so-called working classes. All classes of people have always had indigenous entertainment forms—typically, dance, song, and storytelling. In rural settings, "folk" art was both produced and consumed in local, and virtually noneconomic, terms; it was part of life, not something to be consumed at a price. Urban industrial realities changed all that, destroying the cultures on which participant entertainment was based. Workers were forced to find entertainment to *consume*. That they could afford to consume art at all was virtually unprecedented in history. That they had time for art was a new reality of the Victorian age and the early twentieth century.

Garth S. Jowett has shown that movies were the only art the lowest classes could afford. Reduced working hours brought an increased demand for entertainment:

> In non-agricultural industries the workweek declined by about ten hours between 1850 and 1900, from sixty-six to fifty-six hours. . . . Between 1900 and 1940 the workweek in non-agricultural industries declined from fifty-six to forty-one hours, with the sharpest declines occurring between 1900 and 1920, when the average workweek in non-agricultural industries dropped about five hours every ten years.[12]

The virtual insatiability of urban workers for cheap recreation and the scarcity of such recreation made movies a formidable medium. Movies were cheap, accessible, and required no linguistic proficiency—a large factor in the United States, where immigrants could often speak little or no English. The price? Movies cost a dime. With vaudeville added, the charge was fifteen cents. Vaudeville completely "live" could be had for fifty cents. Regular theater, including melodrama, was a dollar and opera cost two dollars. At a time when the average working family's weekly budget was twelve to fifteen dollars, and when there might be a dollar a week for sundries, movies were about the only recreation people could afford.

Film, once it became a solidly based industry, could compete not only for working-class audiences. It could also undercut theater at its own game, thus drawing in the bourgeoisie as well. The middle class—a money-conscious class if ever one existed—was not going to pay more for what could be had at a cheaper price. Melodrama survived, but the theater of melodrama did not. As Frank Rahill writes:

The triumph of the films was more of a disaster for the popular theatre than it was for melodrama. For melodrama it was no disaster at all, certainly not from the standpoint of survival. What melodrama did when the crisis came was simply to drift over to the ranks of the enemy, taking along its gaudy accoutrements, its raffish side-show manners, and its bag of tricks.[13]

Or, as Rahill entitles the last chapter of his book on melodrama, "melodrama went thataway." It went "thataway" because its audience already had. To put it crassly: art has a way of following the buck.

The development of the cinema was not, however, merely a matter of the meeting of melodrama with the pictorial means for making it cheaply. Looking back, it becomes apparent that several discoveries were necessary for cinema to come into being. First, the mass audience for indoor spectacle had to be discovered and built. Pixérécourt and Daguerre were the pioneers here. Second, the pictorial means necessary for handling large crowds indoors had to be developed. Large audiences are noisy—a verbal theater could not reach them. The development of a theater of pure spectacle took a century to mature, beginning at the time of the French Revolution.

Next, the means had to be found to technologize theatrical distribution. Photography was a start. But photographs originally took hours to expose. Faster film stocks, better lenses, and finally, strong, flexible bases for film stocks had to be invented before photography could be combined with the long-known phenomenon of persistence of vision (which allows the eye to see rapid successions of still pictures as a continuum) to create movies. All sorts of persistence-of-vision toys intended for the parlor or for carnivals were invented before a version of the movie camera, with its mechanism for intermittent film motion, was developed. Finally, there had to be a way to project images so that groups could look at a single movie. When the Lumières developed their first projector, movies became a possibility. Without projection—which itself relied on good electrical or gas light sources, another nineteenth-century development—film could be no more than a toy or side-show oddity because only one spectator at a time could see a movie. But with projection, film could "return to its source," the theater. The theater is a good way of "distributing" a performance in one time at one place. A lot of people can split the costs of the performance. But theater is essentially a preindustrial art form: it requires a performance for every "exhibition." Actors cannot do more than one show a night; they cannot work seven nights a week; they cannot be in more than one place at a time. Film, however, can be printed and duplicated in quantity so that one "performance" can be exhibited simultaneously in any number of theaters, each of which can repeat the exhibition two or more times per evening—each time to a new, paying audience. The theatrical situation made possible the use of one film and one projection setup per theater—film being too expensive to distribute like a book and requiring expensive machinery for projection. When movies became a form of theater—when they returned to the source of the aesthetic that made them possible—the cinema in its basic form could be developed.

The visual and economic advantages of the cinema can be seen in two stills from Abel Gance's *Napoleon* (1927). Though stage managers might have managed a crowd scene like the one shown in the first still (8–3a), they could not have managed to make a convincing version of the second one (8–3b). And even if they could have matched Gance's ability to create spectacle, they would have had to pay their extras for every performance; Gance had to pay only once. Film makers could out-spectacle and underprice the theater with little difficulty.

Pixérécourt built a theater "for the people." That meant two contradictory things—a stage based on visual spectacle and a theater people could afford. The more spectacle theater provided, the more expensive it became. As it became more expensive, it became more vulnerable to competition and price undercutting. The pictorial hunger reflected in and encouraged by melodrama helped, through Daguerre, to create photography, which itself accelerated the move toward a mainly visual form. Until Daguerre, there had been no new media for thousands of years; even Gutenberg's press had merely made print more workable and cheaper. But once Daguerre broke the old monopolies, new media of other kinds became not just imaginable but thinkable. The result, eventually, was the phonograph (which did for sound what the photograph did for the image), movies, radio, and television. Each development was an alliance of previously separated technologies resulting in a new entity, a new medium. Daguerre's primitive camera was the black Pandora's box from which the modern revolution in aesthetics sprang. That revolution—originally a radical redefining of the audience for art—is still continuing.

THE RISE OF POPULAR FICTION

The stage alone did not create the new popular aesthetics. Vaudeville, the music hall, the circus, and the visual arts contributed, too. Above all, public education and the spread of literacy became a factor in aesthetics. The revolution in theater was paralleled by a revolution in literature.

The nineteenth century was the age of the popular novel. Though the novel had roots deep in storytelling history, and had existed in modern form since Defoe, it took a central place as a form of entertainment with the advent of Richardson, Fielding, Smollett, Scott, and finally a wave of nineteenth-century popular novelists, which included Thackeray, Austen, Dickens, and Stevenson in England; Dumas, Hugo, Sand, Balzac, and Maupassant in France; Cooper, Irving, Poe, and Twain in America. From the time of Scott onward, important popular writers became virtual book factories. Dumas wrote hundreds of books; a good popular writer could turn out dozens of huge novels in his lifetime. The middle and even lower middle classes now knew how to read and many people had time to kill. Books and serialized fiction as well as stories in newspapers and magazines functioned as a kind of printed television, a home-based narrative entertainment medium. In unbound

8–3. *Napoleon* (1927, Abel Gance).

Museum of Modern Art, Film Stills Archive

form, literature was cheap entertainment. (Binding a book has always cost as much as or more than printing it.) The nineteenth-century novel was a remarkably dramatic, even melodramatic, art form. Episodic, strongly plotted, peopled by individualized human types, full of intellectual and social commonplaces, and given to cliff-hanging thrills and predicaments, the novel's world view spoke to and fed the aesthetic that was to be taken over by the popular cinema. How many films have satisfied their audiences, as E. A. Dupont's *Variety* does, through the popular novel's aesthetic of thrills (8–4)?

The rise of the novel coincided with the rise of bourgeois individualism: the earliest novels—*Robinson Crusoe, Moll Flanders,* even *Pamela* and *Tom Jones* —were fictional biographies. If one sets aside mavericks like Sterne and looks at the overall patterns of the eighteenth- and nineteenth-century novel, certain conventions emerge. Most novels told the story of a single person or family beset by difficulties. After numerous adventures, trials, tribulations, and reversals, the protagonists emerged victorious—settled, prosperous, respected, fully bourgeois. In Balzac, Dumas, Thackeray, Stevenson, and a spate of others, the plots and settings were often deliberately archaic, and tinged with either adventurous or pastoral romanticism. Dumas's most famous work, *The Count of Monte Cristo,* is perhaps the epitome of the wish-fulfillment fantasy in the popular novel. Not only does the count escape from prison, engage in enough Errol Flynn derring-do to please the most demand-

8–4. *Variety* (1925, Dupont).

ing Hollywood producer, and live in a castle; he also carries a million francs with him as pocket money. The world he encounters is full of corruption and intrigue, but the count is smart and brave, so it is also a world where virtue triumphs. It is no accident that the world of the popular novel is often the world of the past: the popular novelist understood (and taught Hollywood by example) that the nonurban past is a source of romantic gratification. The human values espoused by virtually any popular novelist included moral rectitude, bravery, honor, friendship, and tenacity—all very bourgeois values. With dedication and luck, popular fiction asserted, a good man could succeed in the world. The novel existed to create and reinforce a myth of bourgeois success. Despite the fact that many protagonists were noble by birth, their values were the dreams of the rising middle class.

As John L. Fell demonstrates in *Film and the Narrative Tradition*, a second kind of popular fiction arose alongside the "respectable" sort. This was the dime novel, which appealed to the lower classes—newly, and often just barely, literate. Cheaply produced by what were virtual literature factories, lower-class popular fiction tended to be even more generic in subject matter and form than middle-class popular fiction; often the dime novel was purely formulaic. Detectives, villains, and extreme situations were the common fare. Popular literature aped the plot intricacies of Poe, the emotional extremism of *Uncle Tom's Cabin,* and the world of action of melodrama. Mimed action and strong visual detail were the dime novelist's stock in trade. Simple, direct prose (ready to print in first draft) made the dime novel accessible to even the barely literate.

Just as the movies took advantage of a new, poorer market for fiction, so the mass-market publishers pushed to exploit a newly literate and newly available reading market. Mass popular fiction rose in popularity through the nineteenth century. By the twentieth century, it had writers as prolific as Zane Grey (virtually a one-man industry), and whole magazines, such as *Black Mask,* to purvey its product. Though never studied in literature classes, formulaic dime novels and magazine stories had an undoubtedly huge market and popular effect. They reinforced the aesthetic that made early films potent. It did not matter that the fiction of, or rather for, "the people" was not good by literary standards—it answered a social need. And it is still with us today. The linotype machine and better presses made it eternally competitive with the movies. To find the descendants of the dime novel, one need only visit local supermarket or bus-station bookracks and magazine stands. From the nineteenth century onward, literature, like theater, was no longer monopolized by the upper and upper-middle classes. There were literatures and theaters for just about every group with the money to pay for them. Literature and theater, as consumer entertainment products, responded to social changes in ways which "higher" forms could not, or would not.[14]

In popular fiction were several strains directly relevant to the rise of popular cinema. Dumas, Stevenson, and the dime novelists, with their swash-buckling adventures, directly fed the values of stage melodrama (and through adaptation, provided material for the stage and movies). A large number of nineteenth-century novelists developed the structural and narrative techniques that would become regarded as "film techniques" in our time.[15] Close-ups, cross-cutting, switches in viewing angle, visual narrative modes, the careful detailing of action, techniques of characterization—all were the hard-won products of nineteenth-century novelists developing their craft. But perhaps most important, novelists such as Dickens taught how to create fictional worlds populated by instantly recognizable human types, and an art based on broad emotions and common feelings shared by large groups of people. Characters such as Scrooge and Fagin have become synonymous with human types. Dickens created a popular aesthetic which, however bourgeois, was also populist; in his novels we delight in ordinary people as a source of humor and pathos. The world of Dickens came together with the world of the dime novelists in the early cinema. Dickens's contribution was to teach how to create a recognizable, human world. In the novel of Dickens (and those like him) was a model for entertainment that utilized common feelings as a basis for aesthetic structure. Emotionally, everyone reacts pretty much the same way to any Dickens scene. The assumption of a broad common response became a cornerstone of all popular art forms.

A SENSE OF HUMAN SOLIDARITY?

Dickens himself recognized that his art was dramatic, that reading it silently
and alone was perhaps not the best means of apprehending it. He habitually
and fervently engaged in dramatic readings and productions of his work.
Why? Some of the reasons lie in his work and temperament. And some
reasons can be understood only by seeing how the nineteenth century valued
crowds. In melodramatic theater, as many as 3,000 people would gather to
"feel together." In sporting events, even larger numbers would—and still
do—gather together, for much the same purpose. A love of crowds and of
large gatherings seems fully a part of the last century's aesthetic. That love
helped create the conditions essential to the cinema's birth and growth.
Although that love has not survived except in sports and rock concerts, and
though to a contemporary audience the use of massed crowds in a film such
as Leni Riefenstahl's *Triumph of the Will* seems almost repulsive, we must
understand the existence of crowd feeling—an enjoyment both of being in a
crowd and of seeing crowds—to grasp why the movies came to replace print
as the dominant popular storytelling form. In a group an "everyman" response, a loss of personal individuation, occurs almost automatically. With a
loss of individuation comes both imaginative receptiveness and a sense of
belonging. The receptiveness and sense of security of crowds were keystones
around which the art of cinema was built. When, by using a darkened theater,
a technical way of creating that feeling was achieved, without large crowds
actually being present, the future of the cinema was assured.

Probably nowhere is the sense of being in a crowd more important than in
comedy. Nineteenth-century comedy was not, of course, a one-medium affair.
Caricaturists working in the Hogarth-Daumier tradition published their work
in print, and often in journalistic media. The sense of visualized human types
on which film depends undoubtedly came in good part (as I pointed out in
Chapter 7) from caricaturists. Novelists such as Dickens created verbal
counterparts to Hogarth caricature types. On the stage, dramatists often
parodied the excesses of melodramatic plays. But the main source of popular
comedy was undoubtedly the music hall, which in the United States became
vaudeville. Again, this new art form was a response to the existence of a new
audience for entertainment. Vaudeville and the music hall provided part of
the aesthetic and a lot of the talent for early film comedy. It is easier to laugh
when other people laugh with us.

VAUDEVILLE: THE SPRINGBOARD TO CINEMA

Without vaudeville, cinema might not have become a major art form. Movies
reached their first large audiences by being included in vaudeville programs.
For vaudeville, movies were initially a labor- and cost-saving device, a way of
drawing in more people by being able to charge a few cents less per program.

Filmed comedians did not have to be paid for every performance. And because vaudeville shows depended on variety, films helped flesh out their offerings. Film eventually killed vaudeville by taking over vaudeville's best people—Chaplin, Keaton, the Marx Brothers, Mae West, W. C. Fields, and a thousand lesser performers. In the process, however (and it was a process that took thirty years), the sensibility of vaudeville became as much a parent of the cinema as were the sensibilities of the popular novel and the melodrama.

Even with the help of such books as McLean's excellent *American Vaudeville as Ritual* it is difficult to pin down everything that vaudeville gave to the movies.[16] As with all lower-class popular entertainment forms, little was written about vaudeville when it was in its prime; unlike literature, performance leaves no traces for later scholars to work from. But from reading what is available on vaudeville, and from talking with people who still remember it well (and there are not many still alive), one must surmise that the guts of early film comedy came from the sassy marriage of vaudeville with melodrama.

Vaudeville was a descendant of both barroom comedy and the circus. Its repertory included music, song-and-dance acts, acrobatics, animal acts, mimed and slapstick comedy (done by such as Chaplin and Keaton), juggling (performed by W. C. Fields, among others), skits, parodies, and monologues. Acts followed one another in quick succession. Though stand-up comedians were standard fare, the large theaters (and, in the United States, the immigrants' unfamiliarity with English) prohibited too heavy a reliance on verbal language. Slapstick was the standard form of comedy; the slapstick comedian was an urban descendant of the circus clown. Just as the circus clown traditionally parodies the love-and-danger motifs of the highwire acrobat and animal trainer, the slapstick comedian learned to parody the emotional highwire acts of melodrama. And thus the vaudeville clown, when imported directly into the cinema, had the wit to rescue the movies from the banality inherent in melodrama's myths and traditions. Escapes from death—this time, comic—became a standard part of movie fare. When, in *The Navigator*, Buster Keaton saves the heroine from savages by turning his diving suit into an inflated balloon that she can paddle to safety (with Buster still inside it), he is casting a vaudevillian's eye on the escapes common in melodrama.

In *Our Hospitality*, Keaton not only parodies "revenge melodrama" but puts cliff-hanging into a totally comic perspective. First, he actually falls off a cliff. Then, in the film's climax, he swings suspended from a rock in order to rescue the heroine from certain peril (8–5). Further parodying the chase form in *Our Hospitality*, Keaton at one point even fails to notice that he is being chased (8–6). Keaton found melodrama a source of jokes even as a romantic lover; proposing marriage in *The Navigator*, he makes the conventions of melodrama seem like the hokum they really are (8–7).

We have no real record of Chaplin's mimed vaudeville routines, but his *One A.M.* is the closest of his films to an actual vaudeville "turn." Charlie, a dapper drunk, returns home in a cab. His goal: to get from the cab into his

8–5. *Our Hospitality* (1923, Buster Keaton).

Museum of Modern Art, Film Stills Archive

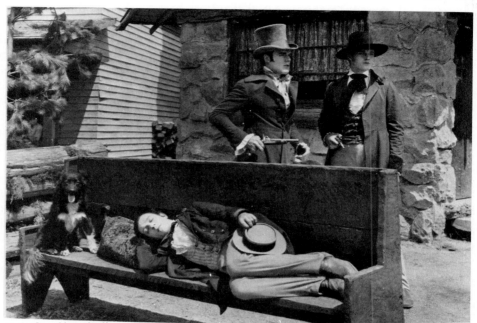

8–6. *Our Hospitality.*

8–7. *The Navigator* (1924, Keaton).

house and up to bed. Charlie squabbles with the cabbie, then goes to the
house. Unable to get in the door, he tries the window. Once in the house, he
encounters a number of obstacles—a goldfish bowl, a circular table, a bottle
of seltzer, a cigarette, matches, a tiger rug, a flight of stairs with a loose carpet
on it, a coat rack, a massive grandfather clock, and finally a demonic Murphy
bed. Each of his opponents assumes the quality of a villainous natural hazard
bent on destroying him. Trying to light a cigarette, he attempts to get near a
lighted candle on the table; as he stalks the flame, the table revolves. When he
attempts to climb the stairs, he ends up rolling back down, encased in the
rolled-up stair rug. At the top of the stairs the clock's huge pendulum wallops
him whenever he gets close. Once past the clock, he attempts to get the
Murphy bed down from the wall. For roughly five minutes the bed battles
him, pulling him up into the wall, slamming down on his head, catching him
in its springs, pinning him to the floor (8–8). Finally, he gives up and goes to
sleep in the bathtub.

In Chaplin, Keaton, Sennett, and virtually every other vaudeville-trained
comic, the bourgeois values of melodrama become something to write small,
even to reduce to absurdity. The mythos of achievement, in the context of
Chaplin's battle with the Murphy bed, becomes ludicrous. The mock-heroic
vision of the little man reduces the banality of the melodramatic to its human,
and most intelligent, dimensions. The cinema may owe melodrama its pal-
pitating and bleeding heart. It has vaudeville to thank for its brains.

Yet it would be mistaken to think that the world of vaudeville was a

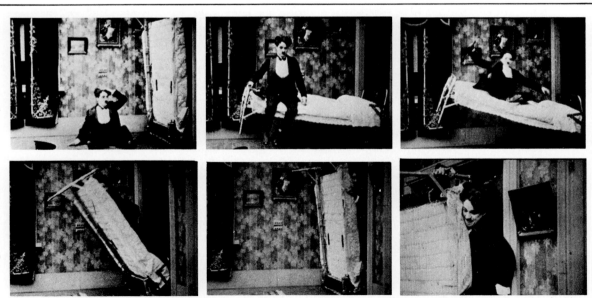

8–8. *One A.M.* (1916, Charles Chaplin).   Museum of Modern Art, Film Stills Archive

complete alternative to the world of melodrama. Vaudeville reveled in sentiment. Child acts, animal acrobatics, singers of sad songs—all were part of a night's show. Even Chaplin and Keaton had sentimental undercurrents in their work. The mentality that made melodrama work was fully necessary for parody to work. An audience that does not feel the pull of a mindless romantic idealism will probably not appreciate the contradictions of that world when prodded by a comedian. What the cinema grew from and took over was a world view that, however complicated, was consistent in its idealism, its romanticism, and its valuing of sentiment.

Probably no film maker has put the romantic sentimentality of vaudeville to better use than Chaplin did in *The Kid* (1920). In *The Kid*, Chaplin, himself destitute, discovers a baby abandoned in the streets and attempts to raise it (8–9a). The two become partners in slum survival, bound to one another by love and by the cruelty of the world outside (8–9b). Though often hilarious, *The Kid* enacts precisely the pathos that made Dickens popular, and ends, again in a Dickensian way, with the discovery and uniting of the child's mother with her child. Tears, along with laughter, were essential to early film comedy and especially to the comedy of Chaplin.

AN AESTHETIC OF EXCITEMENT

In each of the arts that fed into the cinema, there is a single common denominator. None of the cinema's forebears claimed to be great art. Each was primarily an entertainment form. Each was a response to the new (though, by modern standards, minimal) affluence and free time of middle- and lower-class urban residents. Though posterity has canonized a few nineteenth-century popular artists such as Balzac and Dickens, in their own time not a single forebear of the cinema could be called fully respectable—though Dickens came as close to respectability as any. Melodrama, the popular novel, and vaudeville were arts either for the middle classes or for the rabble. No high priests of criticism dictated what those arts did or ought to do. It was a matter of box office or of sales, a matter of satisfying public tastes. Visually the cinema derived not from the art of Michelangelo or even from that of Ingres. Rather it derived from the gauche and tawdry spectacles that one can now find memorialized only in paintings stuffed into the attics of old houses. And to be frank, the early cinema looks it. But what redeemed the cinema and its predecessors was raw energy. The thrills and sentiments and pratfalls worked. Thus there was no aesthetic separation between artist and public. The aesthetic of the popular arts was an aesthetic of excitement, of giving people whatever they thought interesting enough to pay to see.

The cinema was no orphan. Though it strangled its parents by taking their audiences, it fully participated in their values. Furthermore, it coexisted with them for several decades after motion pictures began. Theaters such as the Academy continued to be used for their original purposes until the cinema,

(a)

8–9. *The Kid* (1920, Charles Chaplin).

(b)

the lone survivor of its kind in the performing arts, was strong enough to sustain them. The cinema still coexists with the popular novel and short story. Not until movies were a mature art form did the cinema have to go it alone, without infusions of talent and ideas from its neighboring popular performing arts. The cinema did not have to create and nourish its own aesthetic. And the cinema still borrows ideas, plots, and characters from its strongest surviving relative, popular fiction.

Since the Academy was built, the world has changed a great deal. Smith College stands across the street from it, and the Academy now seats film students as well as townspeople. The movies at the Academy look different from the way they used to. Sound, color, and a wide screen are a long way, technically and aesthetically, from the first movies. But they are perhaps not so far from what the Academy was built to show. Spectacle and the aesthetic of excitement have survived with the building. Sitting in the Academy, one realizes that thousands of others have come there for much the same purposes, and have felt much the same emotions while in the same old seats. And one also realizes that many of these thousands came to the Academy long before there were movies to watch.

NOTES: CHAPTER EIGHT

[1] The best source of information on Pixérécourt is Frank Rahill, *The World of Melodrama* (University Park: Pennsylvania State University Press, 1967). See especially pp. 3–45.

[2] Ibid., p. xviii.

[3] David Grimsted, *Melodrama Unveiled: American Theater and Culture, 1800–1850* (Chicago: University of Chicago Press, 1968), p. 175. See also pp. 228–229.

[4] Rahill, *World of Melodrama*, pp. 297–298.

[5] Ibid., p. 298.

[6] A. Nicholas Vardac, *Stage to Screen* (New York: Arno Press, 1968), p. xx.

[7] The primary source of my information on Daguerre is Alison Gernsheim and Helmut Gernsheim, *L. J. M. Daguerre*, 2nd ed. (New York: Dover, 1968). This quotation is from p. 11.

[8] Ibid., plates 20 and 21.

[9] Ibid., p. 34.

[10] Vardac, *Stage to Screen*, p. 89. See pp. 89–109 for a discussion of Irving's aesthetic.

[11] Ibid., pp. i–xxiii, 63–64, 169, 175, 187, 321.

[12] Garth S. Jowett, "The First Motion Picture Audiences," *Journal of Popular Film*, 3, 1 (Winter 1974): 40. Jowett's full account is in his *A Social History of American Film* (Boston: Little, Brown, 1974). Jowett is my main source of information on early film economics.

[13] Rahill, *World of Melodrama*, p. 297.

[14] John L. Fell, *Film and the Narrative Tradition* (Norman: University of Oklahoma Press, 1974). For Fell's brilliant discussion of the dime novel, see pp. 37–53. For an understanding of the popular arts, Fell's is the best available overview; brilliantly conceived and written, it will be the standard for some time.

[15] Ibid., pp. 54–88.

[16] Albert F. McLean, Jr., *American Vaudeville as Ritual* (Lexington: University of Kentucky Press, 1965).

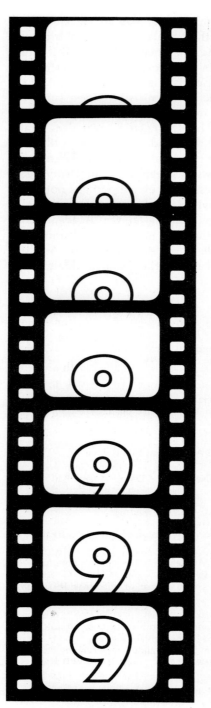

THE ANTIPOPULAR ARTS

The historical processes that brought the cinema into being affected every level of culture and every branch of the arts. The new audience for art, and the new art that developed to please that audience were, in the long view, a consequence of industrialization and urbanization, both of which were in turn the social consequences of new kinds of knowledge. Knowledge, like money, tends to be unevenly distributed among factions in any society. As the popular arts responded to the new audiences and markets for entertainment, more "serious" artists responded to both the new knowledge and the new social realities in ways that split the arts internally. The result was modernism. Understanding modernism is not necessary for grasping how cinema came into being as a synthesis of popular theater, photography, and popular fiction. But to understand the relationships of cinema to its neighboring arts and the ways in which the cinema has evolved, a grasp of modernism's evolution is necessary. Although cinema began purely as a popular entertainment medium, its evolution into a sophisticated art form was influenced by cross-fertilization with literary and theatrical developments outside the bounds of popular entertainment. These developments began long before the cinema came into existence.

FROM PATRONAGE TO PENURY: ART AND THE INDUSTRIAL REVOLUTION

Serious artists until the Industrial Revolution relied on patronage for financial support. The artist who relied on patronage no doubt lived a precarious and often humiliating existence; those with the money to "keep" artists as aesthetic servants often treated them as just that—servants. No box office could be so fickle as a patron on whose whims an artist's career hung. But at the same time, patronage allied artists with those in social and political power. By association if not in fact, artists believed their work to be important and even morally efficacious. Artists and their patrons shared values and outlooks; they belonged to similar social (though usually not economic) circles. With the rise of industrial economies, patronage died as a source of support for the arts. Art became like everything else—a commodity in the marketplace. And while artists could now support themselves independent of the notions of individual employers, the people for whom they had to work in order to stay alive were hardly the cultured elite. It was the bourgeoisie who patronized the art that made money. And so artists were faced with a central, though rarely articulated, choice: work for the bourgeoisie or else reject the bourgeoisie and find some other "public." The choice of Pixérécourt, Daguerre, Henry Irving, Belasco, Dumas, Balzac, Poe, Hugo, Dickens, and innumerable other playwrights, painters, and writers, was to work as popular artists. This meant taking the middle class seriously. It also meant working within the taste structures and conventions of melodrama, decorative and illustrative art, and romantic realism. To reject the middle class meant to make paintings no one bought and novels virtually no one read. It meant working for oneself and for other artists and cognoscenti, and hoping that some day a larger public would appreciate one's work. To a remarkable extent, the important aesthetic developments of the second half of the nineteenth century came from artists and writers who chose the latter path.

For many, rejection of bourgeois values was the only honest choice. Viewed from the perspective of classical aesthetics, the middle class has never been inspiring. Money-grubbing, ambitious, prone to self-justifications out of alignment with reality, and perfectly willing to remain ignorant of whatever is displeasing, the middle class has never been the ideal audience for any art that proposes to be honest. What the middle class wants of art is entertainment after a hard day's work. And what the lower classes want has even less to do with "the truth." After a day on one's feet, it is hardly soothing to be told how rough life is. What is wanted is spectacle, excitement, strong emotions, laughter, and above all, escape. In the nineteenth century as now, it was one thing to deliver entertainment in popular terms and another to work according to the tenets of one's own artistic, social, and intellectual conscience. The revolution in thinking that created and paralleled the Industrial Revolution did not create the sort of ideas that would reap rewards at the box office. To "be" modern, to live according to one's sense of reality, meant (and still means) being subversive. In bourgeois terms, modernist art therefore looks like a product of uncertainty, doubt, and pessimism. It exists in violent opposition to the optimism at the heart of popular entertainment.

A REVOLUTION IN THOUGHT

There have been two major revolutions in Western thought: the Copernican, and the revolution I call, for lack of a better term, "modern." While the Copernican revolution said in essence that humankind is not the center of the universe, the revolution in modern thought went further, saying in essence that we are in no position to be certain about *anything*. Everything is relative, a matter of appearances that are, a priori, untrustworthy. Common sense is no guide to what is real.[1]

No single person was responsible for the modern revolution. It was both intellectual and technological. The steam engine, electric motor, railroad, telegraph, telephone, and automobile (along with the mechanization of industry) were destroying the fabric of social structures while thinkers were throwing bombs at intellectual and religious certainties. The social instability brought by technology altered consciousness as much as did the intellectual changes spurred by men such as Pasteur, Darwin, Freud, Einstein, and, later, Heisenberg. Each major thinker in the last two centuries has subverted faith in common sense. Pasteur showed that much of reality cannot be apprehended by the naked eye; physicians of every stripe have shown that a human being is not something to be understood simply by looking at one or by being one. Darwin exploded the old notions of our place in nature. Freud wrecked our sense of people as reasonable animals. Einstein undermined the rationalistic physics of Newton: not only did reality become relativistic, it became a matter of curves rather than nice straight lines. Heisenberg showed that symbol systems are always inadequate for representing reality; to describe physical elements accurately at the atomic level, one often has to use more than one mutually contradictory mental picture. Nor can one be "objective." One always enters and changes whatever situation one attempts to investigate. A hundred—ten thousand?—other thinkers took virtually every other traditional certainty and turned them into doubts. In the early nineteenth century, most scientists felt that science was progressively reducing the realm of the unknown. But now the sanest of thinkers would have to admit that the universe is a mystery. Everything we find out reveals just how much more there is that we know nothing about.

A NEW KIND OF ART

The result for art? What Keats admired in Shakespeare and called "negative capability"—the ability to function in a world with few certainties—became the badge of the modernist artist. The artist who would be honest at all costs had no choice but to build art on an aesthetics of uncertainty.

The first thing that fell apart was the artist's pose of omniscience. The attitude of the traditional artist was that of a father, guiding his viewer, reader, or watcher toward some sort of higher wisdom. The modernist artist has made a business of proclaiming the limits of any single point of view, even of any single meaning. In literature, omniscience gave way to an ascetic and disciplined pluralistic indeterminism. Everything is seen, presented, and limited by imperfect people in positions where they cannot know the true sequence and meaning of events. In Henry James's fiction, the narrator tells only what *he* knows. Often, as in *What Maisie Knew*, the narrator's biases are so obvious that the reader discerns the story not only through but despite him. In Conrad, how characters see is as important as what they see. Dos Passos juxtaposed the points of view of different social classes and media to try to accumulate composite perspectives on single events. Virginia Woolf, in *To the Lighthouse*, examined a single event from several perspectives and from two points distant in time; from each "storyteller's" mind, the event looks different. In James Joyce's hands, the ironic possibilities inherent in language itself become a way of looking at reality in several ways at once. Writers began to pluralize "truth" and even put it in quotes. For Strindberg, no promise exists that the viewer can know the full meanings of any of the characters' acts. As he puts it in the preface to *Miss Julie:*

> What will offend simple minds is that my plot is not simple, nor its point of view single. In real life an action . . . is generally caused by a whole series of motives, more or less fundamental, but as a rule the spectator chooses just one of these—the one which his mind can most easily grasp or that does most credit to his intelligence. A suicide is committed. Business troubles, says the man of affairs. Unrequited love, say the women. Sickness, says the invalid. Despair, says the down-and-out. But it is possible that the motive lay in all or none of these directions, or that the dead man concealed his actual motive by revealing quite another, likely to reflect more to his glory.[2]

And what an author such as Strindberg "means" can have no single valid interpretation either. The total effect of the new lack of omniscience and the pluralism was to make the viewer's or reader's own position "unsafe." He could never be certain or secure about the realities of the artistic experience. He could posit no false superiority to what he read or saw. He simply had to take it as it came, and find in it what he could.

Dropping the pose of omniscience, artists also dropped old notions of what was properly the subject of art. The Impressionist painters not only offended the bourgeoisie by refusing to pretend that painting should represent common-sense visual realities. They also painted subjects hardly within the canon of the "pretty" in art. The nude had long been a standard subject for painting. But Degas's Post-Impressionist vision of a woman washing her armpit—*that* was a blow at propriety (9–1). Who could be certain of what the proper subjects for art were? Or what the artist's point of view should be? Even Van Gogh, whom the bourgeoisie have absorbed into acceptable decorative art, swirled paint on the canvas so vehemently that none could mistake his portraits for real people or even for the work of a normal mind (9–2).

Picasso not only made the inhabitants of a whorehouse the "subject" of *Les Demoiselles d'Avignon,* but slammed together on a single canvas a synthesis of several points of view and mental states; there is not the slightest pretension of a single illusionistic perspective or perceptual base (9–3). And Dali follows the subconscious by melting time and space into dream fusions not only horrifying in their intensity, but unidentifiable in terms of their relationship to reality (9–4). From the last quarter of the nineteenth century on, even the frames around paintings had lost their function. By the first quarter of the twentieth century, the relationships of art to reality had become so utterly ambiguous that they could be treated as a joke—as Braque showed by painting a nail image into one of his paintings so it would have something to "hang from."

In order to find and create meanings, artists in every medium went outside the bounds not only of politeness but of tradition itself. Manet and his followers ignored perspective, realistic light sources, and traditional painting techniques. The result was a kind of painting that showed subjects not as a camera might, but rather as the artist's consciousness envisioned them. Inhibitions dropped as artists stopped worrying about what was salable or acceptable: working for themselves, artists had the freedom to take on just about any subject, on just about any terms.

And why not? With photography as an alternative source of "realistic" images, painters had lost their monopoly on everything but painting. With the new visual theater and cheap popular literature to satisfy the large buying public, artists with a personal vision of quality had nothing to protect but their own integrity. Artists had to work for themselves and for other artists. As the social situation of art changed, artists began to band together, with writers watching what painters were doing, and painters reading poets, and all of them drinking and eating together in the same cafés. Art became producer-oriented; there was no longer any real difference between producer and consumer. In this context, as André Malraux writes in *Museum Without Walls,* artists became judgeable in terms not of their ability to represent reality but rather of their ability to convey personal visions. A painting became, in Malraux's terms, "not an object but a voice."

Once the world's perceptual significations became something not to represent but to explore and rethink, the world was forced to reveal new meanings. Richard Wasson's description of what happened in poetry is applicable to all the arts:

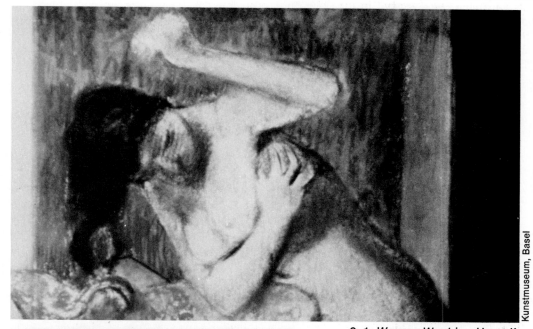

Kunstmuseum, Basel

9–1. *Woman Washing Herself* (1892, Edgar Degas).

Kunstmuseum, Basel

9–2. *Head of a Woman* (1887, Vincent van Gogh).

9–3. *Les Demoiselles d'Avignon* (1907, Pablo Picasso). Oil on canvas, 8' x 7'8".

9–4. *The Persistence of Memory* (1931, Salvador Dali). Oil on canvas, 9½" x 13".

The symbolist poets started with the romantic discovery that landscapes could be used to symbolically project psychological states. . . . The symbolists discovered that every word, every object contained what Joyce called epiphanies and that the careful artist, impersonally and painstakingly juxtaposing words and images, could reveal their symbolic secrets. Every rusty boot on the shore of the snotgreen sea, every smell of steak in passageways, contained a potential epiphany and was part of a symbolic universe, the signs of which the poet was adept at reading.[3]

The only problem was that poets, novelists, and painters had no way of measuring the validity of individual epiphanies. Many poets and painters, ranging from Baudelaire to Rimbaud, from the Impressionists to the Fauves, insisted on their right to be unreasonable—of what use was reasonableness in a world of uncertainties? The only way that issues of style and content could be "decided" was by the intuitions of artists. And so ways of dealing with art became a matter of groups of artists declaring, virtually by fiat, what art should be. The result was a string of "isms," each succeeding the last one and living a short life before becoming outmoded by yet another: Impressionism, Post-Impressionism, Symbolism, Fauvism, Expressionism, Cubism, Surrealism, Abstract Expressionism—the list continues to the present.

THE RESULTS OF MODERNISM

The whole phenomenon of artists being thrown together as antibourgeois outcasts had several interesting results. First, of course, was a great deal of new art and new kinds of art. A remarkable number of maverick artists turned out to be geniuses. Secondly, artists became aware of one another, and one another's arts, in entirely new ways. Before modernism, artists had not been separate from their publics but rather from one another. In their modernist versions, the arts now reverberated in entirely unprecedented ways; one speaks of Symbolism as a movement in painting and the theater as well as in poetry. The third and longest-lived result was that painters in contact with poets became more aware of the potentials of their own medium. Artists became media-conscious. Art became not a matter of reality, or ideas, but of perception, artistic language, and medium. Paul Valêry puts the point in a primitive but apt manner:

> The great painter Degas often repeated to me a very true and simple remark by Mallarmé. Degas occasionally wrote verses, and some of those he left were delightful. But he often found great difficulty in this work accessory to his painting. . . . One day he said to Mallarmé: "Yours is a hellish craft. I can't manage to say what I want, and yet I'm full of ideas. . . ." And Mallarmé answered: "My dear Degas, one does not make poetry with ideas, but with *words.*"[4]

The result of media-awareness was a kind of art that existed to explore a medium. Joyce's *Finnegans Wake* took on the medium of written language, no holds barred. Pirandello's *Six Characters in Search of an Author* was in essence an analysis of theater. A hundred painters asked, "what is painting?" and made the question not only the foundation but the subject of their work.

How much of the modernist revolution came about because of the existence of new forms of popular art and new media such as photography? Did art have no choice but to become "subjective"? I doubt it. Modernism was, in part, a response to the new situation of the artist, of his having lost organic contact with a public. But the real sources of the modernist revolution stemmed from new kinds of knowledge, new social structures, and a new situation in the arts. Modernism was one of three available choices. An artist could be oriented toward the popular. Or he could ignore the new altogether and continue in "academic" or "classical" traditions—and I do not mean to suggest that this choice did not exist, though artists who chose it ordinarily got neither wealth nor the approbation of the avant-garde. So-called "academic" painting flourished alongside both popular pictorial art and modernist painting; and traditional literature was anything but dead during the rise of the popular arts and of modernism. The third choice was to work against respectability and the popular terms of the bourgeoisie, against the decorative and the nostalgic. The modernists chose to be subversives, and probably would have made this choice whether or not figures such as Pixérécourt and Daguerre had existed. They were, quite simply, bored with what passed for either the respectable or the popular in art. The Impressionists and Post-Impressionists had nothing against photography; many of them used it for their own personal explorations.[5] Photography was new. It obviated the necessity of artists' portraying perceptions in ordinary ways and was, in effect, an ally of modernism. What the modernist rebellion amounted to was a rebellion against the nostalgic, the bland, the dishonest, the banal. And this rebellion predated the existence of the cinema by a good half century. It continues even now.

TAMING MODERNISM

The ironies of history have not, however, left modernism alone. Just as new audiences were found for popular arts, so were new audiences created for modernism—or rather, for slightly old modernism. The subversive becomes respectable in time. The Impressionists and then the Post-Impressionists and then their descendants found their way into museums and art history courses. Literary rebels who had hurled challenges at standards of taste were fairly soon incorporated into curricula. Even the bourgeoisie eventually came around. If there is anything the middle class respects, it is financial success; the prices modernist paintings have commanded in the last few decades are staggering. A modernist who lived long enough, and was chosen as a "great," could become rich and respectable. With the rise of universities, the promotion of modernist works by dealers such as Kahnweiler, and the assent of museums and professors, modernism itself became respectable. People who live in middle-class ways—for example, professors—have learned to identify with modernist movements by retraining their eyes and minds to see in modernist ways. In the process, they have come to identify vicariously with the producers, rather than the consumers, of art—especially modernist art. The result has been a revolution in taste and in critical approaches to the arts.

Modernist painters and writers worked for themselves, for a community of artists and cognoscenti. They refused to identify with the bourgeoisie, with the users or consumers of art. As a public for modernist art grew, it learned to assume producers' attitudes toward art, seeing works in terms that are similar to those (or which try to be similar to those) of the artists themselves. If artists would not come to the public, the public had to come to the artist. The triumph of modernism has been in making us view certain kinds of art in terms dictated by its creators.

To identify with modernist art, however, is far different from identifying with popular art, where the producer exists to service the consumer. Ironically, even among those whose business is art consumption—curators, collectors, professors, students—and who are incapable of producing art themselves, the producer's viewpoint has triumphed. This creates enormous problems in any contemporary comparison of modernist art and popular art.

The terms of the battle between modernism and popular entertainment were fairly simple. Modernism advocated honesty; popular art advocated pleasing the public. Modernist art had as its main purpose exploration; popular art existed as a commodity, a way of making money. Modernism promotes radical individualism. Popular forms of art promote what is common to all, and value the crowd.

The cinema inherited the values and purposes of the older popular arts. But modernism triumphed in those circles whose business it is to criticize, explain, and promote art. Thus, though the cinema is the most modern of arts in a historical sense, its value structure has existed virtually outside the bounds of what is thought to be "art." "Art" has become synonymous with modernist value structures.

No art since 1800 has existed in purely modernist forms. But one would hardly guess that by sitting in on literature or art classes. To resolve the contradiction between the modernist and the popular, teachers and critics have learned to ignore the popular branches of theater, literature, and painting, regarding them as "sub-art" species. But film historians and critics have had no way of avoiding a confrontation with the popular, user-oriented history of the movies. Except for a few early avant-garde movements, there was no such thing as a modernist cinema until after World War II. The position of film among the arts has therefore been difficult to assess; from a producer-oriented, modernist perspective, few films or film makers can be regarded as worth studying at all. Film theorists have tried to dodge the problem by creating a producer-oriented approach to popular film makers, the so-called *auteur* theory, which values film directors by showing how individualistic they are—how they resemble modernist artists. But that is only a dodge, which does not solve the problem of a conflict between popular value structures and modernist ones. To identify with the driver is one thing, with the passenger, another.

Thus the conflict between the popular and the modern is double. It involves a conflict between two purposes for art. And it involves a conflict for criticism. How can one see a producer-oriented modernist art and consumer-oriented popular art in terms that are not weighted toward one or the other?

Modernism has triumphed among those who care to think about the arts. The problems this triumph causes for assessing film's place among the arts is the subject of the next two chapters.

NOTES: CHAPTER NINE

[1] For a more radical version of the world view behind modernism, see Amos Vogel, *Film as a Subversive Art* (New York: Random House, 1975), chapter 1.

[2] August Strindberg, Preface to *Miss Julie*, in *The Modern Tradition*, ed. Richard Ellmann (New York: Oxford University Press, 1965), p. 291.

[3] Richard Wasson, "Marshall McLuhan and the Politics of Modernism," *Massachusetts Review*, 13, 4 (Autumn 1972): 574.

[4] Paul Valéry, "Poetry and Abstract Thought," in *The Art of Poetry*, trans. Denise Folliot, vol. 7, *The Collected Works of Paul Valéry*, ed. Jackson Mathews (Princeton, N.J.: Princeton University Press, 1958), p. 63.

[5] See Aaron Scharf, *Art and Photography* (Baltimore: Penguin Books, 1974).

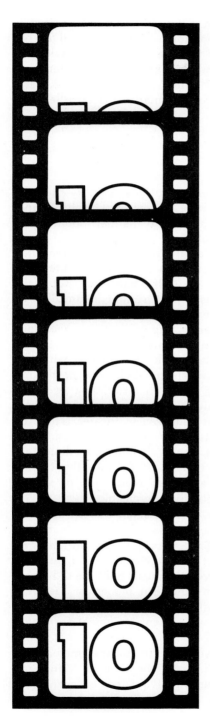

CINEMA AND LITERATURE

It is virtually impossible to write a history of the cinema as anything but a popular art form. Though many of the cinema's greatest works have failed to be popular, the mainstream of film aesthetics has always been bourgeois; film has always been oriented toward pleasing its consumers. But literature, as the term is ordinarily used, has antipopular connotations. Dime novels, stories in mass-market magazines, pulp fiction, and best-selling novels aimed at a popular audience are regarded as little more than sub-literary, except of course by the publishing industry, which, to survive, has had to adapt, if unspokenly, to the realities of the marketplace. When we use the term literature, we use it as literature departments do—as a term that connotes "quality" as much as it does "written fiction and poetry." Quality is defined as what is worth studying. And what is worth studying in the modern period, if course syllabi are any indication, is, in the main, modernist literature. Thus to compare cinema and literature is, from the outset, to compare a popular with a modernist form. Though such a comparison is virtually a priori a comparison of opposites—of apples and oranges, to use the popular phrase—it is still worth making, for two reasons. First, it highlights the differences in the value structures of popular art and modernist literature. And second, it reveals that despite opposed values and functions, the arts have evolved in ways that parallel one another, no matter the taste level of the arts involved.

OPPOSED AESTHETICS

It would be difficult to find arts more different in social sensibility than the early film and modernist literature. Movies were a direct extension of nineteenth-century popular art. Modernist literature was neither popular nor attuned to the Victorian morality that popular art assumed, virtually as a convention. James Joyce's Molly Bloom is a far different kind of animal than D. W. Griffith's Lillian Gish. The moral structures of modernist literature were relativistic and often liberal; liberation was itself a battle cry. But in the early cinema, the moral codes of Victorianism were simply assumed, even though this meant that there usually were only three kinds of women: virgins, mothers, and—horror of horrors—vamps. Similarly, the conventions of melodrama allowed little gray area between heroes and villains (10–1 a, b). Modernist literature was committed, on the whole, to dealing with the present. The cinema was committed to fantasizing about the past. Film comedy was an exception, but even comedy relied on melodrama as a foil. And melodrama was, intellectually, a banal idea system, bankrupt from birth, and in no better shape in the cinema than it had been in theater. Thus the literary critic I. A. Richards could, with little fear of contradiction, lump together "bad literature, bad art, the cinema," and call film "a medium that lends itself to crude rather than sensitive handling." Because the cinema embraced entertainment values rather than a serious exploration of serious problems, most littérateurs felt it to be intellectually indefensible.

There were exceptions, of course. James Joyce loved silent comedy and may even have used it as a source of ideas. Vachel Lindsay was so fascinated by the film medium that, in 1915, he wrote the first important book on film, *The Art of the Moving Picture.* Though T. S. Eliot felt the cinema was a threat to the existence of real popular theater (Eliot loved the music hall), he did praise the Marx Brothers, and even befriended Groucho. But modernist literature was based above all on a valuing of literacy; it was essentially a mandarin art aimed at the elite. The cinema, in contrast, was an entertainment form that accepted the sensibility of those it entertained.

The terms of opposition between modernist literature and the cinema were based on different notions about perception. From the time of Manet on, modernism promoted the idea that perception is individuated: everyone sees differently. The public arts proceeded from the view that people *do* share

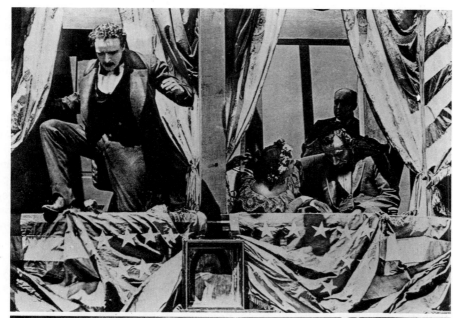

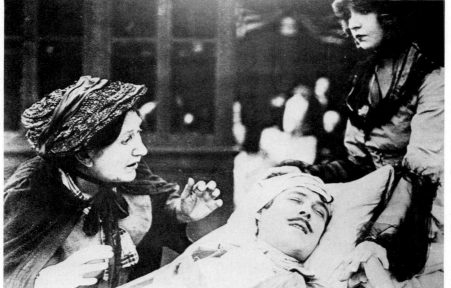

Museum of Modern Art, Film Stills Archive

10–1. *The Birth of a Nation* (1915, Griffith). (a) The death of Lincoln. The distinction between villains and heroes was clear-cut: Who could be more dastardly than Lincoln's assassin? (b) The wounded hero. Here, Griffith used two-thirds of melodrama's female types, a mother and a virgin, both tending a wounded hero.

perceptions; an art such as the cinema could not work at all if everyone saw completely different things in the same series of pictures. Kuleshov's famous experiments proved that people do interpret pictures predictably. A shot of a smiling man followed by a shot of a baby will be taken to be a picture of a proud parent; the same first shot, followed by a shot of a corpse, will be taken to be a picture of a sadist or pervert. If we did not interpret pictures in pretty much the same ways, an art form based on pictures would be a contradiction in terms. But there is truth in both the modernist and the popular view. Meanings are conventionalized. But conventionalization works only if it is accepted by the viewer. The modernist writer made it his business to be exceptional, to see in new ways. And going beyond the conventional, he did go beyond what can be publicly meaningful in predictable ways. To present new visions and to be understood by everyone—*those* are contradictions. It takes time for a broad public to learn new terms in which to see. There are limits to how new perceptions can be and still be communicable to more than a few people. Conversely, there are limits to what can be said using terms that a great many people know.

Because modernist art was, by habit and necessity, producer-oriented, writers accepted unpopularity and often even courted it. In *Finnegans Wake,* to cite an extreme example, Joyce blithely used an invented language based on six spoken languages. Joyce's knowledge of these languages gave him the right to combine them in a work of literature. If it took a reader a lifetime to figure out the book—well then, it took a lifetime. Contrast Joyce's attitude with the attitudes necessary for moviemaking—a movie has to be apprehended and comprehended in a single sitting—and one has, in high relief, the difference between the values of modernist literature and those of the early cinema. Writing for himself and for people like himself, the modernist could assume deep literacy and use it. Joyce's *Ulysses* not only uses Homer's *Odyssey* as a reference system; the last third is virtually a parody of the history of literature. To appreciate *Ulysses* fully, one has to know at least a good chunk of what Joyce was referring to, as well as have a fairly sophisticated vision of what he was doing with it. To understand a modernist such as Joyce, one almost has to adopt Joyce's terms for his own art. The foremost of those terms is a sophisticated knowledge of literature.

In contrast, no early film maker could expect his audience to be literate. In fact, literacy was probably a deterrent to appreciation. Georges Méliès's ten-minute version of *Gulliver's Travels* does leave out a good bit of the original. What matters in popular art is, quite simply, what the audience knows and expects. Film makers such as Porter and Griffith could turn everything into melodrama, and so much the better for audience response. Griffith could even adapt from poets—for example, Robert Browning. Why not? Griffith's audience had never read Browning, and there were good stories to be had in the poetry. Above all, the cinema had to refer to the experiences and ideals of its audience if it was to communicate. Thus Porter's *The Kleptomaniac, The Life of an American Fireman,* and *The Ex-Convict* were tuned to the problems, values, and tastes of ordinary workmen, and, as the following sequence shows, are understandable in the broadest visual terms (10–2).[1] A fire breaks out, the alarm is sounded, the firemen race to the scene, a woman is saved. One does not need six languages to grasp the broad appeal and force of such materials. Nor does one need literary or any other kind of sophistication. The pictures tell a story, tell it well, and leave the matter at that.

This is not to say that early cinema did not have value biases. Rather, the biases were for common experience and viewpoints. Thus, Mack Sennett built his comedies around the familiar figures of urban life, mostly cops and cars. Chaplin built films such as *The Immigrant* around experiences, fears, and hopes shared by hundreds of thousands of new arrivals to the land from which modernists such as T. S. Eliot and Ezra Pound had exiled themselves. Whatever was common coin was usable, as Griffith proved with *The Birth of a Nation*, an immensely popular, albeit morally execrable, masterpiece of racist

10–2. *The Life of an American Fireman* (1903, Edwin S. Porter).

Museum of Modern Art, Film Stills Archive

art, in which the Ku Klux Klan are heroes and blacks are villains (10–3). Rather than the wit, ambiguity, and irony valued by modernists, film makers preferred humor, bathos, and spectacle. A cast of thousands worked as well for Griffith in *Intolerance* as a cast of hundreds had for Belasco: spectacle was box office (10–4). The movies were the stepchildren of Pixérécourt and Daguerre. Although history made movies a modern art, there was nothing modernist about them.

STRUCTURAL SIMILARITIES

The structures and forms of modernist literature, however, do show a striking resemblance to the structures and forms of the silent cinema. Media-awareness and exploration had been factors in literature, as they had been in all the arts, popular and modernist alike, for half a century. Because film and literature are both "printed" media forms, their structural and formal possibilities proved remarkably similar. This has led some critics to claim that modernist literature has been influenced by the cinema. But analysis of literary texts and movements indicates that literature has instead developed in ways parallel to cinema. Furthermore, it might have taken this path whether or not films existed.

The literary revolution that began in the nineteenth century questioned the nature of literary media. It was a radical step for Mallarmé to say to Degas that one does not make poetry with ideas but with words. But in the growth of media-awareness a second distinction became necessary: the distinction between written and aural speech. By the time Edison invented the phonograph, which would do for the world of sound what Daguerre's photographic process did for the visual world, writers had begun to become aware of the choice between print and sound. When we read a sonnet by Shakespeare or a poem by Keats, we have to read "out loud." Even if we make no sound, we imagine the sounds and the feel of the aural textures. Although print can merely suggest the stresses, intonations, rhythms, accents, and idioms of speech, the old prosodies and prose styles were patterned after spoken language. Alliteration, assonance, rhyme, and the rhythm of regular lines all have as their basis a suggestion of spoken language. But in the beginning of this century writers seemed to realize that printed language has *two* sensory possibilities: the aural suggestion, and the graphic. Many writers continued to work on the basis of aural suggestion: Conrad and Yeats are examples. Others, however, chose to work for the reading eye, as well as, or instead of, for the ear. Here the best examples are the novelists Joyce and Hemingway, and the Imagist poets. Joyce (and later Dos Passos) took the mosaic structure of the newspaper and potential control over spacing and typeface, and from it, built part of the aesthetic of *Ulysses*. Hemingway took the monotone of the printed page and made it a keystone of style; with this monotone he could achieve in print what Cézanne had achieved by a radically flattened painting style.

10–3. *The Birth of a Nation.*

10–4. *Intolerance* (1916, Griffith).

It is easy to confuse print-oriented literary structures such as stream of consciousness with cinematic forms. The reason is that film is also a printed form, and is susceptible to the same kinds of organization as print-oriented language. For example, Imagist poetry, in its "standard" format, centered whole poems around visual images that built montage patterns into a single "super-image." In the classic "red wheelbarrow poem" by William Carlos Williams, we see a brilliant example of the form:

> so much depends
> upon
>
> a red wheel
> barrow
>
> glazed with rain
> water
>
> beside the white
> chickens[2]

At first glance the poem appears to be a telegram aspiring to become a photograph. Like a photograph, the poem is ideogrammatic and complete in itself; it draws attention inward, centripetally, rather than throwing attention toward the outside world. Like a film sequence, the language is cut into fragments and restructured into a new composite. The images form an expressive montage in which the total effect is a new idea hardly contained in the sum of the component parts. But the poem is neither photographic nor filmic. The source of its structure is printed language. The wheel/barrow break is solely verbal: barrow is a component in a word concept—wheelbarrow—and is not in itself a separate image. Rain/water and white/chickens are also "purely" verbal breaks; in a photograph, rain water could not be separated into rain and water, and white could not be seen separately from whatever was white. The stanzas separate qualities within the overall image, not objects within a field. In a photograph a red wheelbarrow glazed with rain water would be apprehended in a single glance—not in the two glances Williams uses. Similarly, the breaks within wheelbarrow and rain water would rarely occur in speech —such word combinations are spoken as single words. Even without the purely conceptual "so much depends/upon" the poem is neither a verbal movie nor a poem to be heard; rather it is a testament to the possibilities of poetry as a purely printed form.

Structurally, all visual, printed media are similar. The eye takes in image concepts one at a time. Each one is modified by the next as well as by grammatical signals and conventions. The structures of cinema and of printed verbal language are similar, at least in a few respects. Yet similarity is not grounds for saying writing is cinematic, because if influence does occur, it is virtually impossible to make a formal proof, because the repertories of film and printed language share so much. If Griffith had not carried Dickens about with him on the set, we would have a hard time proving Dickens influenced him. Therefore, as Richard Wilbur warns, attributing this or that writing technique to cinematic influence is dangerous:

> The enthusiasts of the pittoresco at the close of the eighteenth century, rapturously arranging the landscape in their Claude glasses, were conscious of the imposition; the moviegoer walks about taking shots and sequences unaware. The same entrancement characterizes the moviegoer's acquisition of personal style; to put on an Old Vic accent, to ape the gestures of a stage actor or actress—these involve some deliberate imposture, but to smoke like George Raft, to lift the eyebrows like Cary Grant—that is another and more hypnotized order of suggestion.[3]

When influence seems deepest it is often the least provable. For example, reading James Joyce's *Ulysses*, one repeatedly spots images that remind one of cinema, as in the following passage: "Stephen and Bloom gaze in the mirror. The face of William Shakespeare, beardless, appears there, rigid in facial paralysis, crowned by the reflection of the reindeer antlered hatrack on the wall."[4] Knowing that Joyce frequented movies, and remembering that mirror comedy is a film staple (for a post-silent version, see the Marx Brothers' *Duck Soup*), one guesses that Joyce may have been inspired by film. But the guess is just a guess. The movie screen's two-dimensionality can cause images to become synthetic units. But a real mirror is two-dimensional, too. And the image is not purely cinematic: the negative "beard*less*," for example, is achievable only in verbal language; a film image cannot show a beard and the absence of a beard at the same time. On formal and structural grounds and without additional evidence from biographical or other sources, influence from the cinema to literature or vice versa is unprovable. When media have parallel structural possibilities and parallel patterns of historical development, influence can be "found" where none exists. And influence can be missed even though it actually occurred.

THE CINEMA AS LITERARY METAPHOR

The cinema has, of course, become a source of literary metaphor and simile. For example, in Ford Madox Ford's *A Man Could Stand Up*, cinematic experience is evoked to explain Tietjen's sense of time during an artillery explosion. "It was slow, slow, slow . . . like a slowed-down movie."[5] Lawrence Durrell's *Justine* contains a similar example, though one that is more interesting philosophically: "('Are people,' writes Pursewarden, 'continuously themselves, or simply over and over again so fast that they give the illusion of continuous features—the temporal flicker of the old silent film?')"[6] In *U.S.A.* John Dos Passos labels certain sections "Newsreel" and others "The Camera Eye." Though the sections have nothing to do with either real newsreels or what any camera can see, Dos Passos uses the labels to invoke a sensation of movies; he asks his reader to associate cinema with the noncinematic content and form of the sections. The Newsreel sections are collages of doggerel, tabloid newspaper-style headlines, and reportage. The form and content are like a newspaper. What is like a newsreel is the structure. The mosaic of a newspaper page is funneled into a single sequence, with the "news" reeling down the page, though more as a drunk reels down the street than as a film reels off its spool. The Newsreel sections are news nightmares. Similarly the Camera Eye sections take literary content and form as their base and suggest not real film but the film*like*. One sequence goes like this:

> when you walk along the street you have to step carefully always on the cobbles so as not to step on the bright anxious grassblades easier if you hold Mother's hand and hang on to it that way you can kick up your toes but walking fast you have to tread on too many grassblades the poor hurt green tongues shrink under your feet.[7]

There is nothing photographable in the content; the form is literary stream of consciousness. But there is a filmlike quality to the passage. Photography freezes and preserves perceptual fragments, embalming moments in time. Dos Passos's writing photographs and so preserves sensations. The result is a kind of literary pseudo-cinema, a cinema which can exist only in literature but in which awareness of cinema is essential.

Movies have brought new experiences and thus new themes to the modern artist. The influence of cinema on literature has probably had more to do with psychology than with form or technique: the cinema represents a world in which the subconscious can be represented through artifice. Visual art has always provided icons for literature; cinema provides icons of artifice and "non-behavioral" reality. Because film manipulates appearances through technical means, it not only provides vocabulary for the writer who, like Dos Passos, Ford, or Durrell, wishes to evoke the processes of the mind; it also provides models through which writers can explore the vagaries of reality and illusion. For example, in Iris Murdoch's *Under the Net*, a film community serves as a mirror of the problems of a media-oriented age. The protagonist, Jake, has a dog, three girlfriends, and two other friends who are, were, or intend to be in the movie business, a business with a value system based on manipulating appearances. Of all the "characters," Mars, the Wonder Dog, is the most adept at manipulation. Too old to act in films, he is useful to advertisers because he appears to be what he once was, a movie star. He is that modern phenomenon, the celebrity. Mars is a consummate confidence artist. In one scene in which Jake is in trouble, Mars saves him, not in the usual Lassie adventure-story way, but by being an actor. The police raid a political rally held in a movie studio. Chaos erupts, sets fall over, the police try to arrest everyone. Jake commands Mars to play dead, and Mars collapses. Jake "saves" the dog, carrying it past the police (who will not arrest someone engaged in such a humane act). Once past the police, Jake and Mars run for safety. A crowd of spectators applauds, delighted not only in the artifice but in the "movie" reality of the scene, a reality of fictional appearances. For Murdoch the film world provides a model for the larger contemporary world of appearances, in which people (to borrow R. D. Laing's phrase) can even pretend to be what they really are and in which there are no unmanipulated appearances. At a time when sophistication about role-playing has reached the point that no one can be certain about the authenticity of any experience, the film world becomes a vast metaphor for reality: the movies have escaped their screens and come into the streets.

Has film "influenced" modern writers such as Dos Passos and Murdoch? One can answer two ways. Culturally, film's influence is unquestionable. The existence of film has undoubtedly made writers aware of a great deal that they otherwise might have ignored: of the changing roles of literature in society; of the particularities of their own medium; of the problems of a media-oriented age; of the differences between popular and "high" cultures; of the ways in which the visual world and perception are rife with significance. A writer would have to be blind not to be influenced by movies. But to go beyond questions of awareness and ask if film has had specific "technical" effects on literature is different. To that question we must answer that influence is probable but not provable. Film and literature, as printed forms, share many structural narrative techniques. Because films are often adapted from books, and because film has no genres or traditions that cannot also be found in either literature or theater, it is almost impossible to prove that a writer got a technique or sensibility from film rather than from somewhere else. Murdoch undoubtedly spent a good deal of time thinking about film while constructing *Under the Net*. But no film ever questioned appearances in quite the way Murdoch does. Her concern about appearance and authenticity is evident in the philosophical writing she did before she wrote the novel. And in literature Murdoch's kind of questioning is virtually a tradition; the most important precedent for *Under the Net* was probably Thomas Mann's *The Confessions of Felix Krull, Confidence Man.*

It is easier to discuss the ways in which literature has influenced cinema than to treat film's influence on literature. Historically, cinema developed by taking over what had existed in popular literature and theater. Developments in literature have normally preceded similar developments in film; in no case has the opposite been true. Books come into cinema by way of adaptation. And technologically, film is a postliterary medium: except for the portability of books, there is little in print that films cannot simply appropriate to themselves; but the perceptual basis of film is, a priori, beyond the reach of a word-bound medium. No matter how much a writer tries to be cinematic, what he produces will always look more like literature than film. John Updike's *Rabbit, Run* is a case in point. In a *Paris Review* interview, Updike told Charles Samuels that he meant the book to be "a movie" and even subtitled the first version to indicate his intention. But on examination there is nothing technically movielike about the novel. Updike may have wanted to write a movie-novel. But in the medium of print, he simply could not.

THE CINEMA AS SCAPEGOAT

Cultural influence is easier to prove than technical influence. But even here the case is complicated. Serious modern literature has avoided the nostalgia and romanticism that characterize film's history. Serious novelists have, in the main, avoided writing thrillers for the popular book market. And Hollywood has had a bad literary press. The "Hollywood novel" is inevitably a Hollywood put-down, as, for example: Fitzgerald's *The Last Tycoon*, West's *The Day of the Locust*, Mailer's *The Deer Park*. The literary world took T. S. Eliot's comment about the cinema as "cheap and rapid-breeding" for a truth until film makers such as the neorealists, Fellini, Bergman, and the *nouvelle vague* ("New Wave") directors made film respectable. Only in Italy, France, and Russia have literary and film communities had mutual respect for one another. In France intellectuals such as Cocteau, Sartre, and Malraux have involved themselves in film. But the experience of having classic books adapted into thriller movies and the ready money in writing for Hollywood gave cinema a sleazy reputation. Literary people felt superior to the movies, both culturally and morally. The following anecdote by George Garrett, a dramatist and sometime screenwriter, is indicative of literary condescension toward Hollywood:

> Story is that when Peter Lorre first came to this country and did his first, successful picture, he was asked by the Big Boss what he wanted to do next. He suggested *Crime and Punishment*. Boss said: "Gimme a one-page synopsis and we'll see." Lorre looked around the studio until he found a near moron working in the accounting office. Offered the man fifty bucks if he could deliver a one-page synopsis of *Crime and Punishment* the next day. Just skimming, hitting the high spots. Done. The synopsis read like an old-fashioned thriller (truth in that). Boss read it and, in those days when the Industry was prospering and they were making four or five times as many pictures as they do now (though no more good ones), Boss says to get started. Picture was almost finished before Boss got around to reading the "property" and realized, raging, he had been had.[8]

Though Hollywood's money was important to writers, and though adaptation into film inevitably helped a book's sales, a writer was no more likely to admit that film had influenced his writing than that his married life was modeled on experience in bordellos. Writers did go to work in Hollywood in droves from the 1930s on, but Hollywood probably influenced writers *not* to be obviously cinematic. Hollywood meant "selling out." Even though the experimentalist bent of modernist literature faded in the socially conscious 1930s, writers have maintained the antipopular, antibourgeois bias of serious art, an attitude already established in the 1840s. The guiding myths of serious literature and of popular entertainment have continued to be irreconcilable.

Literary opposition to cinema has not, of course, been monolithic. Writers who, for moral, social, financial, or aesthetic reasons wanted to reach a large public, have borrowed freely from the popular aesthetic of the cinema. In the novels he called "entertainments" because they were aimed at a general reading public, Graham Greene openly emulated the cinema's basic "thriller" structure and pacing. Popular writers working for a movie-saturated audience have had little trouble incorporating the conventions of film storytelling into fiction. In the detective fiction of writers such as Dashiell Hammett and Raymond Chandler, Hollywood's glossy romanticism became a component that worked ironically against a feel for the corruption of the streets. Using Hollywood conventions as one part of their technical arsenal, writers could exploit the moral latitude allowed in print to explore wider moral worlds than those available via Hollywood. And, of course, in consumer-oriented popular fiction, there has been little objection whatever to the attitudes of the popular cinema.

Nevertheless, the producer-oriented ethos of modernist fiction has separated even popular writers from a direct identification with Hollywood or the popular cinema. Even in the most blatantly mass-market fiction, the writer's place is higher than that of the Hollywood writer. In popular fiction, an author can become a name brand, a Chandler, a Jacqueline Susann, or, if both popular *and* a genius, an F. Scott Fitzgerald. In film, writers count for little in the total production machinery, however much the story is still the crucial element in a film's being filmable. Popular writers may create user-oriented art. But they usually refuse to identify with the movies. Or at least they did, until recently, when film became a more respectable—because it became a more modernist—art form.

"Literature" remains a value-laden term. A popular "thriller" writer such as John Le Carré is still regarded as a hack in some circles because he writes genre-based best sellers. Popular fiction shares the disapprobation of all popular art forms. Literature is still a term that many would like to reserve for serious—that is, nonpopular and antibourgeois—works. The split in literary aesthetics between the popular and the serious is based on the question modernist artists began asking in the early nineteenth century: can middle-class culture be taken seriously as a basis for aesthetics? There is now, as there was then, good reason to ask that question; there is, now as then, good reason for answering "no!"

The split between a modernist, antibourgeois, and creator-oriented conception of art and a popular, consumer-oriented conception has, I believe, strongly affected film aesthetics. To be respectable, a work of art must be antibourgeois. Above all, it must be "creator-oriented." Film historians, echoing critics of the other arts, have canonized film makers who have used the cinema to express themselves, as if film were like any other art—a producer-oriented form. With the rise of the independent European cinema in the 1940s and 1950s, and the explosion of independent cinema everywhere in the 1960s, advocates of a creator-oriented cinema have had plenty of film makers to "elevate" to the cinematic equivalent of literary stature. And with the tactic of *auteur* criticism, which exists to prove that even in popular cinema, creator-oriented expression takes place, a relatively large number of directors from all periods of film have achieved such elevation to the status of artists. Significantly, this elevation-by-association process began in France, where the literary community (Cocteau, Prévert, Sartre, and Malraux, among others) had long been involved in film making, and where there were no large splits in the artistic community, as there are in the United States. As film directors become elevated to *auteur* status, literary antipathy to the cinema lessens: cinema begins to resemble literature, with its split between the popular and the modernist elite.

Further (as I shall argue at greater length in Chapter 12) the middle class is becoming diversified and intellectualized through the spread of higher education, electronic communication, and the like. It is debatable how long the split between the "serious" and the "popular" can hold up. And, since the 1950s, the cinema has been absolved because of television: the cinema is no longer the most popular, lower-bourgeois entertainment form in our culture. Because film has lost its old, massive popularity, and because its forms have echoed literature's as the market for literature and cinema became nearly identical (the young, the educated, the urban), the old polarities between literature and cinema have lost their punch.

But there is a danger in seeing the cinema in the popular-versus-serious terms of literary aesthetics. And there is a danger in regarding the cinema as a creator-oriented form. To do so distorts the history and primary aesthetics of most films. To grasp the total relationships of film and literature, one must have a sense of their parallel structural development, their sharing of the same historical culture, their differences as media, and the sense that both literature and the cinema should be looked at through the eyes of both the creator and the consumer. To look at film's position among the arts from the perspective of modernist literature is instructive. But at best, it is only a partial way of looking, and gives a partial view of how cinema works, for whom, and why it has been, for eighty years, a vital art form.

NOTES: CHAPTER TEN

[1] See Lewis Jacobs, "Edwin S. Porter and the Editing Principle," in *The Emergence of Film Art*, ed. Lewis Jacobs (New York: Hopkinson & Blake, 1969), pp. 20–36.

[2] William Carlos Williams, "The Red Wheelbarrow," in *The Selected Poems of William Carlos Williams* (New York: New Directions, 1963), p. 30.

[3] Richard Wilbur, "A Poet and the Movies," in *Man and the Movies*, ed. W. R. Robinson (Baton Rouge: Louisiana State University Press, 1967), pp. 223–224.

[4] James Joyce, *Ulysses* (New York: Modern Library, 1934), p. 567.

[5] Ford Madox Ford, *A Man Could Stand Up* (New York: New American Library, 1964), p. 140.

[6] Lawrence Durrell, *Justine* (New York: Pocket Books, 1975), p. 199.

[7] John Dos Passos, *U.S.A.: The 42nd Parallel* (Boston: Houghton Mifflin, 1948), p. 5.

[8] George Garrett, "Don't Make Waves," in *Man and the Movies*, p. 246.

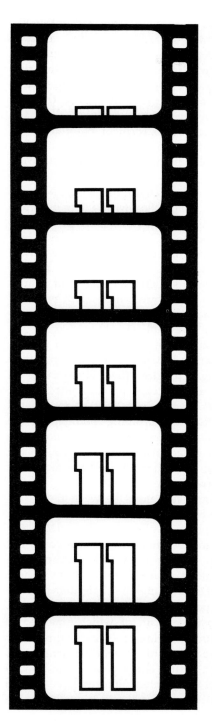

FILM, THE VISUAL ARTS, AND THEATER

THE VISUAL ARTS

The situation of literature vis-à-vis movies is echoed in theater and the visual arts, but with some important distinctions. The early cinema of Griffith and his contemporaries got a good part of its structure and aesthetic from the popular novel, but most of its aesthetics, including its sense of the visual, came from the popular theater. Painting, however, has had little influence on the popular cinema except perhaps in lighting style. With the Impressionists' rejection of bourgeois aesthetics, serious painting moved away from the photographic. Thus potential interchanges with cinema became limited to exchanges with the animated and the optically reprocessed experimental film. In the two periods of strong avant-garde film activity, the 1920s and the 1960s, painting and experimental cinema often shared aesthetic goals. But the history of popular cinema as a visual art can, ironically, be written accurately without reference to modern movements in painting except Surrealism and Expressionism. Surrealist painting has influenced the handling of dream sequences. Expressionism has had a more widespread influence, affecting the visual style of the horror film and of such diverse gothic works as *Citizen Kane* and *The Seventh Seal*. But Expressionism, which involves the projection of mental states into visual terms, is an exception to the rule because it is amenable to theatrical and narrative use, and because it entered the cinema through the theater and thus echoed the previous process through which film acquired visual style, by borrowing from the stage. With the exception of the diorama, painting has never been a form of popular entertainment. Because the cinema borrowed mainly from popular entertainment forms, it evolved with little reference to developments in the modernist visual arts.

Structurally, however, the cinema has shared perceptual concerns with all the other modern arts. All of them have been dissatisfied with a single optical point of view. Movies change shot perspectives sequentially, never sticking with one visual point of view for long. Cubism takes several perspectives into one simultaneously presented picture, juxtaposing subjects and angles without concern for optical consistency. For example, in Picasso's *Violin and Grapes* (1912), objects are fragmented and reconstructed so that their shapes are revealed from a number of advantageous viewpoints; like a film montage sequence, the painting makes sense only when the imagination puts Humpty Dumpty back together into a synthetic conceptual whole (11–1).

Montage in film and literature often is "expressive"—that is, it is a way of juxtaposing different kinds of conceptual reality. In Cubism and Surrealism, a similar juxtaposition occurs, but in a single picture. (See illustrations in Chapter 10.) Many modern painters have also juxtaposed different senses: both Van Gogh and Braque created works with both tactile and visual elements, with the visual forms seen at a distance becoming modified by the tactile and sculptural quality when one moves in close for a good look. The juxtaposition of perspectives and realities is equally important to all the modern arts, whether modernist or popular. Art has come to be a matter of putting fragments of perception together to form new wholes.

Structural parallels aside, it is hard to find resonances between modernist painting and any kind of cinema except the experimental. The visual sense of the cinema originated with theater and photography; by the 1920s, the cinema's visual sense had so evolved along independent lines that it could not be compared with that of the theater, if only because popular melodrama was by then dead and could not follow the cinema in its new directions. There have always been parallels, however, between film makers' heightened sense of the visual and their awareness of other popular visual arts—in particular, cartoons, comic strips, advertising, and poster art, all of which emerged at roughly the same time as the cinema.[1] Just as Hogarth's caricatures and Daumier's satirical drawings helped nineteenth-century narrative artists and stage entertainers find correlations between visual characteristics and social types, so modern illustrations and "narrative" printed pictures have helped inform the cinema, and have also been informed by the movies. With the

11–1. *Violin and Grapes* (1912, Pablo Picasso).
Oil on canvas, 20″ x 24″.

Collection, The Museum of Modern Art, New York.
Mrs. David M. Levy Bequest.

invention of the halftone process in the early twentieth century, photography joined lithography as a source of pictures in print media. Thus the newspapers and especially the magazines of our century have explored the same visual aesthetic as the cinema. (It is a stunning experience to follow the pictorial styles of *Life* magazine and the movies through the period when both were popular; their sense of the visual developed in lockstep.) Commercial photography is commercial photography, whether it rests on a magazine page advertising cigarettes or moves on a screen.

Nevertheless, as the cinema developed it became popular enough to sustain its own visual aesthetic, and its aesthetic would likely have been the same even if other forms of commercial art had not reinforced it. But film was not equally independent of movements in the theater. Particularly since the advent of sound film, the cinema has borrowed writers, directors, actors, and whole plays from the popular Broadway stage. Thus the evolution of cinema and that of the popular theater have coincided, especially in sensibility, throughout this century. But the theater saw the same split between the popular and the serious that occurred in the other arts, and so the relationship between theater and film is double-edged. It has been further complicated by the theater's financial problems. The novel went into paperback to compete with newer, cheaper media forms. Visual art went into printed magazine formats to maintain a grip on popularity. But the theater has never been able to modernize technologically: it is not distributable by mechanized means.

THEATER

Theater has been the only modern art threatened by the existence of movies. It has also, of course, been threatened by radio and television. It is endangered whenever a new medium comes along that is either cheaper for the audience or allows people to be entertained at home. The technology of theater is essentially preindustrial. All media are ways of distributing something, whether efficiently or not, as well as of making it. Theater is a medium that can distribute in only one place at a time; a play must be put on each time it is seen. It takes at least as many people to put on a play now as it did in Shakespeare's time; compared to other modern media, labor costs per audience member are astronomical. Only painting, sculpture, and nonrecorded symphonic music have higher labor costs for the size of their audiences. I can listen to the radio or watch television for nothing or buy a book or go to a film for three or four dollars; except in subsidized theaters, it costs about ten dollars to see a play. And what is more, I have to be there at 8:30; I cannot arrange my viewing according to my leisure schedule. Entertainment is a financial transaction; in our age we have learned not to pay too much for it. We watch trash on television because it's free. A movie has to be worth only a few dollars. But a play has to be worth ten dollars. Only the best popular theater has been able to survive the "hit versus flop" mentality such costs dictate. Though as spectacle (and as a synesthetic form) theater is potentially as powerful as film, attempts to compete on the basis of spectacle have doomed both melodrama and opera—the two most ambitious spectacle theater forms—to be available in only the largest cities or (in the case of opera) in subsidized theaters. The only form of spectacle theater that has thrived has been the Broadway musical, and that has survived by becoming a tourist attraction for New York.

Paradoxically, it is theater's basis of survival that makes it so expensive. The very basis of theater is *not* to fix the performance, not to "print" the performed play. Plays are renewed every night they are performed, and overhauled and updated every time a new performance goes on the boards. The reason Shakespeare still makes good theater is that performances are not fixed in one style forever, like novels frozen in their archaic stylizations. In performance, one can even overcome the handicap of Shakespeare's odd (to us) language. The business that Pound insisted is the writer's—to make it new—is also the theatrician's. The curse and genius of the theater are the same. At every performance the actors come out to see how the audience responds. No two performances are quite alike; no two productions are identical. The production brings the present to the past. And so there is no such thing as archaic theater in the way printed forms such as books and films can be archaic. A ten-year-old film shows its age, frequently looking older than a fifty-year-old play in a fresh production. A time always has its own language; plays continually get fresh translations to keep them new. All plays are adaptations to time. Thus, though sound film should have put theater out of business in 1932 when stage financing became nearly impossible, it did not. A mass-market industry would have been put out of business by film at that time. But theater could hibernate; it could become smaller in scale; it had the habit of perpetual renewal as its base. And so though it could not prosper, it could not be killed.

What happened to modern theater amounts to two stories. Popular melodramatic theater and vaudeville died—or rather, migrated to other media. Film took over melodrama; vaudeville artists survived by going into other media: cabarets, radio, records, movies, and, lately, television. But the serious modern theater—the theatrical branch of the antibourgeois movement in the arts—thrived, not financially of course, but aesthetically. From reading a history of melodrama, one would expect this to be an age when theater was weak because of costs and competition from other media. But in modernist theater, the opposite is the case. John Gassner puts it plainly:

> Until the modern age there were only three truly major periods of dramatic art in some twenty-four centuries of Western theatre: the fifth-century B.C. Athenian, the Elizabethan, and the seventeenth-century French. Ours is the fourth great period. It began in the last quarter of the nineteenth century and has not yet ended.[2]

Gassner points out that our age of great drama has lasted longer and involved more great playwrights and more countries than any of the other great ages of drama. Even if we discount Gassner's view at the usual rate for specialists (to kidney specialists the heart is never the most important organ in the body) his view is strikingly well-founded. The list of important modern playwrights is incredible: Strindberg, Ibsen, Chekhov, Pirandello, García Lorca, Brecht, Hauptmann, Wilde, Shaw, O'Neill, Williams, Miller, Giraudoux, Beckett, Pinter, Ionesco, Synge, O'Casey, Odets, Hellman—the list could go on for a page. What happened? There was enough affluence to support a strong minority theater—a theater of ideas and insights rather than of spectacle. The turbulence and tensions of the modern age have apparently been precisely the right conditions for the creation of great theatrical art.

The stage had been media-conscious since Pixérécourt; the rise of popular melodrama was a self-consciously *theatrical* movement. The literary dimensions of melodrama were never very important; the production, not the play, was the thing. What gave theater its modernist thrust was a little different from the situation in the other arts. Modernist theater began late. The media-awareness of popular theater was an old issue; modernist movements in painting, the novel, and poetry were established. Thus the coming together of theater with seriousness struck with the force of a collision of already-powerful movements. As Gassner points out, the theater movements from which modernist drama evolved were derived from previous movements in the novel. The naturalism and social concern of Zola, Flaubert, and Turgenev, the psychological explorations of Symbolist poetry, and the questioning of perception in modernist painting gave new concerns to playwrights and theatricians alike. Strindberg began to question both the meanings of consciousness and of "real" life; Ibsen and Chekhov followed theatrical realism toward its logical conclusions.

Simultaneous with the emergence of a new kind of playwright, a new sense of production emerged from André Antoine's *Théâtre Libre*, founded in 1887, from the Independent Theatre in London, founded four years later, and from the Moscow Art Theatre, founded in 1897. The "little theater" movement was born, and even in the United States became an aesthetic force by 1915, with the rise of the Provincetown Players and their resident genius, Eugene O'Neill. The modernist stage maintained and explored the theatricalism of Pixérécourt. But it rejected popularity as something to be sought at all costs.

The new theater has not been a spectacle theater, though visual effects have played a large part in its aesthetic. Essentially it has been a theater of ideas and of emotions based on interaction among playwright, acting company, and audience. It has demanded a great deal from its audience: its keystone is intensity. With no orchestra pit to separate viewers from actors, a small elite audience reacts with camaraderie to "its" players. Whereas movies became our large aesthetic supermarkets, with big name brands and cut-rate prices, the theater became a source of specialty goods for the senses, emotions, and mind. Movies became purveyors of dreams; the movie theater became the home of bourgeois voyeurism. Theater became a place to react openly to the modern condition, and to experience an exploration of the interactions between naturalism and the forces of the mind, between public and private realities, between everyday reality and the world of ideas.

The modernist stage is characterized by two qualities: the relevance, even violence, of its ideas; and stylization. At the pivot point between the two has stood the actor: the modern theater has been fully a theater of performance. Sexuality, economics, war, the family—all figure in Brecht and Pirandello as in Strindberg and García Lorca. Our age is a violent one; our theater is its reflection. But the reflection has been in illuminating and distorting mirrors. For example, Bertolt Brecht, in plays such as *Mother Courage,* built an Epic Theater that made no pretense at realistic sets or acting; the audience was to be aware of the sets as stage sets, of the actors as actors playing roles, of the theater as an artificial place, not an imitation of the real world. Brecht's techniques gave playgoers a sense of the difference between theater and reality, and thus enhanced both what could be done with theatrical distortions and what could be said about the reality outside the theater. In Miller's *Death of a Salesman* the characters step through the walls—only suggested by scenery—into the past and into dreams. In Williams's *A Streetcar Named Desire* street scenes appear on the walls as Blanche Dubois becomes deranged. In the theater since 1930 the movements of modernism have been synthesized into an explosive whole: at times expressionistic, at times symbolistic, at times naturalistic, the modern theater has become a place to ask questions of reality, and to ask them from whatever vantage point they need to be asked.

There are no final aesthetic differences between film and theater; every attempt to find some "essential" nature in either medium always founders. But there are real differences in the conditions needed to create theater and film. Theater, reduced to its simplest, involves an actor and someone to watch him. Theater can be done in the street, in a room, anywhere; it does not depend on industrial production. But film requires equipment and film that must be produced by industry; they cannot be home-made. To make film and equipment economically, it must be produced in quantity. One person can go out and make a film alone. But for him to do that, an industry has to exist to provide him with his materials. The larger the industry, the cheaper the materials, as film makers found out when television came into being, and 16 mm. equipment became readily rentable. For an "art" cinema to exist, a large commercial cinema must exist beforehand (a large television industry would have the same effect). Cinema could develop into an art only by beginning as a business, then becoming a mass medium, and then becoming an art. But theater's situation is the diametrical opposite. The more it is "industrialized" —in the way melodrama was industrialized, reliant on the existence of large and mechanically complicated theaters—the more precarious is its existence. Big and complex theaters are expensive to keep going. The rejection of melodrama and the rise of cinema coincided to lift a burden from the modern theater, and to put it back into the hands of playwrights and actors. Film is, first and essentially, a business. But theater is such bad business that it has tended to attract iconoclasts. And that is the strength and source of vitality of the modern stage.

For the theater to be reborn it had to reject Pixérécourt and find new models. Some of those models—Strindberg, Ibsen, the *Théâtre Libre*, the Moscow Art Theatre—were in existence well before the advent of cinema. Others—the Brechtian epic theater, the Pirandellian self-cognizant stage, the modern political cabaret—developed as an antithesis to the cinema. And old models for a freer theater existed and were still viable—above all, the Shakespearean. The result, overall, of the joining of the new models into theater's search for survival has been a theater with three salient features: strong, subversive thought; strong performances by actors; and strong actor-audience interaction. The modernist audience tends to identify with creativity; the modern theater has taken advantage of the identification by making the audience a part of performance itself. Everyone who wants to be simply a consumer for art is watching television or off to the movies anyway. Those who care enough about theater to go are willing to help in its creation.

The proscenium arch of the melodramatic stage is a good place to hang a movie screen. But it is a bad place for the kind of work modern theater requires. The modern theater needs no large spectacle stage. Rather it needs a space for the actors and audience to share their own creativity, their ability to think and react. The cinema freed the stage of its melodramatic past when it took the stage's audience and aesthetic. As a consequence the new theater has become a lively and subversive art. Having no other choice, it made from its dilemma its opportunity.

NOTES: CHAPTER ELEVEN

[1] See John L. Fell, *Film and the Narrative Tradition* (Norman: University of Oklahoma Press, 1974), pp. 89–121.

[2] John Gassner, ed., *A Treasury of the Theatre* (New York: Simon & Schuster, 1963), p. xi.

FUSIONS

Nothing lasts. The cinema began and developed by taking over the aesthetic of melodramatic theater and the popular novel. It became and continues to be mainly a popular art form. But the drive behind cinematic creation is always a drive toward synthesis, toward incorporating everything into the medium of film. Every major film maker in cinema history has done more than simply entertain melodramatically. Every major film maker has gone beyond the main thrust of popular entertainment. The result has been a cinema that has incorporated—albeit slowly, by fits and starts, and in ways that often make borrowing unrecognizable at first glance—a good deal of the sensibility of modernism. When we speak of the art of cinema, we inevitably speak, in part, of the synthesis of modernism with popular sensibilities. The cinema began by stealing the identities of other popular arts. It developed by extending those identities until film could incorporate the "serious" arts into its overall identity.

The story of cinema's assimilation of

modernism is double. Partly it is a story of film makers and movements and changes in the versatility of film production. Partly it is a demographic story: a story of changes in the mass audience at which films are aimed. The immigrants at which Porter aimed his films did not continue to speak their native tongues; films could add sound when everyone in the United States spoke English. The last great waves of immigration were over by World War I; the silent film was no longer necessary by the mid-1920s. Compulsory education raised literacy levels and thus changed the degree to which movements in literature could penetrate popular culture. With the arrival of the paperback in the 1930s and 1940s, and with the spread of magazine-format publications, relatively sophisticated writers such as Ernest Hemingway and Graham Greene could reach a large audience newly ready to read them. Our century's serious literature has become increasingly affordable. Furthermore, affluence levels have risen, and so has the amount of free time available for entertainment. In the last two decades college education has become widespread. Students have met the clash between culture and their bourgeois backgrounds by creating their own syntheses of low-, middle-, and high-browed cultures, and they have demanded similar syntheses in the arts. The grandchildren of immigrants and children of English-speaking middle-class (or would-be middle-class) parents have, in the last few decades, broken down the "purity" of both modernist seriousness and of popular culture; one hesitates to proclaim where the barriers now exist between the two. The cinema has changed because its audience has changed. Television has become what movies once were. With increased urban congestion, the middle class now prefers to stay home at night. Only those less home-bound now frequent films. The cinema still functions as a popular art form, and still carries in every frame its popular melodramatic past. But the meaning of "popular" has changed. Film makers such as Stanley Kubrick, Robert Altman, and Arthur Penn can (and must?) speak in terms unthinkable sixty or even thirty years ago. The result is a cinema not "greater" than earlier cinemas, but great in terms closer to what we consider greatness in serious theater and especially in serious written literature.

The cinema, of course, has never been completely separated from formal movements in serious literature. Directors such as Griffith, Eisenstein, von Stroheim, and Chaplin were hardly illiterates; what was happening in literature and theater has always been a factor in how images are composed and how they are put together. The montage experiments of Joyce, Griffith, and Eisenstein are remarkable in their parallels, and directors such as Eisenstein were the first to point out that fact. Surrealist and Expressionist techniques are as apparent in films as in any other art form: there is nothing in literature more surreal than Buster Keaton's *Sherlock, Jr.* or the end of *Duck Soup*. Expressionistic visuals are as recognizable in 1930s horror films as in the 1920s German stage. Formally and structurally, no art is immune to new techniques, new visions. But the thinking behind modernism—modernism's concerns, intentions, and even preoccupations of a nonformal nature—penetrated the cinema only through an erratic and slow process, largely because it has, until recently, proved antithetical to the aesthetics of mass entertainment.

Four elements have made cinema amenable to influence from literature. Each of the four has involved a response to film's potentials as well as to outside influences. The first is the habit of adaptation that movies inherited from the popular theater. Working from literary models, film makers such as von Stroheim went outside popular conventions to create ambitious films such as *Greed,* which was based on Frank Norris's *McTeague* (12–1). The second element was realism. Film's documentary potential has made it a natural medium for realistic and naturalistic explorations; the influence of literary realism and naturalism (movements that predated the cinema's existence) has been a major force, not only in adaptations—again one might cite *Greed*—but also in more "purely" filmic developments, such as the nonfiction documentary film and neorealism. One of film's greatest potentials has been as a kind of naturalistic literature for the last century. What Zola began and Dreiser continued could be done better in film, if film makers would just do it. Robert Flaherty, the British documentary film makers of the 1930s, Roberto Rossellini, and Vittorio De Sica have been to the cinema what Zola, Norris, Stephen Crane, and Dreiser were to the novel. The *cinéma vérité* movement stands on Zola's shoulders as much as it does on Flaherty's, as much on concern that art respond to its age by describing it accurately as on film's ability to realize that concern.

12–1. *Greed* (1925, Erich von Stroheim).

The third element, again a response both to film's potentials and to extra-filmic factors, can perhaps best be described as the development of an emotionally and intellectually sophisticated populist aesthetic. Good cinema has always spoken to popular concerns in popular terms: it has always respected the intelligence of its audience as well as its desire for entertainment. Griffith, Chaplin, Keaton, von Sternberg, Ford, Hawks, Lubitsch, Clair, Prévert, Renoir, Cocteau, and of course Welles each proved in his own way that film's populist bias is not antithetical to the treatment of serious issues. Genius is genius, forever uncomfortable with the bounds of banality. Serious art has always been distinguished in part by the seriousness of the issues it considered and by the honesty of its viewpoint. In those terms, popular film simply moved into serious literature's territory. There has never been any question whether the greatest film makers were highly literate men. What would have been in question had it not been for a pantheon of great directors was whether the conventions of popular film could "hold" seriousness in the way Shakespeare's popular theater did. Film's greatest directors have proved that film's aesthetic is in no way antithetical to profundity; with that proof film's potentials became increasingly "literary."

The fourth element that made cinema amenable to literary influences was a diversification of cinema's production means. As an industrial system, Hollywood lost its stranglehold on the means of production when television became popular. Both television and technological developments made it possible to produce films outside traditional studio control. Art can be experimental when it is cheap to make. In the last thirty years studio films have become increasingly expensive to produce but, paradoxically, independent films have become cheaper. Werner Herzog's brilliant *The Mystery of Kaspar Hauser,* made in 1974, cost well under $100,000 to complete; shooting costs were under $40,000. *Citizen Kane,* a relatively cheap studio film in 1940, cost over half a million dollars to complete; the same film now probably could not be made for under $3 million. With increasingly portable equipment, a loosening of the studio system, and an audience newly ready for ambitious and offbeat films, an art cinema could develop.

Film makers such as Bergman and Fellini were still products of sophisticated populist film; younger film makers such as Truffaut, Resnais, Kubrick, Olmi, Godard, Herzog, Fassbinder, Kluge, and Bellochio have found it possible to "grow up" at least partially outside the studio system and the bounds of a strictly popular film aesthetic. The result has been a diversified cinema, a cinema with as many aesthetics as there are important film makers. The mainstream narrative cinema is still popular, a form of entertainment. But in a way that it was not until recently, the cinema is now capable of anything. We now can go to the cinema for the same reasons we read books.

Yet the newer cinema has not killed the old. *Jaws, The Sting, The Exorcist, Magnum Force*—the popular melodramatic film is still the dominant film form. Film has not become a modernist art form. Rather, it has finally seen itself split in the same way that theater split and the novel split and painting split long before, into popular and "serious" branches. The split between the popular and the serious is not as severe as in the other arts. It cannot be. For one thing, the new audience for movies is not an elite but rather the children of the middle class, newly educated but still bourgeois. For another film is expensive to produce and distribute; it is a public art dependent on box office. Except in West Germany, France, Canada, and the socialist countries, film is rarely subsidized by government. The cinema is supported financially by those who go to the cinema—mainly the young of the middle class and would-be middle class, who are unencumbered enough by family and inertia to find that going out is a pleasurable activity. Insofar as young people have become intellectualized as a result of education and rising cultural levels, the cinema has been able to become diversified. Modernist elements have found a place in film's repertory. But such elements exist in cinema only in conjunction with traditional popular elements. In cinema, modernism is but an addition to film's mainstream popular aesthetic. What movies have always given the middle class is what most movies still provide. Writers, painters, and play-wrights work in cheaply produced media; modernist writers, painters, and playwrights have therefore been able to reject bourgeois culture and bourgeois values. Avant-garde film makers, by rejecting theatrical distribution and working cheaply with small-gauge film, have been equally free. But narrative film makers have never been able to reject completely the values of those who pay for their art. Narrative film making costs a lot of money. As long as that remains a fact, the cinema's aesthetics will have at least one foot in the popular. Film makers have no choice but to take the middle class seriously.

ART, INFORMATION, AND SOCIETY: THE LIMITS OF AESTHETIC SYNTHESIS

Two themes dominate the history of the arts in the last hundred years. The first is a split between the popular and the "serious." The second is a growth in media-awareness. The effect of the second has been a differentiation between the arts, with painters exploring the potentials of paint, writers the potentials of printed language, film makers the potentials of film, and theatricians the potentials of the stage. The effect of the first has been to split the histories of *each* art: literature has had a popular branch and a "serious" one, and so on. Simultaneously, however, the split between popular and serious has brought the arts together: popular arts have developed in parallel ways; serious explorations in each of the arts have been echoed in the other arts. The linking of the arts has been both thematic and a matter of form because the formal potentials of media such as print and film have remarkable parallels.

Underlying the patterns of art development has been a split in the ways in which society has assimilated new information. New information and ideas in philosophy, psychology, and the sciences have neither penetrated nor affected all segments of society equally. The lower and middle classes have, in the main, chosen the values and dreams of everyday existence as the source of their aesthetic; everyday life is only indirectly affected by new ideas and information. Popular art has taken as its basis the myths, problems, and aspirations attendant on trying to live well, and living well does not, in all probability, require staying abreast of the new. Modernist art has, in contrast, either embraced or confronted the new. Insofar as new ideas and information have challenged the assumptions of middle-class aesthetics, modernism has estranged itself from the popular.

Intellectually, morally, and aesthetically, art has two opposed functions: to affirm and to question. What popular art affirms is different from what modernism affirms; what popular art questions is different from what modernism questions. Pixérécourt's theater and Dickens's novels affirmed the old myth structures on which bourgeois culture rested. Above all, such arts affirm what we have in common as human beings. Part of what we have in common is an appreciation for the archaic, the romantic, and the mythos of success. New ideas threaten our communality, so part of the aesthetic of the popular arts has involved an affirmation that we can do without the new, that the old ideas are still good. Bravery, honesty, decency, the virtues of family life—those are, indeed, very old ideas, and popular art has been their champion.

But popular consciousness has not kept pace with intellectual history. In the last two centuries, virtually every received idea about the physical world, religion, politics, economics, psychology, sociology, and art has been overturned, with a new idea often lasting only a few years before yet another new idea takes its place. Each new idea has eventually affected everyday life. Its immediate impact, however, has been on intellectuals and serious artists. Ibsen's *A Doll's House* predated the women's liberation movement; Flaubert's *Madame Bovary* projected a moral world only recently reflected in high divorce rates. The function of serious art has been to identify what is new, to affirm that we can live with it, and to question the assumption that we *can* live with an outdated world view. Modernism has questioned whether we do indeed have a common life, whether bourgeois capitalism does produce a good life, whether our most basic human relationships can continue in their old patterns. Joyce's *A Portrait of the Artist as a Young Man*, Hauptmann's *The Weavers*, O'Neill's *Long Day's Journey into Night*, and Albee's *Who's Afraid of Virginia Woolf?* are all tormented cries that the most basic assumptions and institutions of life—and the family in particular—have gone awry, and that we had better deal with that fact if we are to make modern history more than the nightmare Joyce believed it was. The problem with serious modern art has been that only those aware of the problems it posed, or willing to face such problems, could respond to it. What most people want after a day's work is affirmation of what they've been working *for*; modernist art rarely offers such an affirmation. For intellectuals, the probes of modernism *are* pleasurable, if mainly as an antidote to the despair that is their alternative. Art pleases by making sense of parts of existence: by questioning what does not make sense and affirming what does, and by integrating the two in single visions. Popular art has not responded to many contemporary dilemmas because ordinary life has not. Modernist art, on the other hand, has not responded to the needs of everyday people leading everyday lives.

Can we expect modernism and the popular arts to merge? Not so long as new ideas do not penetrate and affect all segments of society equally. Though modern mass communication undoubtedly has, along with higher levels of education, partially bridged the gap between the everyday and the new, one must doubt that this gap will cease to exist. As long as it does exist, our arts are likely to remain fragmented, pluralistic, and partial approaches to aesthetic existence.

We pay for art. We spend money and we spend ourselves. We ask specific things from art. What we ask depends on what we need. What do we pay for in movie theaters like the Academy of Music? Not modernist soul-searching—that would break the back of the beautiful old place and mock the provincial elegance and simple notions of entertainment that informed the Academy's builders. No, what we come to the Academy for is to be together in public, to sit in plush maroon seats, and to be involved in the excitement and spectacle of the screen. The Academy is a bourgeois place, a place of bourgeois dreams. In the Academy the world is a spectacle, not a problem. No matter what is on the screen, the world outside will be grittier than the world inside. From the Academy to the state of modern knowledge is a long, long way. Inside the Academy, popular movies are shown. They are the proper extension of the purposes for which the place was built.

PART THREE

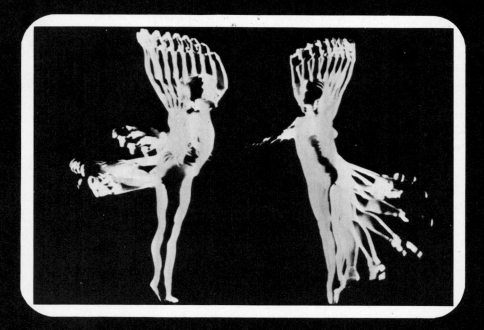

Explorations

The first two parts of *Cineliteracy* were attempts to be both descriptive and catholic. A sense of how films work and of their cultural foundations is essential to a comprehension of what we see on movie screens. To understand how movies work and where they come from one must recognize the claims of all kinds of films. One must, to echo Jean Renoir's line from *The Rules of the Game,* understand that all films have their reasons for being what they are and doing what they do. But when we watch films, not only are we aware of the present and the past; we are aware that film history is in a perpetual state of becoming, of moving in new directions. Furthermore, we are—or should be—aware that we see movies through the filter of our individual ideal expectations, that is, in terms of what we feel they should be and hope they will become. It is impossible to care about the cinema without a personal sense of what kinds of films are most worth caring about. Part Three makes no attempts to be impartial. In it I argue only for those films I care most about—those which as works of art help us find meaning in our lives and enrich our aesthetic senses. And because the films I am most partial to cannot be approached as "just any movie," I propose critical stances aimed specifically at them.

Throughout *Cineliteracy,* I have made no pretense of caring about film as an industry. From 1930 to the present, the story of the film industry has been one of continual consolidation. Today, 90 percent of all film rentals go through seven distributors—Universal, Twentieth Century-Fox, Columbia, Paramount, United Artists, Warner Brothers, and Disney.*Although television has supposedly threatened the film industry, the film industry has in reality taken over almost all television production. Morally, intellectually, and aesthetically, the film industry behaves like an industry, that is to say, with utter indifference to any value beyond profit.

---

* Information on attendance and distribution is mainly from Thomas Guback, "Are We Looking at the Right Things in Film?" Unpublished manuscript, courtesy of the author.

Indeed, the fact that film is an art at all is hardly the result of its industrial base, which has tended to strangle whatever is new, unique, or different in order to deliver a uniform, salable product. During the heyday of Hollywood film, film producers did exactly what they now do when producing television programs. Producers have always gone for what television marketers call the "L. O. Response," knowing that an audience that decides not whether but what to watch will almost invariably consume whatever "product" is "least objectionable." Such products, aimed at offending no one, are the antithesis of art. Rather, film exists as an art form because of the efforts of a few rebels within the system, the innovative work of artists who approach film almost as a cottage industry, and the active support of a minority within the larger filmgoing audience.

Of the nearly 2.7 million people who go to movies every day in the United States, probably only a small minority care much about film art. There are really three distinct film audiences. The largest is a television-habituated audience for whom blockbuster films are a special occasion. That audience is still a mass audience. It allows films such as *King Kong* to open in 1,200 theaters at the same time; it allows over 1,000 prints of *The Omen* to circulate simultaneously. This audience is seasonal, showing up just before Christmas, in the summer, and at a few other times. The films that appeal to this mass audience are mainly old-fashioned thrillers given a few new twists: *Jaws, The Sting,* the two *Godfathers,* and *The Exorcist* are typical of the breed. The second audience is comprised socially of those who have little reason or need to stay at home, and of those who want more than television has to offer. Most of them are young, many are well-educated. Many are urban, not bound to suburban homes and families and therefore free to go to movies at night. This second audience, the habitual filmgoers, is what allows the cinema to remain a popular and diversified form. Its size is large enough so that film distributors must, whether they want to or not, partially cater to it. Its allegiances are unpredictable. Particular actors, known directors, interesting subjects or genres, or simply the rumor that a film is special can bring this group to the theater. The third audience—people who care deeply about cinema—is very small but crucial and is actually a subdivision of the second. This audience often acts as an advance guard for the second, and therein lies their power. Their affinity with good film makers leads them to explore the unusual, the new. They read reviews and film journals, they scout the little theaters. They find films such as Jean-Charles Tacchella's *Cousin, Cousine;* they find film makers such as Lina Wertmüller and Bertrand Tavernier. Word spreads, lines form outside improbable theaters, and new life is injected into film as a popular art form.

Most good movies, of course, are never widely distributed; the industrial system on which film is based sees to that by keeping its exhibition space for its top-selling behemoths. The history of film as an art form is mainly a history of films that lost money. Yet virtually every major shift in the direction of the mainstream cinema has come when a film that should have lost money, that seemed to be too original to appeal to a large audience, managed to do well. In the American cinema of the 1960s, *Bonnie and Clyde, Easy Rider, The Graduate,* and *Five Easy Pieces* fall into this category; however traditional such films look now, at the time of their release they were regarded as too innovative to sell well. In the 1970s, Lina Wertmüller's films—especially *Love and Anarchy, The Seduction of Mimi, Swept Away,* and *Seven Beauties*—have had a similar effect. Internationally, as the case of Wertmüller illustrates, a stream within cinema can become a large-scale phenomenon. I have chosen to explore the dynamic of cinema-changing films through an analysis of two seminal 1960s films, François Truffaut's *Jules and Jim* and Michelangelo Antonioni's *Blow-Up.* Both films illustrate the new adjacency of the arts; both show cinematic currents coming together, clashing, synthesizing, and creating new forms. Both films fuse popularity with intelligence. *Jules and Jim* shows how the popular can be modernized; *Blow-Up* shows how the modernist can be made popular. By juxtaposing the two films I have attempted to illustrate the real diversity of directions from which change in cinema can come.

Yet many changes in film do not achieve easy audience acceptance; they remain the objects of attention only of hard-core film enthusiasts. It is to the unpopular that I have devoted the last two chapters of "Explorations." There is no reason whatever that a film should have to please millions of people in its own time to be worthy of attention as a work of art, even though that is precisely the criterion which one must impose if one is to deal only with "successful" films. In Chapter 15, "Film and Theater," I have approached films unpopular even among *cinéastes,* films which take as their foundation the new emphasis on performance and the new audience roles of contemporary theater. Even devoted filmgoers often resent real challenges to their assumptions about cinema and to their privileged roles as film viewers. Yet if the cinema is to change in directions that make films more meaningful and rich, precisely those films that drill at the foundations of traditional moviegoing will be those that may prove the most important. And in my last chapter, centered on the independent and avant-garde film, I look at several other new directions in film art and examine the symbiotic nature of artistic communities. In film, as in the other arts, change is rarely effected by one person working alone; in the absence of popular acceptance, what is important is the product of movements strong enough to withstand lack of social and economic rewards.

Those films I personally care most about are not those aimed at large, occasional audiences. Rather, they are those that say something essentially new about what film can do, how it can do it, and for whom. In dealing with such films there is, however, a danger. I regard the films in question as works of art. But in the cinema, "art" does not mean the same thing as it does in nondramatic art forms. In art forms such as literature and painting, great works of art are those that are one of a kind, original in conception and execution, and can be considered "immortal." In the cinema, such values are inappropriate, because the cinema is a form of event rather than a class of art objects. The cinema has value structures different from, even antithetical to, the values of "art" as the term is applied to objects. To clarify these value structures and to indicate their consequences for film criticism, I have begun this part with a chapter entitled "Values in Art, Values in Film."

VALUES IN ART,
VALUES IN FILM

Films are meant to be projected in movie theaters, to be unstoppable events with their own rhythms and durations, which will elicit from viewers a special kind of attention. Viewers cannot control the pace of a film; they must follow, attending to the enormously detailed information on the screen and sound track, without being able to flip back a few frames to check past action or to take a close look at important images. The images and sounds that viewers perceive are highly refined evocations of the material world, which require knowledge of perceptual and social languages to be understood; to grasp the sounds and images, the viewer must grasp the film's experiential base and decipher its artifices and conventions. If he can do this efficiently, the film will elicit strong responses, giving viewers experiences unlike those available from any other medium. The cinema's vitality as an art form is inseparable from its ability to give viewers potent experiences. But the elements that make films vital also make the cinema an art with different values from nondramatic art forms such as painting, poetry, or the novel. To expect from films things one expects from nondramatic art forms is to impose values on the cinema that are antithetical to the medium of film. Films function as a special kind of event. That fact, rather than the resemblances between film and older art forms, is at the heart of film aesthetics. That fact must also be the starting point of film criticism.

Parts One and Two have described the processes involved in film viewing and the cultural reasons for film's evolution into its present forms, and so have provided the bases for a functional critique of films. But a critique of films also involves analysis of values. Films are material objects; as such, they invite analysis as art objects. But as art objects, most films are failures, and even the best films have weaknesses, because the values implicit in objects are different from the values implicit in event-based art forms such as performed drama and film. Art objects such as poems, paintings, and novels are meant to be experienced at leisure and kept for a long time. Art events are meant to be experienced dramatically without viewer intervention and to speak to their own moments in history. To be worth keeping, art objects must be tasteful and original; to work well, art events often cannot have either of these qualities. Understanding films requires a tolerance for event-based forms, and that requires a special sense of history.

FILMS AS OBJECTS, FILMS AS EVENTS

All forms of communication become events when they happen. Reading a novel or viewing a painting is an event; so is listening to a phonograph recording, watching a play, or viewing a film. Before film, there were only two kinds of communication events: direct (as in conversation, speeches, and performances of music or plays) and indirect (as in printed language, paintings, drawings, sculpture, and architecture). In indirect communication, messages are carried by and contained in objects. The rhythm and tempo of direct communication when the information flows only one way, as in the performance of a play, is controlled exclusively by the communicator; the viewer must simply follow along. Direct communication occurs as a pure event. It requires no intervening objects; it leaves no residues except in memory. Indirect communication occurs through objects that can be "read." Before the cinema, such "reading" was temporally and to some extent structurally out of the hands of the communicator; it was the "reader's" own activity. One looks at a painting or building or photograph or at the print on a page and, through a process that is essentially analytic, goes from the work's forms to a sense of what it communicates. The "reader" controls the process of comprehension; he controls the "communication event."

Film technology synthesized the two kinds of communication. Films are, like paintings and books, objects that communicate. But because they are projected mechanically by a process that the viewer cannot control, the viewer cannot control his relationship with them. He cannot, as with a painting, take more time if the work demands it; he cannot, as with a novel, skip back to previous pages to make sure he understands a sequence; he cannot slow down or speed up his "reading" so that the work and his mental processes come into alignment. Instead, he must treat the film as a direct event, albeit a fictional and predetermined one. And because films are meant to be treated as events, they have values unlike those of indirect, object-based forms of communication such as printed or painted forms of art, and values very much like those of performed drama and music.

Compare, for example, one's experience of a film image with the experience of any printed sentence or even any still photograph. One can reread the sentence; one can explore its meanings pretty much at leisure. And one can do the same with a still photograph. Seen as a still photograph rather than as a moment that takes a few seconds during the film it is from, the following image (from Abel Gance's *Napoleon*) is easy to decipher (13–1). The revolutionary Jean-Paul Marat is lying dead in his bath. The guns on the wall reflect the values by which he lived; his death reflects what his life came to. One can look and relook, learning more and more. But in Gance's *Napoleon* the image lasts only briefly, and even within the shot, lighting seems to shift subtly; one must grasp the image while it is there, and then go on.

13–1. *Napoleon* (1927, Gance).

Museum of Modern Art, Film Stills Archive

What is worse, once the image has gone by, it can only be recollected in memory or by a complete re-viewing of the film. Although films can, of course, be found in film libraries and can be viewed on machines such as the analyst projector, which allows selective control over film viewing, most films unwind inexorably from a remote projector. What one misses is lost forever; once the film is over, it is gone, at least until the next viewing. And films are meant to be that way—to be events, rather than objects to be studied at leisure.

Because films are events, their temporality is all-important. The rhythm and duration of a film determine a large part of its identity. We take films as a direct form of communication, paying closer attention because they are rhythmic and ephemeral. They exist for us within limited but very important time periods. And that makes the rhythms of moments, and even the rhythms of a time in history, important for film aesthetics in a way they are not for nondramatic art forms. Every film is made for the rhythms of its own age. And that—along with several other elements inherent in dramatic, event-based art forms—makes films more potent but less long-lasting experiences than nondramatic art forms, which exist as forever comparable artifacts awaiting their ideal audiences. Nondramatic art may be for all time. But films are for "now" in two senses: the "now" of the viewing situation, and the historical "now." What makes them potent is the same quality that makes them age badly. As a result of this inherent quality of temporality, a number of expectations we have for nondramatic art are irrelevant to films.

HISTORICITY VERSUS THE ETERNAL

In the arts, we are accustomed to believing that good art is immortal, bad art is ephemeral, "merely" of and for its time. Samuel Johnson, expressing the eighteenth-century view, calculated that it took about a century to decide the quality of a work of literature. Most art and literary historians, many artists, and even some film critics would agree with the spirit if not the letter of Johnson's view. Why do sculptors and architects and painters work in durable materials if not to create objects so long-lasting that they are bound to survive? Why do playwrights have their plays printed? Our whole sense of the arts is that they are something artists have left for posterity, gifts to the future, wagers on the course of history. But a film is different: it is couched so thoroughly in the materials of its own time and exists so completely as an event that it is bound to age, and age badly. It embraces the moment rather than eternity.

Films change more quickly than virtually any other art form, because they contain so much of their own times in them. Styles of behaving, talking, dressing, speaking, thinking—all are historically specific and are contained specifically in films. And much of what we react to in contemporary films is powerful, because locked into the same time period as the film and participating in the same world view, we can "read" the film's images quickly and fluently. In time, any period's style, seen in detail, is apt to appear a bit silly. Thus only film comedies age at all well; most films eventually become comic no matter how serious their initial intentions. My film students greet D. W. Griffith's films with laughter and often cannot seem to take films made more than a few decades ago seriously. The artifices that express a film's time are translucent to that time, but become obvious, like the darkening varnish on old wood, with age; eventually all one sees is artifice. And when that happens, one is in the world of comedy. Most films live and die in the span of a few years or a few decades at most. And that would be true even if film technology did not evolve rapidly in its quest to create more and more potent cinematic events.

Film classics are, of course, exceptions to the rule of "either comic or quickly obsolete." But film classics appeal to a subculture within the larger film audience, a subculture willing to grant old films the signs of their aging. Further, film classics are usually of one of two special kinds: either genre films that employ the conventions of currently popular films, and thus can be taken nostalgically as forebears of current movies, or films that, because of their integrity and the actors' strong performances, give unrepeatably profound renditions of basic aspects of the human condition. Emil Jannings's performance as an aging hotel porter in Murnau's *The Last Laugh*, for example, is so strongly moving and sincere that the entire film, despite its archaic technology and rhythms, must be taken as a valid imaginative world. To take it otherwise would be to take lightly not an old film but a suffering human being.

It should, however, be noted that when films such as *The Last Laugh* or generic classics survive well, they do so in spite of the technology and artifices of film history. They survive because of story and performance elements. Strong stories, solid characterization, and extraordinary performances—the elements film can share with stage drama—give films whatever immortality they have, an immortality based on appeal to considerations beyond film history. In one sense it is accurate to say there are no classic films, only classic genres, stories, and characters.

If the performance aspect of film were, however, improved in quality, films might not become so quickly obsolete. Therefore the recent move toward a cinema of performance (which I discuss in Chapter 15) could change, at least in part, the truth that the cinema is an art with obsolescence built into its aesthetics. But for the present moment and for the theatrical cinema, old films are hardly a question at all. Theatrical films are contemporary films. That is both a curse and a virtue of the cinema as an art of ever-new events.

Art historians and literary critics work against the background of the long histories of their arts, against the sense that every new work competes for readers or viewers with every work from the past. There is never much room in museums for new works, nor, given the competition from the past, is there a great deal of time for reading the new. Thus, critics in fields such as painting or poetry evaluate new works in terms of whether they deserve to survive alongside the best of the old. To merit surviving, a new work must be unique, one of a kind, original, something previously unavailable. But new films do not really compete with old films for attention, at least not in movie theaters; nor are films destined for the same kind of immortality as are paintings or poems. The film critic must, unlike the literary or art critic, recognize that new films compete mainly with other new films.

THE CULINARY ANALOGY

Further, the competition between films exists in somewhat different terms than competition between books or between paintings. Audiences, if my research is correct, evaluate films according to the moods the films evoke, and the moods viewers have after the films.[1] A film is expected to satisfy a kind of consumer appetite for mood-changing experience and is often approached almost as if it were a culinary experience. Just as one goes to an Italian restaurant for spaghetti and a French restaurant for *boeuf bourguignon*, movie viewers seem to choose films generically—according to the kind of experience they want to have. The cinema's aesthetics have a culinary aspect in how they deliver experiences, too. Films are meant for consumption, not immortality. Often they must be evaluated according to whether they provide connoisseur-level experiences for discriminating viewers. Most film reviewers understand this well. But many film theorists do not.

To speak of film experience as culinary may not be merely to employ a figure of speech: films work by arousing and satisfying particular appetites. Expectations are aroused, channeled, directed, satisfied; the initial expectation is not of the new, but of the good. A good meal, even at a three-star restaurant, is not apt to be completely original. Rather, it is likely to be similar in kind to meals available elsewhere, but special because of the quality of its ingredients, the skill and imagination employed in their preparation, and the mood that prevails during their delivery. It would be silly to speak of Picasso, Braque, Gris, or Léger as "master chefs" of Cubism. But it is remarkably accurate to speak of a director such as Alfred Hitchcock as a "master chef" of the horror genre, because in Hitchcock's hands the old conventions of horror movies can surprise and fascinate even the most jaded and sophisticated aficionados of film. Similarly, it may not be inaccurate to speak of classic Hollywood directors such as Ernst Lubitsch as pastry cooks of special merit, or of directors such as François Truffaut as masters of the soufflé, or even of Luis Buñuel's accomplishment in *Belle de Jour* as having gotten away with putting ground glass in what appears to be a meringue. The cinema's dominant pattern is a continual updating of old forms and structures, a continual stretching of old genres and conventions to see to what new uses they might be put, to see if they might be tasty one more time around. And film criticism must, with or without a straight face, take the culinary aspects of film into account. "Great art" may have to be for all time. But a good movie must, first of all, make tonight more interesting.

THE PROBLEM OF TASTE

Perhaps the greatest problem in criticizing films is that the majority of them are hardly specimens of good taste. The movies have made a tradition of satisfying middle-class appetites, and when looked at from the elitist traditions of nonpopular art forms, films inevitably have a tawdry feel about them. Audiences get a kick out of watching a shark chomp bathers in *Jaws*, from watching gangsters decapitate one another with machine guns in *The Godfather, Part One*, from watching, in *The Exorcist*, pea-green vomit, and, in other films, from watching fights, illicit romance, and just about every other kind of vulgar spectacle. The cinema is a popular art, the descendant of popular fiction and melodrama rather than of Keats and Rubens. Its traditions are built on the need to appeal to an audience that, in actual culinary terms, has made McDonald's the biggest restaurant chain in the world. And the cinema's vulgarity is inseparable from its worst and best aspects: though one might prefer the sophistication of Jean Eustache's *The Mother and the Whore* (13–2) to the gross idiocy of the moral view in Griffith's *The Birth of a Nation* (13–3) or even to the sentiment and bathos of Charles Chaplin's *The Kid* (13–4) there is no denying that, in terms of film history, the first is an aberration and the other two are part of the mainstream.

Is questionable taste simply the result of the cinema's history as a popular art form? Partly but not completely, since questionable taste may be an aspect of drama itself. Arts of experience rather than of artifacts are voracious in their appetite for subjects and for sources of new events; fussiness seems antithetical to dramatic art. And that, as Jan Kott points out in *Shakespeare, Our Contemporary*, was as true of the Elizabethan stage as it is of movies:

> The beginnings of Elizabethan tragedy were very similar to the beginnings of film. Everything that was at hand could be included in a tragedy. Everyday events, tales of crime, bits of history, legends, politics, and philosophy. It was a news-reel and an historical chronicle. Elizabethan tragedy did not follow any rules; it snapped at any subject. Just as films do now, it fed on and digested crime, history and observation of life. Everything was new, so everything could be adapted. The great Elizabethans often remind one of film producers looking, above all, for an attractive subject. It is enough to mention Marlowe, Ben Jonson, or Shakespeare.[2]

The quest for ever-new subjects and ever more exciting treatments of them frequently leads the cinema beyond the bounds of niceness and good taste. Films are often vulgar; but one very old meaning of vulgar is "of the world." In terms of the tastes it exemplifies, that describes the cinema quite

13–2. *The Mother and the Whore* (1973, Eustache).

13–3. *The Birth of a Nation* (1915, Griffith).

13–4. *The Kid* (1920, Chaplin).

well. And it should therefore describe the taste range and tolerance of film criticism as well.

Films are not meant to be hung on walls, or to grace libraries as signs of good taste. They are not a decorative form of art. They exist to affect audiences, to be powerful events that reflect and speak to their own times. Film criticism must begin with that fact.

THE LIMITS OF FILM CRITICISM

Films are events, and so film criticism must proceed as a criticism of events. The film critic cannot take literary or art criticism as a model or expect of films what he would of novels, paintings, or poems. Rather, the quality of films as events, and the elements that make films function well for their audiences must be his primary concern. Those elements change continually; the art of cinema is itself in rapid evolution. Therefore the film critic cannot isolate his subject matter from history and dissect it as if it were a purely formal and material entity. Rather, he must always be a historian, concerned with the historicity that gives moments life.

The film critic has only one advantage over the drama critic, whom he resembles in almost every other respect. Films are repeatable events that do not change every night. The film critic can therefore study variant reactions to the same film. He has a constant against which to measure the different audience events created by it. Otherwise, his subject is the dramatic event and the reactions it evokes. His job is to understand how films function. To do that, he must understand audiences and the strategies artists use to satisfy the demand by particular audiences for particular kinds of film events. He must also understand that the strategies used by film makers are never static but always evolving. He must see that the cinema is a vital art precisely because film makers have learned to create events that are powerful in their own times. Therefore the film critic must acknowledge that cinema history, like history itself, is a synonym for change. Film history is in a continual state of "becoming." The processes by which cinema becomes, by which it evolves, must be the background against which film criticism proceeds.

We are a long way from being able to understand quite what it means to say that films are events of a special kind. We know approximately how films function as narrative structures and perceptual mechanisms. We have a rough sense of the basics of the experiential languages films use as a basis for communication. We know the loose outlines of how film has evolved. And we know that, as events, films have value structures different from older and especially nondramatic forms of art. But that is only a beginning. The details of our knowledge are, at best, approximate. And the context of events is always history, always change. But we do at least know what we have to understand to understand the cinema. And that is a beginning.

NOTES: CHAPTER THIRTEEN

[1] In a response study conducted during 1977, involving sixty film students, each of whom gave detailed, anonymous responses to thirty selected films, almost all students reported significant mood changes during and as a result of every film. The ratings that students gave films correlated directly with the moods films produced. In follow-up questionnaires I discovered that even for sophisticated film students the expectation of a mood-altering experience is a primary motivation for film attendance.

[2] Jan Kott, *Shakespeare, Our Contemporary* (Garden City, N.Y.: Doubleday, 1966), p. 349.

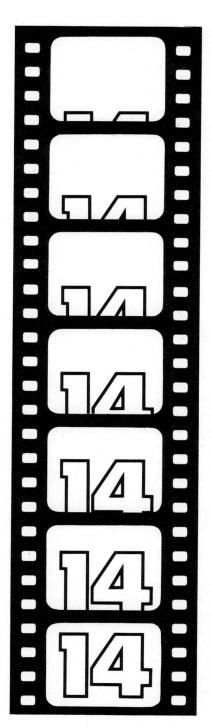

FILMS FROM FICTION

Jules and Jim and *Blow-Up:* Two Ways Toward the Future?

The large popular audience that once was the cinema's now watches television, going to the movies only for large "blockbuster" films such as *The Godfather*, *The Sting*, *Jaws*, *The Exorcist*, *King Kong*, *Rocky*, and *Star Wars*. Had general education and literacy levels remained what they were at mid-century, there might be no audience at all for the cinema, at least not on a regular basis. But education and literacy levels have risen, and a new audience for the cinema has come into existence: the young, the college-educated, and those who behave as if they were. This audience has one foot in the modern, the other in the popular. It wants both entertainment and intelligence, both the popular and the modernist, in the films it goes to.

The problem of the ambitious contemporary film maker is to meet that demand: to find a way of combining the virtues of serious modernist art with those of the popular traditions of film making. The modernist traditionally sacrificed popularity for intelligence. The popular artist traditionally sacrificed whatever he had to—sometimes, though not always, including intelligence—to please the bourgeoisie. The problem of remaining popular while also being serious, relevant, and intelligent, can be approached in two ways. One can either "modernize" the popular or "popularize" the modern. The results of the two approaches are rarely the same; they differ experientially and in how a critic must deal with the films.

To exemplify the two approaches, I have chosen François Truffaut's *Jules and Jim* and Michelangelo Antonioni's *Blow-Up*. Both film makers have achieved perennial popularity; the films they create are marked by intelligence. *Jules and Jim* and *Blow-Up* are among the most popular and respected works of the two directors; both were milestones of the cinema of the 1960s. Both films succeed in making extraordinary demands on their audiences; both refuse to allow their viewers to make easy moral judgments of their characters. Both films study characters and subsocieties that are unorthodox and bohemian, and where the pursuit of freedom means more than conventional goals. Both films deal with violence below the surface of ordinary life. Both films appeal to the audience's sense of beauty more than to the audience's moral sense. In both, society is viewed skeptically, and meaningful human action is regarded as a tenuous endeavor. The two films appeal to audiences, I suspect, for similar reasons: they are studies of youth, freedom, and the attempt to create one's own life in a confusing world. They share their audience, their time in history, and their world, as well as the medium through which they express themselves.

Yet François Truffaut and Michelangelo Antonioni are utterly different kinds of film makers. Truffaut modernizes the popular; while Antonioni popularizes the modern. Their differences as film makers are such that one could not confuse a scene or even a shot by one with a scene or shot by the other. But their differences go even deeper than the differences one would expect between any two important directors. The two have what amounts to radically opposed visions of what man, and therefore the cinema, is. Truffaut sees man as intact in history; for him, all people at all times share their essential problems. Antonioni sees contemporary man as adrift, in a new situation: the past, and especially past "wisdom," can only hinder our accommodations to present realities. Politically, Truffaut is a liberal populist, sympathetic to the bourgeois aesthetic of living well. His films are for everyone and are meant to be enjoyed. Politically, Antonioni sympathizes with the left; culturally, he is an elitist. Truffaut stands close to the mainstream of popular cinema's sensibility; Antonioni stands apart from it. Truffaut is a romantic, Antonioni an antiromantic modernist, a student of alienation. The two men do not even like one another: Antonioni has called Truffaut's films "frivolous"; Truffaut has described Antonioni as humorless, modish, and "terribly pompous."[1] Truffaut stands at the end of a long, long line of entertainers who have combined intelligence with popular appeal: Balzac, Hugo, Chaplin, Clair, Carné, Hawks, Lubitsch, Hitchcock, Welles, and especially Jean Renoir; Truffaut extends and updates a tradition. Antonioni stands alone. He has affinities, but mostly with novelists such as Gustave Flaubert, Cesare Zavatinni, Cesare Pavese. Others in the contemporary cinema are, like Antonioni, modernists—Alain Resnais, Jean-Luc Godard, R. W. Fassbinder, Werner Herzog, Robert Bresson, Jean-Marie Straub, to name just a few—but as is typical of modernists, their commitments to their own individual truths make their films difficult to compare. Among the modernists in film, Antonioni is perhaps not the best, nor the most interesting. But he is unique in that he has found a way of appealing to large audiences without diluting his art. Only Bergman, whose modernism is theatrical, and who was a recognized master before embarking on formal and structural experiment, has matched that feat. Bergman, like Fellini, began in a different tradition than he is in now. Antonioni began as a modernist, and remains one.

The crucial question, however, is not whether Truffaut and Antonioni are harbingers of the future, or are even typical of contemporary directors, though as a modernizer of the popular, Truffaut has many American descendants—Coppola, Lucas, Friedkin, Scorsese. The important thing is to be able to speak of how a film maker such as Truffaut and an entirely different one such as Antonioni work with their medium and their audience. Truffaut and Antonioni speak to different viewer expectations; they guide anticipations and discriminations in different ways and toward different ends. Faced with the same array of possible technical tools, they make different choices—not only of which ones they will use, but of how they will use them. Truffaut relies heavily on verbal language; Antonioni uses language sparingly. Truffaut chooses old-fashioned narration for *Jules and Jim*; *Blow-Up* uses a limited, oblique point of view. *Jules and Jim* is anecdotal, self-consciously a story. *Blow-Up* has a story, but makes the viewer find it. Truffaut began with an old-fashioned novel, a nostalgic memoir. Antonioni started with an experimental short story by one of the most daring of contemporary fiction writers, Julio Cortázar. Truffaut's source, and his film, dwell on the past. Antonioni's source, and his film, embrace a present without past or future. Truffaut's world has easily recognizable ideas and people behaving for fully understandable reasons. But to understand the world of *Blow-Up* one must examine why the characters and the world can be as Antonioni presents them; though we recognize the world of the film, only upon analysis can we understand it. Truffaut's film is about a conflict within the framework of understood terms. Antonioni's is about the problem of trying to understand at all.

And yet there is something that links Antonioni and Truffaut despite their differences. Both understand the perceptual and imaginative situation of the viewer, and both use it to make their films exciting experiences. If Truffaut has given contemporary cinema anything unique, it is the assurance that popular cinema can be intelligent. If Antonioni is important, it is because he has shown that, properly constructed, a modernist film can succeed at what the popular film does—engaging the attention and imagination fully. Both

Truffaut and Antonioni respect the perceptual and imaginative needs of their audiences. And it is this respect, combined with understanding of how film works at the level of perception, that links the two men's films.

IRONY AND ROMANCE: JULES AND JIM

In popular art forms, what we expect is a specific kind of experience. What we pay for is not "the new" but a limited though tasty menu that will please the palate. How well a popular film works depends on whether we think we got what we paid for; how well a popular film is regarded depends on how well it delivers an expected experience. But it also depends on how well it digests. One does not return to, nor recommend, the source of heartburn. The bounds of popular cinema are the bounds of the palatable, the digestible. And those bounds are couched in middle-class terms.

There are as many kinds of popular film menus as there are popular genres. *Jaws, The Exorcist, Carrie,* and *Family Plot* appeal to an expectation of Grand Guignol; in human terms, they are vicarious substitutes for capital punishment as a public spectacle. Whatever audiences are anxious about seems to create a genre. Beauty and love are virtually eternal sources of anxiety. Romance is therefore a perennial film genre; with Grand Guignol, it is perhaps the most popular contemporary genre.

The dominant theme of romance is love, either between friends or between the sexes. Its informing myth has been called by Northrop Frye "the mythos of Summer," the time of vacations and youthfulness. Pure romance, though popular for generations of filmgoers, has not survived whole in our divorce-prone age; it has lost its power to convince. In our skeptical age, romance still appeals but must be tempered with irony. The dominant mood of irony is that summer was nice, but it was also a fool's paradise—it did not last. The informing myth of irony is the spirit of winter, a time of disappointment, of trying to survive, of looking forward to next summer while remembering the last one. It is a time of sudden freezes and thaws, of episodic existence. The subject of contemporary romance is romantic, but the point of view is ironic, and thus the dominant structure is episodic. Enthusiasm turns to doubt, doubt to enthusiasm in a dialectic between optimism and pessimism. Popular audiences once went to romances to celebrate summer. Now they go to be assured that there *will* be another spring, another summer—that winter is not eternal. This is the assurance that François Truffaut gives in all of his films. And it is Truffaut's ability to deliver that assurance, not only excitingly but convincingly (because intelligently) that makes films such as *Jules and Jim* classics of popular cinema.

The following pages examine how *Jules and Jim* delivers optimism convincingly. To understand Truffaut's accomplishment, one must understand the materials and traditions he uses and how he uses them. By emphasizing the artificial aspects of the story, Truffaut gets his audience to treat thwarted love, war, disappointment, and death as temporary, as a subject of play. Winter will not last. By emphasizing the liveliness and resilience of the human through acting, music, quickly paced visuals, and editing, Truffaut convinces us of how quickly—viewed in large terms—summer will come again. We join in Truffaut's playful attitude. And in so doing, we regard life intelligently, fully, and without gloom. Truffaut gives us no "new" ideas whatever. Why should he? The problems the film confronts are as old as the seasons. And as a popular film maker, Truffaut's task is to show us that we already have the materials to survive: the job of popular film is to give us self-confidence through imagination. *Jules and Jim* is about old problems, old ideas, and old solutions. Truffaut, by treating them as play, gets us to experience them as if they were new. We leave the theater humming. We leave stronger than we came in.

TRUFFAUT AND ADAPTATION

As with many popular film makers, Truffaut likes to adapt. If a film is meant to deliver a specific kind of experience, what virtue is there in dreaming up all one's own subjects? The result, in film, will be a new experience anyway. Truffaut has adapted "thrillers" four times: *Shoot the Piano Player, Fahrenheit 451, The Bride Wore Black,* and *Mississippi Mermaid.* He has adapted a psychological study, *The Wild Child;* he has adapted semiautobiographical novels by Henri-Pierre Roché twice: *Jules and Jim,* and *Two English Girls.* Of Truffaut's adaptations, only *Jules and Jim* greatly resembles its original in tone; the others are takeoff points, frames for Truffaut's own interests. In *Jules and Jim,* the materials and tone of the book, as well as some of the characters, are used to create central elements of the film.

The Book

H. P. Roché's *Jules and Jim* is what reviewers sometimes call "a good read." Fast-paced, funny, and self-assured, with an exciting, romantic, somewhat risqué topic—a *ménage à trois* in the artistic subculture of Paris at the beginning of this century—*Jules and Jim* gives readers what François Truffaut gives film viewers: an intelligent, quick, amusingly imaginative romp. The book gave Truffaut his essential narrative strategy. Roché's book is playful, episodic, and quick, held together as an optimistic experience by the tone of the narrative voice, a voice that is both ironic and fatherly. The book gave Truffaut his plot outline and basic themes. It gave him the basis of his characters and the fictional world they inhabit. And it gave him a model for quickly paced shifting perspectives. To read *Jules and Jim* and to see the film is to have remarkably similar imaginary experiences.

Yet Truffaut's *Jules and Jim* achieves its effects in ways and through structures quite different from Roché's. Truffaut compressed Roché's book, rearranged the characters, deleted many elements, and added everything he knew about film making. Truffaut's film is the film of a young man. Roché's book is the reminiscence of a man who, upon retirement, amused himself by writing a novel.

Roché's *Jules and Jim* is a fictionalized memoir. It was written when Roché was in his early seventies, and covers a triangular love affair among two men and a woman between 1907 and approximately 1930. The novel has three parts. The first deals with the friendship of Jules, an Austrian-Jewish writer, and Jim, a Parisian journalist in the *milieu artiste* at the beginning of the century. The second section concentrates on Jules's marriage to and Jim's affair with Kate, a Prussian artist. The third section describes the collapse of the amicable *ménage à trois*, and ends with Kate's and Jim's funeral; Kate has driven them off a bridge into a river. The novel is a picaresque romance with three principals, three parts, and three themes: friendship, love, and aging. Roché complements the ironic symmetries with an ironic verbal tone and sensibility:

> They went North as joyfully as they had come South. In the train Kate drew caricatures of Jim, with captions that doubled him up with laughter. How well she knew her Jim!
>
> In the first buffet they stopped at in Kate's country, they were astonished to find how high the price of a cup of tea had risen. Inflation was still raging. A very old waiter, suddenly defeated by his bills, began crying and then uttering threats in a mounting fury. He had gone mad and was taken away.
>
> This same inflation also permitted them to take a sleeper together for the first time, and to get home quicker to Jules and the children.[2]

In passages like this, Roché plays off pessimism against optimism. Everything has more than one side to it; everyone, and everything, has its good and bad elements. What holds the whole thing together, and makes optimism dominant, is Roché's voice, which convinces the reader that all will turn out all right; Roché is a father figure who *knows*. And he forgives because he understands. Further, he understands in almost universal terms; in accord with time-honored tradition, Roché employs nature as a metaphor system.

> They came back along a stream which was turbulent in parts; in one place there was a waterfall. They decided that the mass of falling water was like Kate, the uneven surges were like Jim, and the succeeding calm stretch was like Jules.[3]

The characters in the novel are both individuals and types; Roché is a sketch artist like Daumier, setting up a world of colorful and witty vignettes through compressed prose.

Jules and Jim is a nineteenth-century novel in method, a twentieth-century novel in its risqué subject matter. Roché wrote the book so his grandchildren would know what life was like in the golden age of his youth. And, since he wanted it to be a good experience for them, he wrote it in terms they would understand—the terms of popular art. Roché had been a friend of Picasso and Gertrude Stein; he knew the modernist world by heart. But he had never found alienation in that world. Rather he had found old things: love, friendship, pain, hope. It is these things that he uses for the core of his book, and that Truffaut used when making it into a film.

TRUFFAUT'S INTENTION: A POPULAR FILM

François Truffaut became acquainted with *Jules and Jim* during the mid-1950s while he was still a film critic for *Cahiers du Cinéma*. When he filmed it in 1962 he saw it in popular-film terms.

> I hoped to give *Jules and Jim* the atmosphere of one of those little films that MGM used to produce twenty or twenty-five years ago: *Mrs. Parkington, The Green Years*, etc., films whose only fault was that they were conventional, but which *did* give the impression of a fat 800 page book, with the years going by and people's hair going grey.[4]

Roché's format, quick pace, and flair were ideal for such intentions. Combining entertainment values with the artifice of omniscient narration and a mood of nostalgia, Roché's work also met the requirements of Truffaut's temperament.

> My films are circus shows, and I'm glad of it. I never put on two elephant acts together. After the elephant, the juggler, and after the juggler, the bears. I even allow a sort of intermission toward the sixth reel, because by then people's attention is flagging. At the seventh reel I take them in hand again, and try to end with a flourish. . . . I swear I'm not joking; I think of the circus while working. I'd like to see people hiss and boo the unsuccessful sequences and clap those they liked. And since in order to see my films people have to shut themselves up in the dark, I never fail, toward the end of the film, to take them out into the countryside, beside the sea, or in the snow, so they'll forgive me. . . . I think constantly of the public.[5]

A *ménage à trois* covering two decades *is* a circus. While Roché's nostalgic tone suits Truffaut's aversion for the prosaic, his episodic structure fits Truffaut's circus aesthetic perfectly.

The bohemian "adult children" of Roché's novel also fit Truffaut's temperament. "I've always preferred transposed life to life itself," he has said; "I was a child who huddled forgotten in the corner and dreamed . . . I still am."[6] A memory—a dream—the two have remarkable affinities. And the complexity of the novel also undoubtedly appealed to Truffaut, whose films always celebrate life's complexities and our ability to live with complexity:

As soon as one interpretation seems to be winning out, I destroy it, to avoid intellectual comfort, both for the spectator and for myself. I try to be objective, so I present a thousand different facets of reality. . . . For me the man can and must judge. The artist, never. . . . Life must escape all the ideas that the spectator may have formulated about it. . . . One must dissuade the spectators from judging the characters.[7]

By keeping intellectual discomfort high, Truffaut maintains the viewer anxiety on which narrative tension depends; by keeping spectators from judging characters, he leaves the thrust of his narratives open-ended. Roché's novel provided him with the means to accomplish these narrative ends.

THE SPECIAL LANGUAGE OF JULES AND JIM

In conception, strategy, and theme, Truffaut's film is close to Roché's book. As adaptations go, *Jules and Jim* is not "close," though it is a film that works its source hard. What Roché could give, Truffaut accepted. But in turning *Jules and Jim* into a film, Truffaut did not borrow, he *used*. And what he used—the strategy, some incidents, the three main characters, the device of a ringmaster-narrator—he transformed into purely filmic terms. The language of a book is made up of words. The language of a film depends on actors, sound, cinematography, and editing.

The Actors

A novel is not cast. A film is. For Truffaut, actors are a film's central ingredients. Truffaut had long conceived of *Jules and Jim* as a vehicle for Jeanne Moreau; he wanted to show her exuberant side. Casting an actress of Moreau's stature had consequences. To utilize her talents and provide time for her to perform, Truffaut had to make several changes from Roché's book. First, he had to cut down the novel's first section, eliminating most of Jules's and Jim's other women, and giving some of their characteristics and dialogue to Moreau's character, Catherine. Second, he had to eliminate Kate's Prussian qualities and ability as a swimmer. Moreau is thoroughly French and, on the evidence of the scene in which Catherine leaps into the Seine, not much of a swimmer. Third, since Moreau can sing charmingly but hardly professionally, and probably could not portray a professional sketch artist convincingly, Truffaut eliminated Kate's profession, making his Catherine an amateur singer rather than a professional artist. All this required adding scenes (Moreau defending French wines, Moreau singing) and tailoring themes to match; it also required eliminating other scenes and other themes.

To play opposite as strong an actress as Moreau, Truffaut needed strong actors for Jules and Jim. The best Austrian actor Truffaut knew was Oskar Werner. To fit Jules to Werner, Truffaut had to cut out Jules's Jewishness and exploit Werner's special talents: a set of winsome expressions, evocative gestures, and a gentle voice. Truffaut chose an unknown actor, Henri Serre, for Jim. (He needed someone tall, French, and bookish-looking as well as handsome; since Jean Gabin's heyday in the 1930s there have been few such actors in France.) Serre has a good voice but not much range; his face is handsome but has basset-hound undertones. He was not as experienced or versatile an actor as Werner. Thus Truffaut had to adjust the relationship between Jules and Jim to allow Werner's charisma to work freely. In the book Jim is Roché's surrogate. In the film, Jules seems to be Truffaut's. Serre speaks more lines than Werner, but serves mainly as a foil for Moreau and Werner. But all three actors are good with their bodies, so Truffaut could capitalize on their physical possibilities.

Each actor moves in ways which embody attitudes and ideas. Moreau plays a volatile character. She snaps her head into quickly changing attitudes, switches facial moods with mercurial speed, and seems always about to leap from wherever she is. The accompanying sequence, from a few seconds in the film, shows Moreau's speed (14–1).

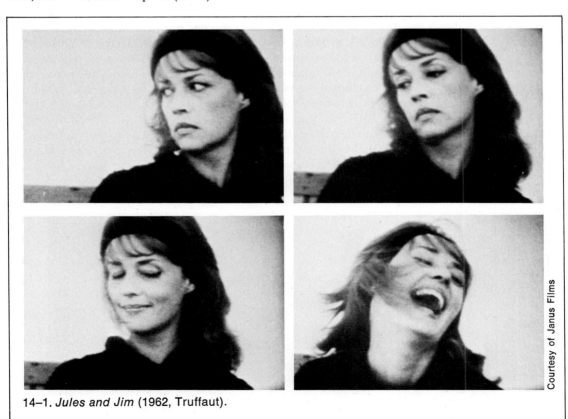

14–1. *Jules and Jim* (1962, Truffaut).

Courtesy of Janus Films

Moreau would probably have been the center of the film whether or not Truffaut wanted her to be: she is a force. Her expressions and movements are statements with no subordinate clauses. She tilts her head to one side or the other. When she wears a hat, she perches it on her head like a jaunty mascot. Though physically short, Moreau plays Catherine "tall": when she looks up at the tall Serre, she does it with her eyes rather than her body. When she rides a bicycle, drives a car, or even walks, it is with extreme concentration, the concentration of a thoroughbred, nervous when not in motion. She never talks; she proclaims. She never strolls; she marches. She is a woman going somewhere, it does not matter where, in a hurry.

In the novel and in the film, Jules and Jim search for a statue; finding it, they search for a woman to match. The statue's stillness counterpoints Moreau's quick changes (14–2). Because they see the statue in Catherine, the audience attempts to see it too. The conflict within Catherine's character becomes such that the audience searches for a constant in all that motion, searches for the center of a whirlwind. The search is fulfilled only when Catherine is dead; the difference between Moreau's portrayal and the statue is the difference between the animate and the inanimate.

Jules and Jim provide contrasts to Catherine, and to each other. Werner, as Jules, leans forward to talk with or look at others. When he is with either Catherine or Jim, he looks up at them—not with just his eyes or his head, but twisting back from the shoulders. When he walks, even alone, he struts. He is a short man accustomed to walking with people taller than he. When he gestures, it is with emphasis and theatricality. He is no athlete: his feet clump on the ground, flatfooted and in shoes that seem too heavy. Physically he is most at home with his child, Sabine. Like a child's, Jules's body appeals for approval, for equality in a world where the strong are physically big. To underline the effect, Truffaut even had Werner's hair cut like a boy's. In

14–2. *Jules and Jim.*

Courtesy of Janus Films

contrast, Henri Serre's Jim is a tall, relaxed athlete, physically sure of himself to the point of being passive. He slouches, glides, sprawls. He is stiff only when he is dressed in a suit, or meeting people shorter than he is. But even then he does not act; he is acted upon.

Voices support bodies. Moreau's is dynamic, capable of quick mood shifts, but always commanding. Werner's is thickly accented, modulated between exuberance and sadness. Serre's is a "storyteller's" voice, laconic, quick when necessary, smooth.

By building his film around his main actors, Truffaut substituted performance for characteristics emphasized in the book. To exploit Werner's skill at evoking humor and pathos—Chaplin's *The Kid* is echoed in many of Werner's scenes—Truffaut changed Jules from a novelist to a scholar who writes about insects, and who threatens to write a novel about them. Jim becomes a novelist as well as a journalist; this accords with his storyteller's voice. To exploit Serre's passivity, Truffaut borrowed a concept from Roché's *Les Deux Anglaises et le continent,* the book on which *Two English Girls* is based: Jim becomes a "curieux," a man who makes his living by being curious about other countries and other people.

To set off his main actors, Truffaut used other performers as the basis for his minor characters. Roché's Kate has several "spare lovers." Truffaut condensed them into one, Albert, who could be played by the musician-composer Bassiak, a logical accompanist for Moreau's singing. Roché's Jim has several lovers as well as a mistress. Truffaut left in the mistress but compressed the book's secondary women into one female "picaresque" played by Marie Dubois, the female lead in Truffaut's *Shoot the Piano Player.* Dubois's brilliance as a comedienne helps establish the film's rollicking opening mood when she does an imitation of a steam engine, using a cigarette. Later Dubois helps break down a mood that has become too serious by relating, as a monologue, her erotic autobiography. In Roché's book, Jules and Kate have two children. Truffaut, simplifying, compressed them into one. The child actress, Sabine Haudepine, dominates Jules and echoes Catherine. She is the only actor or actress in the film who can really compete with Moreau's almost overpowering cinematic charisma (14–3). To complement and complete his film's fictional society, Truffaut employs several brilliant actors, including Jean-Louis Richard and Bernard Largemains, to contribute strong bit performances and give a sense of the bohemia from which Jules, Jim, and Catherine spring.

The job of Truffaut's main actors was to play the friendship and love triangle themes at full intensity. The job of his supporting actors was to expand the film's themes and keep the film from becoming too consistently serious. In a novel there is no such thing as major characterizations that are "too good." In film there is such a danger: actors such as Moreau and Werner are stars precisely because they can make themselves the centers of attention in any film they play in. Moreau in particular can make even banal moments compelling, whether or not the film's rhythm needs compelling moments at that place. Truffaut's solution was to allow his main actors to

14–3. *Jules and Jim.*

Museum of Modern Art, Film Stills Archive/Courtesy of Janus Films

work "wide open," and to balance their seriousness with amusing interludes provided by supporting actors. In one scene Jim waits for Catherine in a café. A drunk slouches over a table, his saucers piled high, continuing to drink. Another customer obnoxiously explains why he, unlike his wife, has no sense of humor. By the time Jim leaves, and Catherine appears (their missing one another allows Catherine's and Jules's tragic marriage to occur), we are distanced by laughter. Later in the film, Jim, now completely in love with Catherine, goes to Paris alone. In a café he meets old friends. Marie Dubois sees him and begins an exuberant monologue on her amours, ignoring everyone who comes to shake Jim's hand. Then Jim meets a friend who says of Catherine, "Wouldn't mind having a go at her, myself." Finally a friend introduces his mistress as a woman with no mind, who is "pure sex." Each encounter undercuts the romantic seriousness of the Jim-Catherine love affair. By the time our attention goes back to it, our serious mood has vanished. Truffaut builds moods with Moreau, Serre, and Werner; when these moods have gone far enough, he destroys them through the agency of supporting actors. The balance of themes and moods in the film does not derive from the book but from Truffaut's use of actors.

In Roché's novel, controlling ironies are provided by narrative wit. In novels, direct and omniscient narration is an accepted albeit archaic convention. Truffaut was faced with a choice between dropping narration and fully "dramatizing" the film, and maintaining the narration as a deliberate artifice, with the narrator as an unseen character. In film, narration is almost always a joke, intended or not. Truffaut emphasized artifice in order to make the joke intentional. Truffaut's narrator bridges episodes, tells characters' thoughts, and comments ironically on the action. Michel Subor's narration is neutral and fast-paced, adding layers of exposition and irony to dramatized incidents. The effect is one of comic compression, seeming to double the speed of the film's quick action by allowing actions to begin and end in midscene. Subor's neutrality distances the viewer by carefully calculated degrees. As an offscreen character looking back in time, the narrator allows Truffaut to carefully control emotional intensity at a level "higher" than that of dramatic action.

The essential tension in *Jules and Jim* thus becomes one between romantic intensity and ironic distance. Truffaut enhanced the tension by his treatments of sound and visuals: the film's music and photography each echo the tension, sometimes enhancing intensity, sometimes providing distance. Of the two, music and photography, *Jules and Jim*'s music is by far the simpler structurally and in effect, and can be considered most quickly.

Sound

The film has two musical styles. The first is fast and "popular," the other, smooth, orchestrated, and conventionally romantic. They correspond to a dichotomy between exuberance and sadness, the two dominant moods of the film. The film opens with calliope-like "café" music, abrupt, light, a signal that the film is set in the golden age before World War I. The tone is a jovial accompaniment to Jules and Jim's friendship and bohemian life style. That musical style recurs later in the film when Jim returns to his café to meet his friends. Akin to, but more personal than, the café music is the Bassiak-Moreau song "Le Tourbillon" ("The Whirlwind"), which is lilting but expresses the romantic intensity of Catherine's life. Georges Delerue, the film's composer, used deliberately haunting music to provide the sound track's second style. Instructed by Truffaut to keep the music "light," Delerue paced his music to accord with and comment on the action. Before the war it is light and cheerful; after the war, sad. The beginning is written in mostly major chords and uses a full orchestra. Later, woodwinds—bass, clarinet, flute, and oboe—become dominant, with instrumentation a source of sad undercurrents in major keys. Delerue locks musical mood into the hopes of the characters, and at the film's end, modulates Bassiak's "Le Tourbillon" to make it a sad comment on human aspirations. Working at the level of the heart (and in contrast to the narrator's intellectualizing), Delerue shows off the romantic dimension of *Jules and Jim* as a tale of impossible love.

Cinematography

Truffaut offset the romantic appeal of Delerue's music with antiromantic photography geared to demand full perceptual participation in the film's visual action. Four elements in Raoul Coutard's photography contribute to perceptual activity. One is the lighting, flat and gray. Another is the use of the cinemascope format. Thirdly, odd compositional patterns often lead the eye away from its "natural" object, the actors. And fourth, Coutard's camera movements often "chase" rather than predict or synchronize with the action. The four elements, along with Truffaut's gray-on-gray wardrobes and cluttered sets, force the viewer to work at seeing Truffaut's story, preventing the eye from becoming passive.

Coutard's lighting is the antithesis of normal studio style, the normal mode of film romance. There are no "modeling lights" or backlighting or rimlighting; the general illumination is soft. Normal "dimensional" lighting uses a four-light structure: a "key" light illuminates the scene; a "fill" light models shadows; backlight and a "rim" light "kick" the composition, giving it more life and making the actors stand out from their surroundings. Coutard's style looks documentary in approach, more like the still photography of Cartier-Bresson than like a traditional film romance. The effect is to turn *Jules and Jim* into a documentary on a fictional event.

Coutard's use of the cinemascope format is as unusual as his lighting. Normally wide screen is used to enhance spectacle. For Coutard wide screen simply provides a shape in which to compose. Part of the time he even ignores its dimensions, composing in only part of the screen. Once (in the café scene where Jim waits for Catherine) he even masks off the left side of the picture. A good part of the time, Coutard deliberately unbalances compositions, letting motion shift away toward the side, playing motion against composition in a spatial-temporal counterpoint. The total effect is to offset the emotional quality of the action by drawing attention to the way Coutard is playing with his camera. While Coutard involves the eye he reminds it that what is being watched is "only a movie."

To reinforce visual drama, Coutard and Truffaut play with lines. Pictures with no otherwise striking features often have railings, wall decorations, window frames, or doors to "aim" the viewer's eyes. Jim sits writing a letter to Catherine. There is no motion to speak of. But the viewer's eyes are riveted on Jim by the railing behind him (14–4). When Jim comes to Catherine's hotel room to tell her their affair is over, Coutard photographs him from below so that the molding in the top corner of the room forms a triangle; on the wall behind Jim as he talks, a spearlike ornament "aims" at him (14–5 a, b). When Jim moves to look out the window, the spear—two-headed—again points at him, while window supports frame him from the other side (14–5c). All lines (literally) lead to Jim. And in the scene in which Moreau will sing "Le Tourbillon," Moreau and Bassiak are at screen left, Werner and Serre at screen right. The slats on the bench and the paneling on the walls lead our eyes be-

14–4. *Jules and Jim.*

tween the characters (14–6). From a purely visual point of view, *Jules and Jim* is almost an essay on paneling, tiles, railings, and fences.

Coutard frames within frames, leading the eye toward whatever is of most importance (see p. 206). Catherine, returning to Jules and Jim, peeks through a window; the window frame gives Coutard his subframe (14–7a). Early in the film, Jules, Jim, and Catherine are together on vacation; a balcony provides a frame for what is important in the composition (14–7b). And when Catherine awakens Jim by driving outside his window, the frame of French doors allows the viewer both to see Gilberte and Jim together and to see the possibility of their physical separation (14–7c).

Considering his background as a still photographer, Coutard uses his camera in a surprisingly mobile way. Outdoors, he dollies the camera ahead of the actors, enhancing their forward motion. (The effect is like looking backward while riding in a car.) Indoors, he usually pans rather than dollies, but his pans often include slight tilts upward, which increase the feeling that the action is quick. Coutard often allows action to move ahead of his camera. Thérèse (played by Marie Dubois) moves to the right to light a cigarette for her "smokestack" act. She turns quickly, going from screen right to the left while puffing. Coutard lets her move well into the frame before he begins to chase her with the camera. The effect is to make the action more vital, impulsive, and quick. The viewer *must* remain perceptually involved.

Editing

The film's sense of playfulness is reinforced by editing, transition techniques, and switches in visual style. Truffaut provides irises to get into and out of scenes; the iris, used "straight," died in the 1920s. Truffaut burns in titles (in

14–5. *Jules and Jim.*

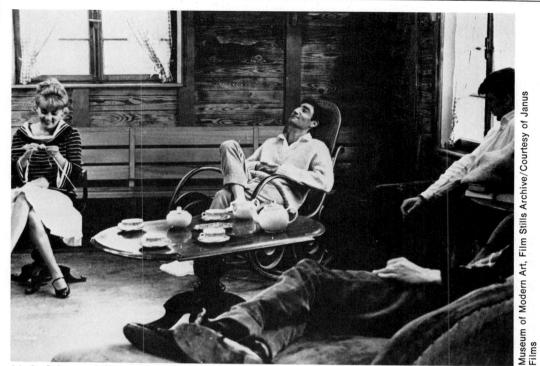

14–6. *Jules and Jim.*

French) over empty shots of the sky to reinforce the artificiality of the device of narration. He uses aerial shots of Jules's country house in a witty way. When Jim's and Catherine's love is going well, the camera rushes forward; when it suddenly goes badly, the camera moves backward. Truffaut cuts from cinemascope action to "period" documentary footage, establishing distance between the film as fiction and the time historically represented in the film. He even "stretches" documentary war images to give them an expressionistic, nightmarish effect. He superimposes shots, dissolving from Jules singing "*La Marseillaise*" in a German accent to a war-recruitment poster; he dissolves from Catherine's letter to a double exposure of her face over a moving landscape (see 14–8, p. 207).

This film, Truffaut is saying, is to be taken playfully. And Truffaut reinforces the mood of artifice by refusing to age the actors with make-up, despite the long time span of the fictional events. The viewer of Truffaut's film knows he is to take the film lightly, to look at it as an artifice. The viewer of *Jules and Jim* participates in a fiction while remaining perceptually aware of it *as* fiction. And, perversely, because the film's surface *is* so playful, involvement is more concentrated than if it were not.

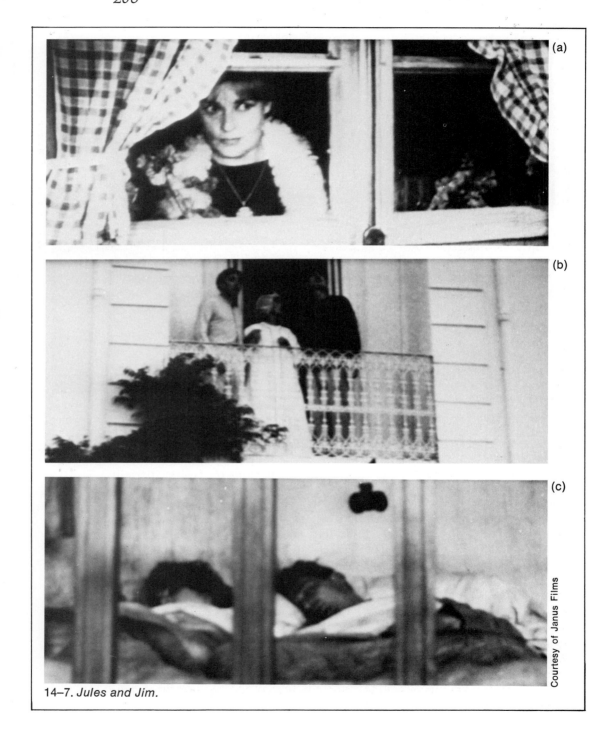

14–7. *Jules and Jim.*

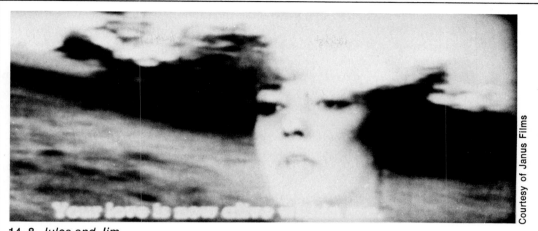

14–8. *Jules and Jim.*

Courtesy of Janus Films

MOMENTUM AND SPECTACLE: A SPORTING AESTHETIC

Each of the major ingredients in *Jules and Jim* (including the novel) provided Truffaut with means by which to balance romance and irony, the claims of the heart and of the mind, while they all work to propel the film forward. Using the book's episodic structure and narration meant no time was wasted on exposition of the basic drama. The actors rush through their roles, playing them wide open; they do not have to provide bridges for scenes. The sound track pulls at the viewer, urging involvement. The cinematography demands full and active use of the eyes. When the film does have quiet moments, it is to break the rhythm and provide rest before the next brisk sprint. Truffaut's genius was to treat romantic love structurally as a sporting event.

As Susan Sontag has pointed out in another context, "The cult of love in the West is an aspect of the cult of suffering—suffering as the supreme token of seriousness. . . . The sensibility we have inherited identifies spirituality and seriousness with turbulence, suffering, passion."[8] The dominant characteristic of romantic love is pain. Extreme forms of romantic love are not only emotional athletic contests, but, like boxing, football, bullfights, and most forms of racing, they involve their participants in agony. Athletics—whether physical athletics, the spiritual athletics of the saint, or the passional athletics of characters like Jim and Catherine—requires of its practitioners extraordinary skill (what athletes do would kill anyone else) and a proclivity for violent absolutes. The tightrope-walker's dictum, "to live is to be on the wire," expresses the athlete's contempt for ordinary life's relativism. But the point of athleticism is to provide spectacle. The difference between "pure" romance and a film such as *Jules and Jim* is that pacing and irony keep spectacle values foremost in the latter.

The relationships among the characters are volatile: one moment the characters are passionate; in the next incident they fight; five minutes later (in actual film time) they meet, having been apart. However compelling each moment is, the viewer cannot identify with so much seen so quickly; all he can do is become involved with the characters and follow the action. The narrator, like a narrator of a sports event, helps him keep it all straight and fills in background. The music helps keep emotions in order; the cinematography keeps the eyes involved. Every time minor characters come on there is an intermission—then the event resumes. The whole process drives toward the finale, which provides structural and thematic resolution to the entire film.

Jules, Jim, and especially Catherine are people who will not play by the rules. Catherine marries Jules; she shouldn't. Their marriage is doomed but still they have a child. Catherine has affairs. She and Jim fall in love; Jules tolerates—even encourages—his best friend's affair with his wife. Catherine wants children with Jim. They can't have any. She rejects Jim. Then she wants to resume the relationship. Jim by now wants to marry his mistress, Gilberte, and have children. Catherine tries to shoot Jim; he escapes. A performer intent on ending the show only with death, she is aware of the sadness of aging athletes and lovers. She and Jim meet again. She invites him for a drive. She drives off a bridge into a river. They die. Jules has their bodies cremated. (We watch this, too, as if it were spectacle.) The narrator intones:

> The ashes were collected in urns and put into a pigeon-hole which was then sealed up. If he had been alone, Jules would have mixed them together. Catherine had always wished hers to be scattered to the winds from the top of a hill . . . but it was not allowed.[9]

Jules walks down the steps, and goes toward the exit.

As in any spectacle, *Jules and Jim* affirms the value of "rules." As with any romantic spectacle, it wisely waits until the end to do so. What Nick Carroway in *The Great Gatsby* calls "riotous excursions with privileged glimpses into the human heart" is also the subject, and central focus, of *Jules and Jim*. Once we have had those excursions and privileged glimpses we are set back down into our own world, a world presumably of sanity, responsibility, and order. Truffaut takes us out of our prosaic lives, entertains us, and then returns us to normality.

TRUFFAUT'S ACCOMPLISHMENT

The point of *Jules and Jim* was not to be original, but to reauthenticate the optimism that has been the trademark of the popular arts since the nineteenth century. Truffaut's use of nostalgia, of old ideas and situations, is essential to his accomplishment. To be optimistic, one must have confidence in oneself, in people, in the patterns of history—in something. Truffaut creates confidence in a number of ways. He implies that *he* has it through the bravado of his film style and his grasp of his materials. He reinforces the viewer's confidence by sharing his playfulness with him, by reminding the viewer just how much he knows, and by expressing confidence—through his uses of the narrator and the sound track—in what remains constant in time. The events, narration, and music of *Jules and Jim* never really move from one fixed point to another; they go in spiraling fashion, with bits of old songs and old motifs coming back in ever new forms. Whatever is over will be back again; whatever is new will be a variant of the old. Summer will come again. It will not be entirely new, but it will be fresh. And the old will weave its motifs into every new song. If characters die, the narrator survives; if the narrator stops, there will always be narration and song. And because the pace of history implied in the pace of the film is so fast, if summer and love die quickly, then so will winter.

Popular art reassures. It says that some things, if not eternal, are at least recurrent. Thus there are very few new elements in *Jules and Jim*'s ideational structure. What did not come from Roché's book came from other books or films, or from tradition. The theme of impossible love is as old as Greek mythology; the love triangle is standard French fare. War as the destroyer of human relationships—one finds that theme in *The Iliad* as well as in contemporary works. *La vie bohème* and nostalgia for the turn-of-the-century "Golden Age" were trademarks of both Marcel Carné and Jean Renoir. Romance mixed with spectacle and irony is a standard formula of popular fiction; one finds it in Tolstoy, in Balzac, in Hugo. *Jules and Jim* is a new variation of a very old story. And there is comfort in seeing and hearing old stories told again.

What Truffaut does, however, is to modify the old so that it can be watched with fresh eyes, and with fresh, modern intelligence. Donald Sutherland has said that Casanova's appeal was in making women feel it was the first time, though they knew it was not. Ezra Pound wrote that the artist's task is "to make it new." Truffaut makes the old new; what he makes new, however, is as old as love or eating. What makes a master artist, lover, or chef—the techniques, though not the medium, are the same in all seductive, imaginative arts—is his love for and enthusiasm about what he is doing and whom he is doing it for. Truffaut respects and loves his audience. He includes them in his jokes, his ironies, his enthusiasms, his nostalgia. The result is infectious. The audience responds by willingly looking at *Jules and Jim* through Truffaut's eyes. And it is precisely the willingness to look at art through the artist's eyes—to conspire and collaborate with the artist's viewpoint and activities—that is the essential element of modernist response.

The techniques used in *Jules and Jim* are deliberately self-conscious; one cannot watch the film without continually being made aware of the artifice. But Truffaut's self-consciousness, however "modernist" it is in structure and form, is unoppressive because it is playful. The reason large audiences have difficulty with modernist treatments of structure, form, and perception, with the aesthetic of indeterminacy, is not entirely the result of the newness of what modernist artists are dealing with. Rather, the arrogance of much modern art is such that viewers or readers feel they are outside the ingroup for which a work was made. Art is always a form of play. But because of the antibourgeois stance of modernism, artists have let popular audiences know that "I'm not going to play with *you*." The effect is that those not in the ingroup reject the standoffishness of modernism. Truffaut gets around the problem very simply. He uses the Transactional Analyst's ploy of reaffirming again and again "I'm O.K., you're O.K." Doing that, he can get an audience to respond with full intelligence to his self-conscious narrative device, his camera techniques, his fragmentations, his playing with film itself. And at the same time, Truffaut can get those who expect intelligence and modernism from a work to take his essentially nostalgic and old-fashioned materials seriously. If Truffaut is a genius of popular cinema (as I believe he is) it is because he is a master strategist.

But the effect of incorporating modernist intelligence in popular materials is also to increase optimism. College-educated audiences as well as the general public have come to regard modernist approaches to art as a little too sacred, a little too sanctimonious. The playfulness of modernist art—a playfulness evident in the works of Picasso, Léger, Duchamp—coexists with the deadly seriousness of its tasks. In colleges and other educational situations (museums and libraries) playfulness is forgotten, submerged in professorial intonations. Roché ate, talked, and drank with Picasso, Stein, and Matisse— he knew there was an amusing side to all this experimentation. Truffaut, building on Roché, plastered his sets with Picasso prints—even used them to signal the passing of time. Roché's and Truffaut's characters are "modernists." Roché and Truffaut say simply that such people are human too. They live in the same culture we do; they fall in love; they die. There is universality in impermanence, humanity in the artists—and implicitly in the art—that Ortega y Gasset and others have described as "inhuman." Even artists eat, love, and sleep as we do. We are connected by the basics of our experience. By incorporating a modernist surface and intelligence in *Jules and Jim* and by making "modernist" characters the film's subject, Truffaut reaffirmed the essential playfulness of all art, and the communal experiential base on which society rests, despite its absurd rules and violence. By embracing the modern as well as the past, Truffaut reaffirmed the continuity of all experience. That reaffirmation is, to any audience accustomed to believing in split culture, optimistic and reassuring.

In *Jules and Jim* there are two messages. One is that we must try to understand. "Everyone has his reasons"—Truffaut quotes Renoir's line from *The Rules of the Game* more often than any other. The second message is that we *can* understand. Our differences are temporary, episodes in a fast-paced film. Our intelligence and humanity are permanent. That Truffaut managed to make those messages convincing makes *Jules and Jim* a landmark of modern popular cinema.

If the cinema of the future did nothing more than expand on Truffaut's example, did nothing more than make the popular intelligent and the intelligent popular, I, for one, would not grieve.

BLOW-UP

If the nineteenth century is François Truffaut's spiritual home, the twentieth is Michelangelo Antonioni's. The problems Truffaut's characters encounter could, in the main, have been encountered in any age. But the problems of Antonioni's characters, especially in his *The Red Desert, Blow-Up, Zabriskie Point,* and *The Passenger,* are specifically modern problems stemming from our modern urban, technological, capitalist age. Antonioni is a unique phenomenon in the archaic milieu of commercial film. Virtually alone among important contemporary film makers, he refuses to take us out of town and out of our time. Further, in films such as *Blow-Up* he refuses to let us view our time from any perspective other than a radically modernist one. He refuses us definitions of reality that will make our human condition easier to bear. Instead, he forces us to face it head-on and without excuses.

Blow-Up was, in 1966, the first film to be both avant-garde and truly commercial. It played everywhere—in Aberdeen, South Dakota, in White Plains, Idaho. It made money. It got talked about. It got imitated. Culturally it was as if Joyce's *Ulysses* had been a Book-of-the-Month-Club selection that people actually read. With *Blow-Up,* modernism, the major art movement of this century in every medium except film, reached a mass audience.

The more closely one analyzes *Blow-Up,* the less one understands how it could have been popular. Antonioni's previous films were not. They were so dense, difficult, and slow that they played only on the art film circuits. *Blow-Up,* superficially, is different. It is fast-paced and loud, and deals with a popular subject—youth culture. But the closer one gets to the film, the more it becomes a film not merely to be watched but to be pondered. And one has to try hard not to use terms such as "epistemology," "phenomenology," and "ontology" in describing what the film says and what it is about. *Blow-Up* is a film in the form of an inquiry into the nature of our knowledge about contemporary reality.

There are no easy answers to what *Blow-Up* "says" or even to what it is "about." Critics whose business is art have claimed it is about art; critics whose business is media have claimed it is about media. Critics who like youth culture agree with Antonioni that it is favorable to that culture; critics who dislike youth culture have cited it as a condemnation of the values of youth. I believe such interpretations fail to recognize both the modernity and the complexity of the film. *Blow-Up* descends not from the moralistic cinema but from the urban novel of Joyce and Pavese. The film is a loose adaptation of the most experimental of modern fictionalists, Julio Cortázar. *Blow-Up* takes on more than media and art; it takes on technology as a state of mind. Technology is Antonioni's home territory, a main concern in all his recent films, and *Blow-Up* uses a point of view that denies us superiority to its contents. We are as limited as its protagonist in our knowledge of what it contains. To understand the film we must understand where it came from, what it does, and how it does it. Antonioni said while making *Blow-Up:* "I put reality itself in question." We have to do the same for the reality of his film.

THE INSPIRATION: CORTÁZAR'S STORY

Blow-Up was (as the titles inform us) "inspired" by a short story by Julio Cortázar.[10] Cortázar, though little known in the English-speaking world, is an Argentine living in Paris, and in the top rank of young writers. His work combines virtually every stream of literary experiment. Pivoting on the ambiguities of fiction, fantasy, and behavior, his stories and novels unfold in eerie jazz rhythms of words layered in an unsecured way. The reader is never certain of his own position or of the main relationships of the story materials. In his most famous novel, *Hopscotch,* the reader even has a choice of how to read: he can proceed sequentially through the chapters, read them in an alternate order suggested by Cortázar, or make up his own order. How the reader tackles the chapters determines the novel's meaning as well as its structure; structure becomes meaning.

In the story "Blow-Up" (originally titled "The Devil's Spittle," a colloquial Spanish expression meaning "a close shave") the narrator, a professional translator and amateur photographer, debates how to tell the story. Standard modes of storytelling, even standard grammar, cannot capture the narrator's meaning. As the story unfolds, it relates the incidents stemming from a walk through Paris intended as a picture-taking excursion. The narrator, after taking a number of other pictures, frames a picture of the Pont Neuf. In the picture, a blonde woman seems to be seducing a teen-age boy. The narrator fantasizes about how the seduction will proceed; he snaps the picture. The woman objects; the boy takes the opportunity to run off. As the photographer leaves, he discovers that outside the frame of the picture a middle-aged man has been waiting. The woman has been seducing the boy for him. The photographer, pleased at having "saved" the boy, returns home. After blowing up the picture and hanging it on the wall of his apartment, the photographer cannot ignore the picture; its contents begin to move and take on life. The story, unstoppable, unfolds, and the narrator watches it. As before, the boy escapes. But the man, now at the center of the frame, becomes a lump that blots out the island they are on; the narrator cries. Now, as the narrator tells the story, the blow-up has become a window through which he can see clouds, a few birds, and the sky. The narrator's subjectivity has taken over the experience. The story as a whole becomes an analysis of the indeterminate barriers between experience and imagination, and of the holes in the barriers.

The story itself bears little resemblance to Antonioni's film. Wherein lies Antonioni's "inspiration"? Part of it probably came from the incident of a photograph's seeming to mean one thing and turning out to mean something else. Part of it may have come from Cortázar's pose as a writer writing about a photographic experience; writing and cinema posit a time element lacking in still photography, an element of imagination not contained in the artifacts produced by still photography. And part of it probably came from Cortázar's concern for the interpenetration of perception and imagination: this is a perennial Antonioni theme. But above all, I believe Antonioni was attracted by the indeterminism, the uncertainty that Cortázar showed could multiply whenever a fragment of experience is looked at closely and imaginatively. Cortázar, like the Impressionists, Symbolists, and Cubists, questions the "facticity" of apparent facts; he shows how meaning depends on what is hidden, on clues, on what is imagined and put together in the mind. He shows that events—what was happening, what it means—are impenetrable except through the imagination. And Cortázar shows that single events can have many—dozens, hundreds?—of possible meanings. The photographer believes meaning is to be "found." The writer, like the film maker, knows that each of us has to create it. Events are, in themselves, irrevocably enigmatic. Cortázar's story is Heisenberg's "uncertainty principle" fictionalized; we never know where events came from or where they are going. We know only, and maybe, that they "seem."

THE ABSENCE OF A PAST

Antonioni's characters in *Blow-Up* have no past; we glimpse them as they are without knowing how they got that way. Antonioni's protagonist, Thomas, simply *is*, and we have to deal with his situation as he does—as he encounters it. Antonioni does not tell us about memories. Thomas has no lost innocence to recapture. In *Jules and Jim* there really was a golden age of friendship and freedom before World War I. The war and time, like the snake in Eden, destroyed a good world. If the old world and its values could have been retained, things might have turned out well, or at least better. In Resnais's *Hiroshima, Mon Amour,* the heroine's wartime love affair with a German soldier was blissful; after his death and her ostracism, she was not able to recover paradise by really loving again. In Bergman's *The Seventh Seal*, the knight's life was good before he went on the crusades, but this experience ruined his chances of living happily. In the same director's *Wild Strawberries*, things might have gone better if the old doctor had been different as a young man. In Fellini's *La Dolce Vita*, Marcello's ruin comes from having sold out; at one time his life had promise. In Welles's *Citizen Kane*, Kane is taken from his home; a boy who might have turned into a decent man instead becomes the media lord, "Citizen Kane." In each of these films (and one could name a hundred more), the protagonist's difficulties come from having to deal with past mistakes. The far past is treated by the characters (and film makers) as a haven of values, and so the job of the protagonist (or audience, often) is to undertake a dredging operation to bring up what has been lost. These films say: "if only we knew the mistake, it could perhaps be corrected or at least not repeated by others."

Traditional cinematic treatments of time make for a villagelike relationship between a story's characters and the audience. Modernity imposes human relationships quite unlike those to which people in previous centuries were accustomed. In a city, we know few friends well or for a long time. Most relationships involve indeterminate acquaintances. We meet someone— metaphorically, we bump into him. He comes in and out of our lives in a fragmentary way. We know a few things about him: profession, mannerisms, social group. We don't know where he came from, and have no real expectations about what will happen to him. Eventually (unless he becomes a friend) he disappears. Relationships are, on the whole, tangential; there is nothing to bind us to the majority of people we meet. Modernist literature has long recognized this social reality: in both Joyce's *Ulysses* and Dos Passos's novels from *Manhattan Transfer* on, most of the characters have only a circumstantial relationship with the main characters, and we know *them* only in an incomplete way. But the cinema has always promoted the feeling that we can really know people in the way villagers know each other, knowing their families, their backgrounds, their aspirations, their destiny. Part of the appeal of traditional cinema is that we can return to the archaic village for two hours and really know people.

What is wrong with that? From a modernist point of view the past is simply over. Our lives are different now, and therefore our art must deal with what *is*. Not only was the past a fool's paradise from a scientific point of view. We simply cannot return to it. Art is useful (to paraphrase William James's view of ideas) insofar as it helps us get into satisfactory relation with other parts of our experience. Therefore art must deal with urban, technological reality.

In an interview with Charles Samuels, Antonioni stated bluntly: "I'm an admirer of technology." He pointed to some television circuitry, and remarked on its beauty. "In my films," he told Samuels, "it is the men who don't function properly—not the machines." He argued that we no longer know what concepts such as morality mean: "We are saddled with a culture that hasn't advanced as far as science. Scientific man is already on the moon, and yet we are still living with the moral concepts of Homer." But of *Blow-Up* he said: "[the film] is favorable to the youth of that particular moment and place."[11] Is that to say that its characters attempt to get into satisfactory relation with their experience without recourse to the outmoded concepts of the past? To answer that question requires a detailed analysis of the film.

THE STORY OF BLOW-UP

Blow-Up is the story of a photographer, Thomas, who inadvertently photographs a murder being committed. He does not realize he has photographed a murder until he enlarges his photographs. He returns to the scene and sees a corpse. He returns to his studio to find all but the most ambiguous of his enlargements stolen. He attempts to communicate his experience to friends but cannot. He returns to the scene a second time the next morning; the corpse is gone. The story is told as Thomas himself would see it, were he watching his own story on film. *Blow-Up* is thus a study of Thomas's behavior *and* his mentality. Because of the restricted point of view, we must deal with the story as it comes, without predigestion or an outside reference point.

The story proceeds without obvious breaks. For analytic purposes, however, it is useful to treat it in three parts. The first section shows Thomas's "normal" life. The second section shows Thomas growing dubious about his photographs as a technician, a man gifted at problem solving. The third section shows Thomas facing both the raw fact of being a witness to murder and the consequences of his having discovered it alone and through a process of technical detection. He must face the fact that he cannot communicate what he knows.

Thomas's "Normal" Life

The opening section of the film establishes Thomas as three very modern things: a sophisticated role-player, a hustler, and a "pro." Thomas treats situations as technical problems that can be solved by intelligence. Part of Thomas's problem-solving technique involves manipulation of his own persona. When we first see him, he looks dirty, unshaven, tired, merely a young man holding a paper bag—from all appearances, a real derelict (14–9).

Then we see that he drives a Rolls-Royce and that the bag he carries conceals both money and a Nikon camera, and we recognize that his clothes are a costume that allowed him to photograph surreptitiously in the flophouse where he spent the night. Students pretending to need money stop him; to their "needy" act, he laughingly responds as a benefactor. Later, when a peace marcher needs a place to leave her sign, he volunteers the back seat of his car. He is whatever the moment requires. For a first-rate high fashion model, he plays voyeur to her exhibitionist, flirting with her to bring out her sexuality (14–10). But with sullen clothing models, he is a tyrant, turning them into living mannequins for a stylized advertisement shot (14–11). With his assistants, he is a perfectionist boss. With his agent he is a businessman. With an old man in an antique shop, he is a customer. With the shopowner, he is, like her, a hip young person given to irrational whims. Thomas isn't a chameleon, just an actor who role plays in order to get results. He does it almost instinctively.

The results Thomas aims for are double. On one hand he is a businessman. On the other he is a professional. As a businessman, he is an art capitalist engaged in three (perhaps four) kinds of art work. He does glamour photography; he does clothing advertisements; he deals in retail outlets (an enterprise suggested by his nonchalance when buying a "junk shop"). The docu-

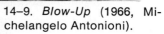

14–9. *Blow-Up* (1966, Michelangelo Antonioni).

14–10. *Blow-Up.*

14–11. *Blow-Up.*

mentary photography may, or may not, be a business venture. Photography books sometimes make money, and often raise a photographer's reputation. But Thomas's documentary photography should be regarded mainly as an expression of his professionalism.

Thomas is a "real pro." Professionalism is, of course, an important modern mythology, combining as it does the puritan work ethic, pragmatism, and an older European respect for quality. Professionalism can be found in craft unions, the arts, and what are normally thought of as the professions, as well as in fields such as writing, photography, and film; the mythology of professionalism, however, has mystical intensity in artistic fields. A pro is more than a competent craftsman, though competence and craftsmanship are cardinal articles of faith with him. A pro has managed to integrate his personal life with his work; his self-image is nearly identical with his work. (Thomas in fact lives at his photo studio.) In certain respects a pro is a modern transmutation of a medieval craftsman, but without an institutionalized guild to support him. For support a pro has his tools and his ego. A pro like Thomas uses only the best machines: he photographs only with Nikons and Hasselblads and drives a Rolls-Royce. He treats the machines with an offhand familiarity. Like his tools, he is utterly reliable. Although he might be detained by a job, he works well despite fatigue and impediments (such as surly models). He is both an artist and not *merely* an artist. Thomas does all kinds and aspects of photography well; photography is his craft, and he is therefore at home with documentary, glamour, fashion, or any other kind of photography he attempts. Versatility is not merely pragmatic; it is a kind of noblesse oblige that is part of being a pro and the consequence of believing in technical rigor. Thomas treats other pros well; his editor (Ron), his painter friend (Bill), the model (Verushka), and the old man in the antique shop are also members of a kind of modern aristocracy. Thomas treats those who are less than pros quite badly, behaving like a tyrant to his assistants and the clothing models. His egotism and elitism amount to the same thing.

In certain respects Thomas's professionalism functions as a kind of asceticism, as a limit to his personality. He lives so totally through his work that he seems to have no permanent outside commitments. To a certain extent his professionalism is a success-oriented neurosis. I doubt he would be capable of a good home life. Decency, politeness, and honor are outside the code by which he lives. But he is not a bad person. He has merely adapted to his profession's demands. Photography is a profession that demands perfectionism but still is as precarious as any other creative art. If Thomas were to react to the derelicts in a fully human way, he could not photograph them; if he were to treat his clothing models politely he probably would not be able to produce good fashion photographs; if he were to acquiesce to the demand by the woman in the park that he give her his negatives, he would lose the photograph he wants for the end of his book. Just as a doctor cannot treat his patient in a fully human way while performing surgery, Thomas cannot be a good person and a good photographer at the same time. Thomas's tragedy is that he has no life other than as a photographer. His profession has taken over his life.

Antonioni presents Thomas's normal life neutrally. One cannot help but be ethically appalled by Thomas's tyrannical methods in his studio. But one also cannot help being fascinated by his energy. He is vital, alive, fun-loving; he *does* things, and with élan. Thomas jokingly summarizes the speed of his life when he tells two would-be models that he doesn't have two minutes to have his appendix out. The speed of his life is brutal, so much so that Thomas's dominant mood throughout *Blow-Up* is fatigue. It is not that he has to run; he simply does not know any other way of being. He drives fast, photographs fast, runs rather than walks. Even when he sits down, he fills moments by playing with coins, fidgeting, and looking around for distractions. He lives quickly, energetically, but in terror that he will find a moment with nothing in it. The only moments he stops are those he photographs. And then it is not Thomas but his camera that freezes moments.

As a photographer, Thomas's job is to embalm moments of time on film. He collects moments. But his photographs are the only still centers in his life. Everything else is transient. Insofar as photography attempts to stop time, preserving moments, Thomas's life and his profession contradict one another. In terms of his life, Thomas is a professional liar. But a photographer is never sure how photographs will turn out until they are developed; he does not burn his flophouse clothes, or suggest they be burned, until he has seen from the contact sheets that he will not have to return there; thus Thomas is also professionally a sleepwalker who, like his friend Bill—or like Antonioni himself—never knows what his work means while he is doing it. And it is around that fact that the second section of the film revolves.

Discovery and Disquietude

Thomas leaves his studio to look at an antique shop he is interested in buying. The owner of the shop is out; after talking with the old man who runs the shop, Thomas goes into a nearby park to photograph. He snaps some pigeons, and then sees what appear to be two lovers, a young woman and an old man, walking in the park. He photographs them, thinking the pictures will make a good ending for his otherwise brutal photography book (14–12). The woman runs up to Thomas, objects to having been photographed, and attempts to grab Thomas's camera. When Thomas bullies her, she runs away in panic. Thomas treats her as just someone who does not want to be photographed. He goes back to the antique shop, talks with the owner about her urge to escape antiques, and buys an old wooden airplane propeller from her. He drives to meet his editor, Ron, on the way radioing to his agent that the shop seems to be a good deal. He meets his editor in a restaurant. They discuss the flophouse photographs. Thomas says he has just taken some photos in a park, "very peaceful . . . very still." The park incident is merely an incident to him; he thinks nothing of the woman's objections. Then he sees a tall, blond young man spying on him through the restaurant window. When the man realizes that he has been noticed, he hurries off. Thomas sees him trying to open the trunk of his Rolls-Royce. Thomas runs to catch him; the man disappears. Thomas drives off (meeting the aforementioned peace marchers), and is followed by a gray Rover. It is at this point that Thomas feels there is something wrong; the second section of the film begins.

When Thomas reaches the street where he lives, no one is in sight. He parks his car and honks his horn (to see if anyone can hear him? to prove he exists?). A man looks at him. Thomas skips off and calls a friend, asking to be called back in a few minutes. Thomas seems to suspect he is in danger, perhaps (I assume) of being mugged or robbed. He goes to his door and

14–12. *Blow-Up.*

encounters the woman from the park, who runs up to him, asking for the negatives he has taken of her. He seems relieved at finding only her.

The following sequence is basically a psychological duel between Thomas and the woman. She is nervous, even desperate. She pleads for the photographs, tries to steal the camera, offers sex in return for them. Thomas plays a cat-and-mouse power game, playing the role of famous photographer: he makes her stand and sit and pose as if she were a model. He forces her to respond to music as he thinks she should. He gives her the phone when his friend calls, and says, "It's my wife." He tells stories about his fictional private life to get her interested in him. He complains about his work, trying to elicit sympathy. In other words, when she offers sex in return for the photos, he wants her to model for him instead. His response is as a studio photographer accustomed to getting results by establishing a mildly sadomasochistic psychological relationship with his subjects. The two are interrupted by the delivery of the propeller. They discuss it; it obviously means two different things to them. The woman leaves after he has persuaded her to write down her phone number for him. He sits down, thinks for a few moments, and then runs to his darkroom to develop and enlarge the park negatives.

Faced by a confusing situation, Thomas's response has been to assume his social role, to force a master-servant photographer-model dynamic on the situation. His ploy told him nothing about the nature of the now-fascinating photographs. So his private response is to employ the resources of a pro, developing, enlarging, and examining the photos. He is accustomed to things out of context, and attracted to them (for example, the propeller, photographs in general). But he is also trained to dissect fragments, making appearances reveal truths. He has faith in detection, in the processes of making appearances interrelate in order to learn new insights. And so the blow-up sequence is almost a paradigm (or parody, since it is simplified) of the faith and methods of post-Renaissance man.

Thomas's faith in his blow-up technique is essentially the faith of the researcher accustomed to divining the "true" nature of things by progressively performing technological tests in a laboratory. The informing belief is that if one can reduce something to its component parts, revealing their nature by technical analysis, the end result will be information that can be related back to raw, untransformed reality. By following a sequential process, the testing is coherent. By reversing the steps of the process, one can return to the original, relating the trivial and the profound. The researcher has faith that first, if the information is gained correctly, it will bear on its original context, and second, that the insights gained by taking something out of context in the laboratory can be brought back to the original context. Each stage of laboratory process requires intelligent hypothesizing in order to guide the following analytic steps. Each stage reveals new information and provides the basis for the next hypothesis, which will reveal new clues.

Thomas's first blow-ups seem peaceful, except that the woman seems to be trying to steer the man toward one side of the field, and has a tense expression on her face. She seems to be looking toward the nearby fence (14–13a). Thomas has the clues for a hypothesis that there is something important about the fence. He enlarges a segment of the fence (photographing the enlargement and blowing up the new negative) and discovers the vague impression of a man with a pistol, hiding behind the fence (14–13b). (He interrupts the process to phone the woman; she has given him a false number.) He believes his photographing has interrupted a murder. The doorbell rings; two

(a)

(b)

14–13. *Blow-Up.*

teenyboppers who want him to photograph them come in. Thomas stops his work for a little fun, after calling Ron to tell him he has saved someone's life.

Thomas accepts the interruption. As a collector of discrete and unconnected moments, interruption is a normal process in his life. A peace march interrupted his drive to the studio after he left the flophouse. There, a phone call from his agent interrupted him. He interrupted his stay at the antique shop to photograph in the park. His talk with Ron was interrupted by the man trying to break into his car. His second encounter with the park woman was interrupted by the delivery of the propeller. His life is a series of "ands" which he deals with as they come. And he believes he has finished the blow-up sequence.

Lying on the floor after a comic mutual rape with the teenyboppers, Thomas looks at the blow-ups and realizes there is an unexplored clue: a clump partially hidden by a tree. He kicks the girls out, and pursues a new hypothesis. He makes a negative from the enlargement, and then makes an extreme enlargement from the negative. The clump vaguely resembles a human head. Perplexed, he wonders if it is a corpse. He goes back to the park and, in the dark, sees a body on the grass. Frightened, he goes back home.

Technically, Thomas's blow-up research has been successful. It has led him to the discovery that he has photographed a murder. But his mentality does not provide him with resources for processing what to do with his information. The mythos of research, like the mythos of photography, assumes an interruption between "real" contexts and the contexts of the laboratory. One is not ethically responsible for what one discovers in a laboratory. Research proceeds from a fiction: that laboratory realities are distinct from outside realities, and that the researcher can (or must) suspend judgment of discoveries achieved technically. Thomas can handle interrupted processes. But he has no resources for handling the kind of connections implicit in there being a real body in the park. Though he has satisfied his curiosity about why the woman wanted the negatives, he had not been prepared for what lay beneath the innocuous surface of his pictures. Ordinarily, the researcher can safely assume a kind of immunity from the ethical implications of his curiosity. But by going to the park and confirming the connection between what he has detected and "reality," Thomas has violated the assumption of artifice—the assumption that research is a matter of "pure" curiosity—on which his confidence as an analytical detective had depended. Now he is a witness to a murder he had no intention of witnessing, and is in danger. Ordinarily the first act of a researcher who has made a discovery is to share his discovery with other researchers, thereby sharing the responsibility for the discovery. But Thomas is in an untenable situation: he cannot merely share the analytic process because the murder was real; and he is a loner. Bill—who is accustomed to not knowing what things mean when he makes them—is Thomas's closest counterpart. But Thomas discovers, in the third section of the film, that he has no community with which to share his information, or responsibility for what he knows.

Confronting Subjective Experience

The first two sections of the film are anything but studies of alienation. Thomas is perfectly adapted to his world, and very competent to deal with it. But the third section of the film shows Thomas's growing awareness of his limitations and of his aloneness. Awareness of being alone comes first. Thomas returns to his studio, but instead of getting the pictures, he goes to Bill and Patricia's apartment. The door is ajar, and he goes in. The place is a mess. In the bedroom, seen through a window, Bill and Patricia are making love. Thomas, startled, withdraws a little; Patricia signals him to stay, and watches him, excited by his presence, while he searches for something else to look at. Although he has had no qualms about playing "three on the floor" with two teenagers, Thomas is embarrassed. His eyes go to one of Bill's abstract paintings; it looks remarkably like an extreme photographic enlargement, pure grain in a vague pattern. He leaves, and returns to his apartment-studio. It has been ransacked. The negatives and blow-ups, except for the last, extreme blow-up of the body on the ground, are gone.

Patricia's kinky request that Thomas watch her having sex is the first time in the film that he is repelled, or embarrassed by a voyeuristic situation. He is a professional voyeur. But his voyeurism ordinarily is a matter of *his* deciding what to watch. He seems not to be able to deal with voyeurism as an act of friendship. Patricia's exhibitionism is too personal for him, and he does not have his camera as a mask or excuse. It seems unlikely that he would have qualms about photographing someone making love. But without a camera he has to confront the situation raw. He seems to realize that he is out of his depth, or (what amounts to the same thing) what his voyeurism means to others. It is an invasion of private, subjective worlds. As is his habit, he withdraws to the world of photography: his studio.

When Thomas finds only the least intelligible blow-up left, he has to confront his own subjectivity, the privacy of his world. He no longer has publicly communicable information on film. Without the contexts for the final blow-up contained in the original photographs, or the sequence between first and final pictures intact, his knowledge is unprovable, unsharable. Without artifacts to shore him up, he is alone. For research insights to be "valid"— something that can be agreed upon—the record of process has to be intact, or reproducible. Thomas is afraid. He hides when he hears footsteps. It is only Patricia, but she acts as if the scene in her apartment had not occurred. In his mental state, Thomas has to accept not discussing the strange scene. He shows her his remaining blow-up, and tells her he photographed a murder. Who? Why? He doesn't know. Patricia is dubious: the blow-up "looks like one of Bill's paintings." Thomas agrees. Patricia asks for help, and then ignores Thomas's question about what is wrong. She changes the subject back to the murder, and then abruptly leaves. Her subjective problems, like Thomas's, are too intense to share. But Thomas has not given up; he calls his editor's place. Ron is not there but Thomas finds out where he is. He wants to show him the body, to share at least the "corpus" of his experience.

Thomas drives into town. He brakes violently when he sees the woman from the park. She disappears into a crowd. He tries to find her, and winds up in a rock music club. She isn't there, but Thomas becomes involved in the scene. The guitarist has trouble with his amplifier, and in anger, beats the amplifier with his guitar, breaking the guitar. The guitarist tears the neck off the instrument and throws it to the crowd. Thomas (unable to resist fragments torn from their natural contexts?) fights for it, and runs out of the club. He throws away the guitar neck; getting it seems to have been more a reflex than a matter of obtaining something he valued. Thomas goes to the party where Ron is. Ron, stoned on marijuana, is in his own world; Thomas's problem doesn't make sense to him. Thomas sees the model, Verushka; in the morning she had told him she was going to Paris. "I *am* in Paris," she says. The party is a study in intentionally dissociated subjectivities, of people engaging in parallel play without really connecting with one another. They have chosen not to communicate; Thomas, wanting to communicate, is out of place. Ron finally remembers that Thomas said something about a park:

Ron: What did you see in that park?
(Thomas looks away and shakes his head hopelessly.)

Thomas: Nothing.
(Ron goes off. Thomas trails after him with an expression almost of dismay.)[12]

At Ron's insistence, Thomas joins the party. He is not a man who can stand opposed to whatever surrounds him; in social situations, he is sociable, even if being sociable means being self-absorbed.

In the morning, Thomas awakens in an empty house. He goes to the park, this time with his camera. But there is no corpse, and no trace of there ever having been one. There is only the sound of the wind rustling the leaves. Thomas leaves, walking along a path that leads by tennis courts. There, Thomas meets the student-clowns he gave money to the morning before. They are acting out a mime of a tennis game, complete with spectators. Their "ball" bounces into the field where Thomas stands. They implore him to throw back their ball. He does so, participating in their reality. He continues to watch the game, and begins to hear the sound of the "nonexistent" tennis ball. He stands alone (seen in long shot) on the grass. Then Antonioni optically erases him from the scene, and the film is over. Once again Thomas has melted into his environment, and this time it is he himself who has disappeared. Antonioni leaves his audience with its own disappearance to deal with; for Antonioni, Thomas's story is over.

Thomas's role as a photographer stops being effective or functional once he has finished his blow-ups. He does not bring his camera when he first returns to the park and sees the corpse. He sees confirmation of the murder as the end, not the beginning, of a process. He could have photographed the corpse at night; to photograph a still object at night is not technically difficult. The first time Thomas does not have his camera with him, he confronts the oddity of being a man without his mask. From then on, the situations he confronts are unphotographable. Patricia and Bill's bedroom situation is too intensely subjective to "understand" on film. Patricia and Thomas's conversation, the rock concert, and the party are auditory or internal at base; visually, there is not much to them. The corpse is gone when Thomas returns; time makes it unphotographable. (Photography is always a matter of making artifacts of moments, of being at the right place at the right time. Thomas should have expected, and perhaps did expect, the corpse to be missing in the morning.) The mime tennis game is visual, but its reality is a matter of social agreement; its essence has nothing to do with what can be "objectively" recorded. A man who is little else than a photographer, confronting the unphotographable, is a man out of his place in the world.

Yet the ending of the film is radically and necessarily ambiguous. Has Thomas, by learning to "hear" the tennis ball, learned to appreciate the positive side of subjectivity? Or has he once again lost his identity in a crowd? Has he been defeated by the ludicrousness of carrying a camera to do battle with unphotographable situations? Or has he learned a new way of being? By the time of the party he had lost his imperialistic "winner's" sense of himself. When he needed other people, perhaps for the first time in his life, they did not help him. When Thomas participates in the wishes of the mimes, is he joining their world, or simply admitting his susceptibility to suggestion? Or does he realize that societal definitions of reality determine what can be regarded as real? Or is he succumbing once again to the figurative? (Mime, like photography, relies on the figurative quality of impressions.) Thomas's expressions are ambivalent; he seems uncertain about where he finally is.

ANTONIONI'S METHOD

We cannot know the meaning of the ending because Thomas does not know. Antonioni allows us no superiority to Thomas, no greater time perspective, no greater amount of information. Although in intense moments we hear what he hears and see as he would see (as in the still frames when he photographs Verushka), Antonioni abjures the superiority of a traditional storyteller. Therefore we can only witness Thomas's story. Traditional cinematic methods make the viewer of an ordinary film almost godlike: the camera's "fly's eye" ability to move about, the sound track's choric comments, and the omniscient point of view predigest the meaning of events for the viewer, thereby making him superior to the characters in what he can see and know. But in *Blow-Up* (just as in a story by Cortázar or a novel by Virginia Woolf or Cesare Pavese) we know no more than a character could. Rather, we must see the film as a still photographer would: as much *found* as created, a matter of surfaces, movements, sounds, behavior. We must hear the story as Thomas does. And because Thomas is a still photographer, we must accept even a jagged editing style. Each shot is a separate perception that makes its own statement rather than being part of a continuous whole. Thomas's perceptual style is so much the style of the film that (in contrast to Antonioni's usual long-lens visual style) we see the film through normal and wide-angle lenses, with a feeling of space between objects. (*Blow-Up* would have been an entirely different story if Thomas had been the kind of photographer who liked long lenses, and if he had brought a telephoto lens to the park. He either would have seen the murder happen, or, if he had missed it, he would not have had the material to discover the murder during the blow-up sequence.) Therefore *Blow-Up* is as much about a way of seeing as it is about Thomas's way of life and experience.

Antonioni's method is not to make us *identical* with Thomas; without losing the technical arsenal of cinematography, Antonioni could not have limited our perspective solely to what Thomas sees from his own eyes. There is no such thing as first-person cinema. In contrast to verbal fiction, the camera must always stand outside its protagonist. (And in contrast to the sound track: because sound in film has no precise location, we can listen through Thomas's ears, hearing the rustling of leaves in the park during the blow-up sequence, and later in the park, hearing the tennis ball.) Our position as viewers is as characters who are *like* Thomas in how we see. We are forced to role play visually and therefore to identify partially with Thomas. The identification is never complete because, despite the sound track, we never know what he thinks. His interior life is private; he is always an "other" person to us, and we don't know enough about his past to believe we really know him. He is an acquaintance. In a village he might be a friend. But in London, he is (like so many people we encounter in a city) someone whom we run into, keep track of for awhile, and then lose. We never have so much as a good conversation with him. His friends are his, not ours. The restrictions of our acquaintance with Thomas are both modernist and urban.

By avoiding nostalgia and limiting the point of view, Antonioni both exploits and departs from the techniques he developed in his previous films, particularly in *The Red Desert*. Antonioni photographed *The Red Desert* from the protagonist's point of view; neurotically heightened color gave us the world through her eyes, in a kind of color expressionism. But in *The Red Desert* Antonioni also presents one of Giuliana's fantasies about the ideal past, in which she is alone as a child on an island. The fantasy is the most beautiful thing in the film; therefore one has to compare the industrial world in which Giuliana lives with her dream world on the basis of *beauty*. In a world of perceptions, aesthetics always precedes ethics. *Blow-Up*, like *The Red Desert*, relates beauty to knowledge, with ethics as a kind of third, and minor, force. But in *Blow-Up* there is nothing with which to compare or contrast Thomas's perceptions.

Thomas, like a movie watcher, is a gatherer of insights through perception. He sees, knows, and then acts. Therefore he is faced with a paradox: the more beautiful something is, the harder it is to act on. The more beautiful something is, the harder it is to know what it means "figuratively"—recognizably and humanly. Three years before he made *Blow-Up*, Antonioni wrote:

> We know that under the image revealed there is another which is truer to reality and under this image still another and yet again still another under this last one, right down to the true image of that reality, absolute, mysterious, which no one will ever see or perhaps right down to the decomposition of any image, of any reality.[13]

The more Thomas looks into the nature of his images, the more mysterious, and beautiful, they become. His final blow-up resembles the abstract paintings of his friend Bill. Antonioni's point is to bring the purely figurative photographer's eye into alignment with the ambiguity-ridden eye of modernist art. Thomas undergoes the art revolution of the last century during the film. At the film's beginning, everything is figurative for him. If he can get into the right relationship with reality's significations (the derelicts' destitution, the park's pastoral atmosphere) he can simply reveal them through his Nikon F "epiphany machine." Thomas believes in the ability of surfaces to reveal their information casually. But as he blows up his negatives, he realizes how much his photography simply creates fiction. He realizes what the Impressionists realized a hundred years before: that all art is a fiction. The derelict photos had been an attempt to escape fiction, to get away from his studio glamour creations. Now he has to face the fact that there is no security in appearances. They always have other appearances beneath them, and others beneath those, each more beautiful and ambiguous than the last. Thomas can no more act on the basis of his final blow-up than he could on the basis of Bill's abstractions or a painting by Jackson Pollock. He has re-created the history of modern art in his darkroom. And that (in terms of perceptual knowledge) is why he must return to the park without his camera. He has to start over, to rethink his situation. Which means he must re-see it.

By giving us Thomas's world through an eye like his, Antonioni has, at a stroke, attempted to bridge the gap between cinema's archaically figurative conventions and modernist art's radically ambiguous current state. To see the present in context amounts to seeing it in a modernist way, with fiction treated as fiction, and reality treated as a source of mystery. Do Thomas's discoveries make him free? Not at all. He is still a photographer, a hustler who must have the guitar neck, a role-player who parties when he is at a party. Do Thomas's discoveries paralyze him? Not at all. He returns to the park in the morning. He plays the imaginary tennis game. He can still act. Do Thomas's discoveries make him more honest? He does not ask that question in any way that we can see, so we do not know. And if we could see, could we be certain of knowing? For Antonioni, perception provides no sure guide through ambiguity. In his world, intelligent seeing is synonymous with uncertainty.

THE POPULARITY OF BLOW-UP

One question remains. How did Antonioni manage to make *Blow-Up* popular? The questions *Blow-Up* asks, the procedures it follows, and the nonanswers it gives are certainly not the materials of popular cinema. Yet the sheer popularity of *Blow-Up* is a fact, and is precisely what distinguishes Antonioni's later work from that of dozens of equally intelligent, equally probing modernist film makers. To answer that question, we must ask again not what the film is doing, but how it is doing it.

All films involve their viewers in imaginative hypotheses; all films seduce the viewer, and then lead him toward a fictional denouement. For the process to work well, it must be regarded as play. For the viewer to follow fictional events with discrimination, the processes and conventions of that play must be clear. Antonioni's film rejects normal viewer expectations, but only in part. And the *process* of hypothesizing in *Blow-Up* does not—except in the ways in which "clues" turn out to be false, and in the ways in which the viewing process echoes the film's themes—differ significantly from the process used in all films.

The first section of *Blow-Up* both seduces the viewer and establishes the ground rules for what follows. The viewer inquires into Thomas's identity; in trying to unravel the paradoxes of Thomas's multiple role playing, the viewer directs his attention to visual surfaces. The viewer's consciousness puts together a Cubist portrait of Thomas. The portrait is playful because Thomas's world is a world of play. For most viewers, the frontier between commercialism and art that Thomas inhabits is a world that exists only in the imagination. The viewer asks about—and gets clues to—Thomas's identity. Then the hypotheses change; the film, at a simple, banal level of interpretation, moves from an exposé to the edges of murder mystery. Again the viewer follows. How will Thomas unravel the clues? What will he do when he does? What will happen to him afterward? The plotting of *Blow-Up*, though it is revealed only implicitly, is strong. And the process of unraveling Thomas's identity becomes the process of viewing the rest of the film. Though the film's genre keeps shifting, the structure of the perceptual and hypothesizing processes in the film remain constant. Because attention is fully engaged by those hypothesizing processes, and because the pace of the film is swift and flashy, the viewer does not ask where he is going; he is on too swift a vehicle to do more than stare straight ahead. Perceptual involvement takes the viewer out of his own world just as surely in *Blow-Up* as it does in ordinary popular cinema.

Blow-Up proves a very simple point. If the viewer can be seduced, and *if* his hypothesizing and perceptual processes can be established so that he will be able to "follow" the narrative, and *if* the narrative "ride" is able to absorb full attention, a film maker can take the viewer virtually anywhere. Provided that the film maker pays attention to, and respects, the viewer's position, there is nothing antithetical about popularity and modernism. Antonioni succeeds because his understanding of perception is profound; he is able to allow the viewing process itself to take precedence over the popular audience's wish for comfortable conclusions. Having agreed to play Antonioni's game in the first parts of the film, the audience plays fair: it goes with Antonioni's hypothesizing to its unsettling conclusions. And because Antonioni plays fair himself—he does not change the rules of the perceptual game once he establishes them, nor does he bore the viewer—the viewer is pulled into sympathetic collusion with Antonioni's examination of contemporary reality.

The cinema has no limits. It can do anything; it can say anything. But to do so and have a popular audience—the *sine qua non* of the feature film—it must respect the viewer's intelligence and the processes by which he imagines and perceives. *Blow-Up* works for popular audiences because Antonioni respected and used what a viewer does when watching a film as part of his narrative strategy. Like Truffaut in *Jules and Jim*, Antonioni reached out to his audience and included them in what he was doing. The audience responded. The result is a phenomenon in film history—a popular modernist film.

The cinema is an audience art. Antonioni was the first hard-core modernist to understand that fact and take advantage of it. If others follow, the future of the cinema could be intellectually, morally, and aesthetically exciting indeed.

NOTES: CHAPTER FOURTEEN

[1] Charles Thomas Samuels, *Encountering Directors* (New York: Capricorn Books, 1972), pp. 27, 53.

[2] Henri-Pierre Roché, *Jules and Jim*, trans. Patrick Evans (New York: Avon Books, 1967), p. 185.

[3] Ibid., p. 115.

[4] "Interview with François Truffaut" in *The New Wave*, ed. Peter Graham (Garden City, N.Y.: Doubleday, 1968), p. 92.

[5] C. G. Crisp, *François Truffaut* (New York: Praeger, 1972), pp. 54–55.

[6] Ibid., pp. 9, 67.

[7] Ibid., p. 62.

[8] Susan Sontag, *Against Interpretation* (New York: Dell, 1966), p. 47.

[9] François Truffaut, *Jules and Jim*, trans. Nicholas Fry (New York: Simon & Schuster, 1968), p. 100.

[10] Julio Cortázar, "Blow-Up," in *Blow-Up and Other Stories*, trans. Paul Blackburn (New York: Collier, 1967), pp. 100–118.

[11] Samuels, *Encountering Directors*, pp. 19, 21.

[12] Michelangelo Antonioni, *Blow-Up* (New York: Simon & Schuster, 1971), p. 110.

[13] Samuels, *Encountering Directors*, p. 23.

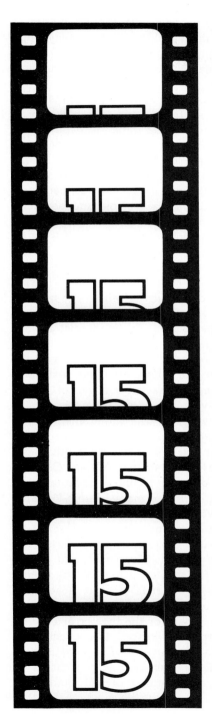

FILM AND THEATER

What has the theater to offer the cinema? Certainly not popularity; modern theater is not popular theater. Modern theater is a theater of experiment, of ideas. It appeals to a cultural elite. But because the theater and the cinema are both performed dramatic arts that depend on audiences, the cinema has more in common with the theater than with the novel, still photography, or painting. The cinema can borrow ways of seeing from the older arts; it can borrow traditions, sensibilities, techniques, ideas, and even whole stories from printed fiction. But the cinema can borrow all those things from the theater, too. And whereas the cinema almost never gives painters employment and only rarely converts photographers into cameramen or novelists into screenwriters, it can, and regularly does, borrow all kinds of production people from the theater—not only writers but directors, actors, and technical personnel. Theater and film are humanly symbiotic. The analysis of cinema's relationship to writing or the visual arts can proceed on largely structural and formal grounds. But to handle film's relationship with theater, one must deal with adaptation in a human sense. One must look at what happens when people adapt themselves to the cinema, bringing from their theatrical backgrounds their personal visions of what cinema can do and be, as well as their talents, traditions, training, and techniques.

Cinema and theater share their performance aspects, their personnel, their need to excite audiences, and their "spirit." Both forms have rejected purity in favor of a quest for inclusiveness. Theater and film are imperialistic, even (as Susan Sontag suggests) "apocalyptic" in their attempts to become total and synesthetic art forms. If one is to speak of a "model" for theater-film relationships, one cannot speak of competition or a one-way flow or even, to borrow an electronic metaphor, of alternating current, with pulses flowing back and forth along a single wire. The only model that fits is a very old one: so-called Chinese boxes. Each box contains smaller ones ad infinitum; each can fit inside larger ones, also ad infinitum. As each art evolves, it encompasses its own past, the past of adjoining arts, and its own past *as* encompassed by the history of adjoining arts in a continuing quest toward incorporating the whole history of all the arts.

This complicates theater-film relationships enormously. Neither the modern theater nor the cinema started from zero. The cinema depended heavily on the traditions and forms of melodramatic theater. But the modernist theater was created from many of the same forces that caused the cinema to evolve. And theater's most radical innovators have found inspiration in the cinema. Of the major instigators of modernist theater, only those who, like Stanislavski, began working before the cinema's inception have been free of its influence. Pirandello's plays, for example, were an exploration of theater aware of itself as theater. But Pirandello knew a great deal about cinema, even writing a novel (*Shoot: The Memoirs of a Cinematograph Operator*) exploring the implications of the new medium. Bertolt Brecht's antifictional theatricalism evolved fully aware of the cinema. His revolving stage in *Mother Courage* brought swift scene changes and a number of other technical advantages of film to the theater. Brecht worked on one film in Germany, *Kuhle-Wampe*, and later worked as a screenwriter in Hollywood. Though he used films in his plays largely as "documents," his quickly changing scenes and sense of emotional structure reveal more than casual borrowing from film. The Bauhaus theater group, which included Vsevolod Meyerhold and Erwin Piscator, openly advocated "cinematicizing" the theater, using "all the means available to the other arts." From the time of Wagner on, the theater has attempted to be all-encompassing, to be the outside box in the Chinese boxes of art evolution. Even Antonin Artaud, spokesman for the theater of cruelty, involved himself in cinema, writing two surrealist film scripts and acting in films such as Gance's *Napoleon* and Dreyer's *The Passion of Joan of Arc*. In Paris in 1976, the most popular play in town was a stage adaptation of Eisenstein's film, *Potemkin*. Nothing is sacred, nothing out of bounds in theater's perpetual attempt to renew itself.

Susan Sontag, in *Styles of Radical Will*, credits Filippo Marinetti, the proponent of Futurism, with founding the idea of a cinematic theater: "Writing between 1910 and 1914, he envisaged the theater as a final synthesis of all the arts; and as such it had to draw in the newest art form, movies."[1] It was at almost the same time that Porter and Griffith were drawing on the techniques of the melodramatic stage, making it the foundation for a popular film aesthetic. But while innovators such as Griffith were drawing on theatrical techniques, they were also moving away from theater, using close-ups and quick cutting. And while theatricians were borrowing from the cinema, they were also moving toward areas the cinema did not monopolize: an emphasis on acting and on overt theatricality—a deliberate staginess. Cinematic innovators from Griffith to Bergman—who shows what Griffith's close-up can do when expert acting accompanies it—have attempted not to imitate theater but to do what the theater can do while exploiting to the maximum their resources as film makers. Theater innovators have done much the same thing: giving up none of their own advantages, they have attempted to do what the cinema can, plus what "only" theater can do. Beyond basic differences in technical means, there is nothing in either art that makes it inherently the "larger" performing art, nothing that stops either art from encompassing the techniques of the other. Plays can include whole films; films can give the feeling of liveness that theater has made its trademark. One must, finally, question whether there are any irreducible differences between these two performing arts. Theory leads nowhere; only their different histories finally distinguish theater and cinema.

A voice for our age's ambitions, fears, and taste for risks, the modernist theater does, however, have a vastly different history than the cinema. The modernist theater thrived not on cinema's formula of nostalgic values in new settings but on a search for new values. The theater has been in a state of identity crisis for over a century—from the time of Antoine's *Théâtre Libre*, of Strindberg, of Ibsen, and of Stanislavski. The cinema has been in crisis only since the advent of television in the 1950s. The rethinking of cinema's identity in recent years follows that of theater, which, long before, had had to encounter the problems of unpopularity, of dealing with a new, smaller audience. In the theater, not only new plays but a new sense of drama emerged from modernism. It may be that a similar new sense of cinema will result from the cinema's current crisis. In the new theater, there emerged new relationships between actor and audience, between actor and role, between performance and reaction. If the historical process of the past eighty years holds true, it may be that, once again, the future of the cinema will echo the past history of adjoining arts; the future of one art is often contained in the past of another. And thus, a consideration of the cinema's future possibilities must take into account the possibility, even the probability, that cinema's evolution will resemble the theater's. Because of the human interchanges between theater and film, the chances of the cinema going where theater has are great indeed.

In the old drama and in the cinema that developed from it, the actor was merely part of the spectacle, the audience merely the viewers for the performance, and the interchange between performance and audience largely a matter of perceptual and emotional content. Norman Holland's description of Charles Kean's 1850 *Macbeth* could as well be a description of a scene in a spectacular Hollywood epic: "*Macbeth* . . . had an enormous eleventh-century banquet hall complete with hundreds of retainers, roasted oxen being carried about, and all the rest."[2] But the modern theater has moved beyond simple spectacle, stressing the actor's primacy and new forms of interaction with the audience. Members of the audience are not there merely to be entertained; they are there to be assaulted, to think as well as feel, to stretch their own abilities to comprehend. Myth, magic, and ritual stand alongside realism as working ingredients in the new theater of the imagination, the "poor theater" as Jerzy Grotowski has dubbed it. The stage itself has become part of drama; ideas and language have become intermeshed with spectacle. With everything stageable and nothing safe, the profound rather than the entertaining has become serious theater's central commodity. If the cinema follows the example of the theater, we are in for an exciting but disturbing time.

Or, rather, it will be exciting if the evidence of the last ten or twenty years is any indication. The revolution may have already begun. Not only through adaptation but through theater-trained directors such as Bergman, the new theater's sensibility has begun to have a strong influence on the cinema.

Unquestionably, one of the greatest "instigators" of modern cinema has been Ingmar Bergman. A good deal of what he has brought to the cinema came from his background in the theater. He began his career by attempting to revive the Swedish stage. While he was at it, he revived the Swedish cinema as well, bringing to it most of the revolutions in modern theater. Only rarely has he adapted works from the theater. He has not had to. He adapted himself and his actors instead. The rest of modern theater came with him as part of the package of his personality. A forceful man, he made the cinema fit him as he learned to fit into the cinema.

What has Bergman, in over three dozen films, given the cinema besides perhaps a dozen masterpieces? His main contribution, I think, has been to bring the new theater's emphasis on actors into the cinema. The cinema has never, of course, been without good actors, but acting has traditionally been subordinate to story and spectacle. Cinema actors have often been little more than mannequins whose visual charisma rather than their acting ability was their stock in trade; the star system even insisted that an actor maintain his or her image no matter the role. (When advertisements proclaimed "Garbo laughs!" audiences flocked to see the star's new-found emotional range.) Constructed in shot-by-shot "setups" that force actors to keep getting into character for a few moments, with no audience to respond to, films have traditionally demanded very little creativity of the people in front of the lens. They have made do with whatever actors could conjure up during short takes.

Revolutions in cinema have often been revolutions involving acting: neorealist directors such as Rossellini accepted the difficulty of acting on film and used amateurs as "themselves." Welles changed the face of the cinema by bringing his Mercury Players—essentially a repertory company—to Hollywood. Godard, Truffaut, and Cassavetes have brought new styles to the cinema by encouraging their actors to improvise, to get involved in the creative film process. Bergman solved the problem of the actor in a different way: he made the potentials of individual actors the starting point of most of his films, going so far as to write roles specifically for the people who would play them, not to exploit their images but to explore their range and potentials. Working with the same actors for a dozen or twenty years, Bergman has created standards of performance virtually unknown in cinema history.

Bergman, by his own account, has spent his life studying actors.[3] He has created what is, virtually, an actor's cinema. Although he has made many weak films, he has never made a badly acted one. He sticks the camera where it will show the actor's work; he rehearses the technical approach to a film assiduously so that filming will not get in the way of performances; he searches for characterizations in the personalities of his company. Bergman told Charles Samuels why he had Liv Ullmann use a crutch in *The Passion of Anna*: "All the time I was writing the part I knew Liv Ullmann must play it, and I knew that the crutch would have a powerful effect on Liv Ullmann's feelings."[4] If an actor sees a part differently from Bergman, Bergman is apt to change the role. As he puts it: "You always have the script, your intention, and the actress. All the time, a fight goes on among those things. It is very fascinating, this struggle. Often it makes things come alive. An example is *Persona*."[5] Working in close-ups and long shots, depending on whether an actor's face or whole body is needed to convey meaning, Bergman takes advantage of the fact that in films what we watch most closely are the people. Bergman's cinema is a cinema based on people, built around the art of acting.

Is Bergman's emphasis on the actor really all that radical, or even theatrical? Oddly, yes. For all the money Hollywood spends on stars, and for all the good performances actors manage to give despite circumstances, the people in front of the camera have only too rarely been asked to communicate directly with the audience through the medium of film. Bergman and his repertory company of actors have shown what is missing in conventional cinema. They have shown what actors can do. Since Bergman developed the techniques of writing for specific actors, new directors have taken up the practice. For example, in Alain Tanner's *Jonah, Who Will Be 25 in the Year 2000*, Tanner and his screenwriter first chose the actors, then wrote the film. Lina Wertmüller writes for her lead actors. Her films exploit the talents of Giancarlo Giannini and, from their inception, are designed to. Acting is becoming a force in contemporary cinema beyond, but in part because of, the example of Bergman.

Bergman is but one example of what theater can bring to the cinema. We cannot know whether his emphasis on acting will transform the cinema as Stanislavski's transformed the stage. But this much is certain: we expect more of actors in film than we did before Bergman. New standards have been set. New directions have been initiated. And if that is not a revolution, it may be the beginning of one.

But Bergman is not the only example of the theatrician-turned-film maker. Nor has he brought the whole of modern theater's experimentalism into the cinema. That has been a job in which others have done much, too, though in less spectacular fashion than Bergman. Bergman's contribution, his "actor's cinema" has become part of the cinematic mainstream. But a good number of theater directors have brought other things. Accustomed to a perpetual questioning of "what is theater" many theater-trained film makers have challenged traditional definitions of the cinema. They have challenged the standard structures of film. They have challenged old notions of what a film can be "about" and what it can do. They have challenged even the spectator's traditional role.

Of national contemporary theaters, two in particular stand out as hurlers of challenges to film aesthetics: the British and the German. Of the two, I have chosen to focus attention on the British because neither German modernist theater nor film makers trained in German theater—such as, for example, R. W. Fassbinder, rated by many as one of the half-dozen best young film directors in the world—are well-known (or even known at all) to English-speaking audiences. Although the most interesting films being made anywhere are now being made in Munich, I must unfortunately limit my present analysis to films that readers have had a fair chance of seeing, merely alluding to what is going on elsewhere. Fortunately, the British theater does reflect international currents. What is happening in British challenges to film aesthetics reflects directions, if not the total genius, of directors elsewhere.

In the recent cinema, one theatrician has been of particular importance: Lord Michael Birkett. Birkett has produced or helped produce virtually every important film adaptation from theater in the last fifteen years. Associated with the National Shakespeare Company and more recently with Britain's National Theatre, Birkett has backed experiments by Peter Hall, Clive Donner, and Peter Brook. The films I will analyze here—Hall's *A Midsummer Night's Dream*, Donner's *The Caretaker*, and Brook's *Marat/Sade* and *King Lear*—are the work of a group of theater-film innovators aware of, if not working directly with, one another. All had the backing of Birkett. Thus the following essays are a consideration both of what theater can bring to film, and of the force of a single group and, indirectly, of a single man.

Beginning a revolution in the arts takes very few people. Sustaining a revolution in the arts takes very many, most of them in the audience. Birkett's group is not alone in challenging film aesthetics. Whether new developments will gather momentum is too early to tell. But something has begun. And if it continues it may change the face of cinema.

The theater has lost its mass audience. But it has not lost its power to challenge the cinema to go where it has gone, and to evolve to meet the needs of our time.

THE SUBVERSION OF SPACE: PETER HALL'S A MIDSUMMER NIGHT'S DREAM

It is no accident that the cinema's technical resources and conventions are geared to describing us by what we do rather than by what we dream, want, or think. Even the philosophical systems of our century—pragmatism, behaviorism, phenomenology, existentialism—are philosophies of action which treat our inner life as less important than our behavior. People are what they do. For portraying us in those terms, the traditional cinema is admirably suited.

But what *of* thought and dreams? Are they beyond the reach of the cinema? Cinema has long been praised for its ability to portray dreams. But does it do so accurately? And what of thought? Is there not some truth to Descartes's "I think, therefore I am"? The cinema has given us little in the way of real dreams, little in the way of what would ordinarily be called serious thought. And the reason may well be contained in the cinematic uses of space. Dreams and thoughts are physically free. But in film, space is functional. When we watch a film, our attention is directed by two kinds of expectation. Genre, story, theme, and motif provide narrative structure and a guide to what is important within scenes. The structures of space and setting provide organizational patterns and limits to what we can expect to see. With both narrative and locational expectations fixed, a director can change angles, focus, and lenses, and move around to reveal details without disrupting overall coherence. Location "integrity" fixes the viewer's attention, assuring him that what he is watching makes sense. To break from the convention of location integrity without providing an adequate substitute is to flirt with confusion, chaos, and incomprehensibility. Images must be organized to make sense. The problem is: how to achieve both the freedom of the mind and coherence. That problem has not been solved by traditional feature film makers. But it may have been solved by Peter Hall in *A Midsummer Night's Dream*.

Until recently, the Shakespeare adaptation was the dullest of all film types. Failing to realize that Shakespeare did not tell realistic stories about realistic people in realistic places, and that his métier was not space, but rather the imagination, directors made one dreary Shakespeare film after another. Recently the situation has changed; a new vision has emerged, indicating what might happen if "Shakespeare" met the cinema. Here is Peter Brook's version:

> If you could extract the mental impression made by the Shakespearean strategy of images, you would get a piece of pop collage. . . . I think the freedom of the Elizabethan theatre is still only partially understood. . . . What people

do not fully face is that the non-localized stage means that every single thing under the sun is possible, not only quick changes of location; a man can turn into twins, change sex, be his past, his present, his future, be a comic version of himself and a tragic version of himself, and be none of them, *all at the same time.* . . .

The problem of filming Shakespeare is one of finding ways of shifting gears, style, and conventions as lightly and deftly on the screen as within the mental processes reflected by Elizabethan blank verse onto the screen of the mind.[6]

Brook suggests that collage, montage, and split-screen techniques could bring a Shakespearean mobility to the screen. Brook understood what Shakespearean imagery might look like on the screen but not the problems involved in achieving it. Shakespearean imagery achieves mobility because there is no fixed physical space to contradict it. Space in Shakespeare, and by extension, in all verbal language, is purely imaginative. Could space be treated that way in cinema?

Film makers have long known that location coherence is not a necessary feature of cinema but rather a convention. Méliès's "magical" cinema, as early as 1896, ignored location coherence whenever doing so would produce laughter or amazement. René Clair's 1924 *Entr'acte* made a Dada joke of locations, turning audience expectations about location integrity into a source of humor. In 1928 Luis Buñuel and Salvador Dali's *Un Chien Andalou* made the joke surrealistic. Shots and scenes are structured according to "psychic automatism." In one scene a room looks out onto a Paris street; in another it looks out onto the seashore. The room is the same. In the Marx Brothers' *Duck Soup* a call for help is followed by a collage of shots of jungle animals, running children, and other absurdly inappropriate—and obviously differently located—shots. Audiences find such jokes about location hilarious. In the American underground cinema, Stan Vanderbeek's 1950s collage films organized shots ideationally and associatively rather than by location. Gregory Markopoulis and Stan Brackhage structure images in ways that do not allow viewers to *expect* location coherence; no one misses it after the first few minutes. In the European New Wave, Alain Resnais (first in *Hiroshima, Mon Amour*, then more extensively in *Last Year at Marienbad*) used visuals as if they were a form of internal monologue. Objects within locations, even locations themselves, changed between shots. At least some audiences are able to accept the dislocations as part of the overall ambiguity. Even mainstream film makers have developed conventions for temporarily portraying consciousness in a visually free way. As long as it is obvious that we are watching a dream sequence or reverie, we accept the lack of localized visuals without confusion.

The overcoming of location coherence is a two-step process. First, the audience must be signaled not to expect rooted visuals—through stylized imagery, music, or some other deviation from the film's style. Second, location "rationality" must be replaced by some other principle of organization.

Neither presents problems in short cinepoems meant for sophisticated audiences. And neither presents problems for short reverie sequences in commercial films. Film makers often merely tint the film to indicate that a mental state is being portrayed, and organize images thematically so that the overall concerns of the film determine the pattern of the dream. But neither underground cinepoems nor short reverie sequences need sustain themselves for any length of time. Cinepoems do not even need to be intelligible to large audiences. For a film of standard length, the problem of finding a substitute for location intelligibility is not in the first, signaling step. It is in the second step: finding a principle strong enough to sustain lengthy deviation from intelligible locations. What can be brought off for ten minutes and what for sixty are two different things. What will be accepted by elite audiences and by general cinema audiences are equally different.

Peter Hall, a theater director by profession, has the advantage of not regarding the visual element of film as having an organizational primacy. Film makers habitually dislocate sound, especially music and narration, without problems. But especially in sound film, verbal language (though it may often be richer than the visuals) is organizationally subordinate to visual location. Need it be? Most film makers, accustomed to the organizational as well as the perceptual primacy of the visual, do not even ask. During most of *A Midsummer Night's Dream* Hall simply organizes the visual elements to counterpoint Shakespeare's language. He so stylizes his images and so fragments his montage that the viewer has to rely on language to sustain coherence. By making the visual organizationally subordinate to the verbal, Hall manages to represent Shakespeare's world of sheer consciousness (or unconsciousness) without restrictions. Images that do not have responsibilities can be free.

Hall's Method

Except for one soliloquy and the middle three acts of Shakespeare's play, Hall's treatment is of no cinematic interest whatsoever. The beginning and ending are mere filmed Shakespeare, realistic and deadly. The reason is that in Shakespeare's play the beginning is sheer exposition and the end is a tying together and resolving of the plot. The world is the Athens of Theseus, representative of rational order. Hall represents that world anachronistically, setting it in an eighteenth-century manor. His treatment mirrors the unimaginativeness of that world, plodding through the exposition of Shakespeare's version of the old comedy plot of "young-love-out-of-whack" (which is too well known to rehearse here) as if it were merely a chore. It is only Shakespeare's world of sexual desire that interests Hall and is of interest cinematically. Perhaps significantly, the film is most imaginative when either Diana Rigg (Helena) or Judy Dench (Titania) is in front of Hall's camera.

Helena's soliloquy (at the end of act 1, scene 1) shows the ease with which Hall's method works. Diana Rigg bemoans the problems of being an ugly virgin. Flirting with the camera, she exudes an almost palpable sexual hunger;

15–1. *A Midsummer Night's Dream* (1969, Peter Hall). (a) Theseus's court;
(b) The world outside; (c) Rigg's soliloquy; (d) The world of the dream-forest.

this virgin has the soul of an erotomaniac. The twenty-six-line soliloquy is continuous. With our attention on the contrast between the soliloquy and Rigg's delivery of it, we barely notice that Hall jump-cuts from location to location, placing Rigg now by a pillar, now by a tree. Without the aid of the stylized lighting in the forest sequences, Hall uses location simply as if it were musical counterpoint, enriching and complicating what works as a pivot of attention—Rigg's presence—while her voice and clinging gestures provide continuity. The effect is electric but subtle: inattentive viewers probably do

(c)

(d)

Filmways, Inc.

not even notice the location switches. Those twenty-six lines of inventiveness are an essay in perception and a preview of what will follow.

·Beginning his film with ordinary, unimaginative visuals, Hall accustoms his viewer to focusing on Shakespeare's language (15–1a). Then he brings the scene outside, releasing it from stagelike confines (15–1b). Next, he moves to Rigg's soliloquy, and, after that, to the full-scale dream world of Oberon and Puck (15–1 c, d). By stages, the nature of the visuals changes until they bear little resemblance to the world of ordinary perception.

15–2. *A Midsummer Night's Dream.*

Filmways, Inc.

15–3. *A Midsummer Night's Dream.*

Filmways, Inc.

Filmways, Inc.

15–4. *A Midsummer Night's Dream.*

Stage and film directors have always had trouble with Shakespeare's forest from the time that the young lovers enter it. Shakespeare layers his dream world with verbal abandon. Puck's and Oberon's manipulations of the plot via love potions (which make Titania love ass-headed Bottom, both young men love Helena, and so on) create a comedy of confusion that makes for a large, single, but far from homogeneous dream. Hall adjusts his visuals to modulate the dream. The lovers enter the forest clean, but soon become muddy (15–2); Rigg, but not the others, is treated with unobtrusive jump-cutting. The craftsmen bring their color tone with them into the forest. Grayish-brown tones go to black as Bottom enters as a lover into Titania's world. Darkness and fog machines create the requisite visual confusion (15–3). The plot—almost farce—casts attention on Shakespeare's language by making it the only reliable element in a comedy of confusion. Significantly, Hall accelerates the pace of speech to a near machine-gun speed. Forced to listen even harder than before, the viewer holds on to the language and lets the visuals run free. Because both the language and the visuals are comic and somewhat erotic, the thematic layering effect works well.

Hall's method works best when his actors are visually and audibly commanding. The difficulty of Shakespearean language helps enforce concentration when it is rapidly delivered, comes directly off the lips of the actors, and is accompanied by compelling visuals. Hall used a nearly full text of Shakespeare's play, accelerating the pace of the delivery to maintain concentration. He shot most of the film in close-up in order to keep concentration from wandering. The viewer has limited resources. By requiring that all his attention be focused on language and freely changing visuals, the film successfully manages to keep the viewer from asking questions inappropriate to the film. Absorption is a matter of consuming all of a viewer's energies.

Hall's method works well with Shakespeare. Would it work with lesser language? Probably, but within limits. Essentially it is a dream-technique, a way of portraying consciousness. It requires strong linguistic power and subjective story content. It requires charismatic voices and visuals; acting is perhaps even more important in free-image cinema than it is in more mimetic, realistic genres. But the method does work. Hall's *Dream* is no small accomplishment in overcoming the strait-jacket of fixed locations; it opens to cinema new possibilities for portraying dreams in visual terms. A technique that can handle Shakespeare's complex *Midsummer Night's Dream* can surely be applied to the dreams of lesser creators. Without Shakespeare's language to order the film, the visuals would be merely underground Walt Disney with a touch of madness. The language works against the grain of the visuals. But again the technique works best when Hall focuses on a woman. Titania's soliloquy (played by a seminude Judy Dench as a comic vamp scene) shifts from greenish to natural colors, to red tones, to darkness. Dench's slightly whispery voice and her gestures compel our attention (see 15–4 on the preceding page).

A CINEMA FOR THE AGE OF WASTE: CLIVE DONNER'S THE CARETAKER

The cinema depends on the world's making sense. It depends on our believing in our senses. And it depends on our believing in culture, in the objects of our culture making sense when the eyes reach out for them. As no other art does, the cinema can exist only in a world where what meets the eye has a reason for being.

But the fact is that our culture is full of junk. Our civilization wastes objects just as it wastes lives. Walking around our cities, we learn not to notice dereliction. But art, especially cinematic art, must make languages of the materials in its reach. The cinema may well have to recognize that fact. And if it does, Clive Donner's film of Harold Pinter's play *The Caretaker* may prove both seminal and prophetic. A venture from the theater of the absurd into the cinema of the absurd, *The Caretaker* shows that if we cannot avoid the deterioration of our civilization, we can at least make art of it.

Absurdist drama, one of the strongest forces in contemporary theater, takes as its starting point a sense of language as a junkyard of irrelevant and inappropriate forms with significations out of joint with experience. It assumes, in Beckett's terms, that there is nothing to be done; we might as well play. In plays such as *Waiting for Godot* and *Krapp's Last Tape*, Beckett's protagonists spend their stage time jousting with language and objects. The tree on stage in *Godot* is too small to serve to hang the characters; they cannot die. Their shoes do not fit; their pants will not stay on. And the tape recorder in *Krapp's Last Tape* never delivers what it should. Nothing provided by nature or culture functions for the purposes for which it is needed. And language too has become a machine that will not work; it has lost its power to communicate, to change the world.

In Ionesco's version of absurdist theater, characters collide and fall in a comedy of miscommunication. In Pinter's version, things are more sinister: human wrecks strut the stage playing power games with one another, aping normally "significant" human gestures and language until one or more characters slip and are destroyed. For Pinter, the world of misplaced significations is a jungle in which language, objects, and other people are treacherous. Only luck allows one to survive. Perception and language have lost their power to explain and so control reality. They can only postpone, not prevent, disaster. Pinter's drama is the most paranoid vision in contemporary art. If it is funny, our laughter is a laughter of recognition and desperation. Taken seriously, it makes us shudder, not laugh.

Absurdist theater has existed since the 1940s. But very few absurdist feature films have been made. In Eastern Europe, dozens of short absurdist films have surfaced; the best known is Roman Polanski's *Two Men and a Wardrobe*. Though Polanski is a devotee of Beckett, he has managed to make only two absurdist features, *Cul-de-Sac* and *What? Cul-de-Sac* is Polanski's best film, but neither of his ventures into the cinema of the absurd has been financially successful. Most of his work in feature films has involved the subversion of commercial genres. In Germany, several film makers have ventured into the absurd—Werner Herzog's *Even Dwarfs Started Small* is the best-made example—but in the main, film makers have not been able to get the money to put together feature-length absurdist films. Why? Because the absurdist vision is the most nihilistic and subversive of comic visions, the most savage about what culture has become, the most pessimistic about the future. To hypothesize from a junked culture toward its imaginative conclusions is no way to make money. It is in this context that Clive Donner's filming of Harold Pinter's play assumes importance as one of the few feature-length absurdist films in existence. That it was made at all is surprising. That it is a good film is amazing.

The Donner-Pinter *Caretaker* uses as its setting a virtual junkyard of unused and unusable objects. Except for five brief interludes, the whole film is set in a single room. Donner refused to "open up" the play, refused to let us take our eyes off the people and objects in the room. Instead he treats his central location as a miniature spectacle. The room belongs to a man who intends to refurnish it and rehabilitate the house it is in, which is supposedly owned by his brother, a building contractor said to live "elsewhere." The man has collected the things he needs for the job: lumber, a stove, a sink, old clothes, tools, a toaster. Nothing works. The stove is not connected. The toaster has something wrong with it, and the man, though he tries often enough, cannot fix it. There is hardly any room for people. The man will begin his remodeling project after he has built a suitable workshed in the back yard. He has not yet begun the shed. He probably never will; his time is absorbed by measuring the lumber for the shed rather than putting it to use (15–5)

The film opens with the man bringing a derelict home for the evening. The derelict sleeps on the spare bed. He intends to go get his identification papers the next day so he can get work; he left them with someone twenty years ago. He never goes. He has no proper shoes for the journey. The shoes the man offers him are too small, do not have shoelaces, or are the wrong kind. The man and his brother hire the derelict as a caretaker for the house. Though he smells so bad that the man cannot sleep well with him in the same room, the derelict is a vain, racist bum whose conception of himself has no relation to his position. But the man, traumatized by previous shock treatments at a mental hospital, wants company; his brother enjoys terrorizing and humiliating the derelict. So the derelict stays on, lying to himself about his usefulness, confronting but never coping with the world of useless objects in the room. Unlike the brothers, the derelict has never learned that derelict objects can be lived with; he still believes in a world of material quality and orderliness. To him, the fact that windows leak and faucets give no water or have no hoses connecting them to water is perplexing (15–6). He lives in terror that the disconnected stove will gas him.

15–5. *The Caretaker* (1963, Clive Donner).

Arthur Cantor, Inc.

15–6. *The Caretaker.*

Arthur Cantor, Inc.

The room is small and unbelievably cluttered. The one window isn't covered by its curtain. Near the window is the stove. Next to it is the caretaker's bed, surrounded by broken chairs, ladders, lumber, fixtures. A single light hangs from the ceiling. So does a pail, there to catch water from the dripping roof. The characters walk, climb, and crawl through the mess, too large for the room they are in, all investing their hopes in its potentials. For the caretaker it could be a permanent home; for the owner, a swank apartment; for the man who lives there, a place to begin working with his hands. But the room is comically out of proportion and ill-suited to what is wanted of it: situated in a run-down neighborhood, its roof leaking, too small for the junk and the dreams that clutter it, it forces the characters to meet its measure.

So what do the characters want? More objects. The owner wants (or claims to want) decorations in "teal blue, copper and parchment linoleum squares," the colors "re-echoed in the walls." His vision of suburbia imposed on the room is as absurd as the room itself. The man who lives in the room wants more tools—as if they could transform him into a craftsman, a builder. The caretaker also believes objects could transform his life. If he had a clock he could get something done. If he had a bread knife—how can he cut bread with just any knife?—he could cut bread. Objects that signify what they should, objects that could transform the room and the lives of its inhabitants

15–7. *The Caretaker.* (b)

—that is the dream. The reality is junk. Junk piled up; junk strewn about. The room echoes the occupants' junked lives. Though the world outside is a frightening wasteland, inside it is full.

Against a background of objects, a drama evolves. The characters use one another as they use the room—as excuses, as reasons for hope, as tools for self-gratification. The caretaker bullies the man who lives in the room; the brother bullies the caretaker. They squabble about trifles. They resist making

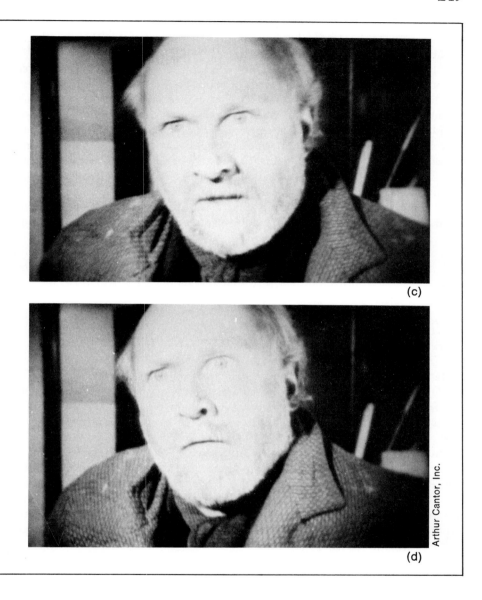

(c)

(d)

Arthur Cantor, Inc.

real contact. When the man reveals he has been in an institution, the derelict regards him as subhuman. Finally, the man's Buddha is broken. The man says the arrangement will not work. The derelict must leave. And at that point, it becomes apparent that the three men are not just unfeeling clowns. In the small room, we have had to watch them in close-up for two hours. They have become, oddly, friends—people like us. And the tragedy of wrecked existences becomes evident in the film's last frames (15–7, a–d), as the derelict's face registers every emotion he knows: cajoling smiles, anger, shock, and finally a recognition of what awaits him outside; though the world in the room is absurd, outside it is worse.

The final irreducible, the final thing we have left, is realization that even in a room full of junk, people are still human: the face has not become absurd. In that affirmation there is something that makes *The Caretaker* fully human, and therefore bearable as well as funny.

The Caretaker is built on what we will not look at in ordinary life. It is on one level a comic parable. On another, it is a bleak vision saying that in our wreckage we will still feel pain. The vision behind the film is apocalyptic. Donner's presentation is convincing. *The Caretaker* yokes the theater of the absurd with the cinema of closely watched performance. It exists in tension with itself and with the cinema's sense of civilization. It exists as a warning. And it exists as a model for what the cinema may have to become if we do not take its warning seriously, or in time.

Following film convention, *The Caretaker* proclaims its final frames with the title, "The End." Few films mean that title as seriously as *The Caretaker* does.

THE ANTI-CINEMA OF PETER BROOK: MARAT/SADE *AND* KING LEAR

Peter Hall's *A Midsummer Night's Dream* is innovative in one sense only: it finds a new structure for ordering viewing perceptions, allowing the cinema to show dreams and thoughts without tying them down to particularized settings. Hall's friend, Peter Brook, is innovative in deeper, more far-reaching ways: he has attempted to bring the whole of modernist theater's development into the cinema. In *King Lear* and *Marat/Sade* Brook has extended into the cinema the thinking of modern theater's three most important innovators—Pirandello, Brecht, and Artaud. He has challenged not only what a film should be "about," but also how it should work; ultimately, he has challenged traditional ideas of what a good film *is*. Pirandello, Brecht, and Artaud created what could be called an "anti-theater." Borrowing and extending and combining their ideas, Brook has begun to create an "anti-cinema."

The crucial difference between normal theatrical art and "anti" art is in the attitude the spectator must take. In ordinary theater and film, the viewer implicitly "trusts" the maker of the work. Anti-theater and anti-cinema ask the viewer not to *trust*, but to *think*. Believing that what is not started inside the theater will not be continued on leaving it, directors such as Brook insist that the viewer begin thinking while the film is in progress. For this to occur, the viewer must be distanced from the work.

In the theater, both Brecht and Pirandello created viewer distance by making theatricality so strong that the viewer had no choice but to be aware of the play as a play and therefore of himself as a viewer. Rejecting the idea of full immersion in a fictional world, and taking a recognition of artifice as a starting point, Brecht and Pirandello, for different reasons and in different ways, placed their audiences "outside" their works. Attempting to inoculate audiences against naïve immersion in worlds of fiction, they argued that all media are to be distrusted. So much of modern experience is fictional! Pre-processed through magazines, novels, movies, television, newspapers, and establishment-controlled educational facilities, our information about the world must be distrusted. The only way to intellectual, moral, and political freedom is through complete sophistication about media-derived experience. Such is the battle cry of anti-theater; such is the theme of the anti-cinema of which Brook is a part. The point of anti-art is to get the viewer to question himself and the processes by which he gains information about the world, the processes that define reality for him.

Brook is not, of course, alone in creating an anti-cinema. A number of other frankly intellectual and often politically engaged film makers are working similar paths. Jean-Luc Godard, Vilgot Sjoman, Alexander Kluge, and Glauber Rocha—to name just a few anti-cinema directors—have challenged "involvement cinema" directly. Godard has done so the most energetically: in 1962, with *Les Carabiniers* and *Vivre Sa Vie*, he began a search for anti-fictional techniques that reached full fruition in his 1975 *Number Two*, probably the most sophisticated, brilliant, and intellectually demanding feature-length film in the history of cinema. But Godard did not invent anti-fiction; he mined the same veins Brook did—those developed forty years ago in the theater. Unlike the recent Godard, Brook shows his intentions directly; unlike Godard, his cinema has not reached the state of "modernization" that makes it watchable only from an artist's perspective. Brook's films are, even for the relatively uninitiated, still watchable. This is especially true of his version of Peter Weiss's play, *Marat/Sade*.

Marat/Sade

Brook's *Marat/Sade* is not a conventional adaptation; it makes no pretense of being anything but what it is: a film of a play. As such, it is true to the spirit of anti-fiction. Using cinéma-vérité trademarks such as a restlessly panning camera, slightly overexposed high-contrast film, and grating sound, it parodies the "you are there" cinema of truth while being an obviously manipulated film. Where the film takes you is an artifice: Peter Weiss's play. Weiss built his drama around a fiction: a performance of a play by the Marquis de Sade supposed to have been staged in the insane asylum at Charenton, France, in 1808. Sade's "drama" plays on the murder of Jean-Paul Marat by Charlotte Corday in 1793. Sade, its "writer" and "director," is on stage to debate with Marat in an encounter that Weiss has called "entirely imaginary," an attempt to bring together "the conflict between an individualism carried to extreme lengths and the idea of a political and social upheaval."[7] Sade's dialogue is culled from Sade's writings, and Marat's from his. Actors playing Charenton inmates perform Sade's play on a stage designed to appear as an asylum bathhouse; nurses and the asylum director are on stage. The inmates waver between being inmates and being Sade's actors, and finally riot at the end of the play.

The filmed play has three levels of artifice: as film, as modern play, and as the "Sade" play. It has three historical reference points: the modern era; 1808 (the time of the supposed play, the time of Napoleon's rise); and 1793, a crucial year for the French Revolution. Brook's, Weiss's, and Sade's presentations are stylized so that the film spectator must sort out levels of theatricality, ideas, and, above all, the work's "meaning" by sifting through artifices (see 15–8a, p. 254).

The core of the filmed play is the dynamics of contradiction. Contradictions occur at every level. The audience is a film audience, but because the film is bluntly a filmed play, it takes the role of Weiss's audience, which in turn plays the role of the 1808 Charenton audience for whom Sade's play is being staged. When the "inmates" riot, assault their "keepers," scream "freedom!" and attempt to scale the bars separating them from their "1808" audience, the film viewer is reminded that the artifice of cinema "saves" him from them— just as the fact that actors are playing the part of inmates "saves" a theater audience watching the play (15–8b). Yet the viewer is aware that the artifice of acting that separates the "inmates'" roles from their lives has broken down, with violence resulting; thus he is reminded that other restraints (for example, the restraints on behavior that keep people from assaulting one another when angry) are almost equally fragile. The film illuminates the borders between seeming and being. In Sade's play, he has himself whipped by the inmate who plays Corday (15–8c). She whips him with her hair, but he acts as if it were a horsewhipping. At the same time, we hear, not the swish of hair on bare flesh, but the whine of a saw blade against metal. One artifice cancels another; the scene is more shocking than an actual beating.

Weiss's play allows Marat to express his revolutionary idealism; it also allows Sade to point out the mechanical bloodiness of postrevolutionary purges. Their arguments bear on 1793, on 1808, on now. But the real point of the violence is brought out by inmates miming slaughter-by-guillotine. The sight of a mime cheerfully guillotining one finger with another somehow seems more revolting than the real thing. Everything that is said is both "meant" and parodied, proposed seriously and mocked, seen new because of its new context, and undercut. The revolutionary, Marat, is played by a paranoid. Charlotte Corday is played by a somnambulist melancholic; she must be awakened, reminded of her lines, told she must come to Marat's door three times before "killing" him. Despite its staginess, the idealism of Marat and Corday is oddly compelling. And the artifice of having a revolutionary played by a paranoiac and an idealistic assassin played by a melancholic adds a layer of associations to their actions. How many revolutionaries *are* paranoid? How many political assassins *are* somnambulistic? Artifices both undercut and give new meaning to what they treat. The artifices of anti-fiction slam together contexts ordinarily seen as separate. They suggest associations speculatively, tentatively, as ideas rather than as truths to be accepted.*

Brook modulates each level of artifice to keep the audience off balance. Sade's "chorus" is made of singers and mimes who appear to be intoxicated, not caring about the play when they are not "in character." They gambol by themselves when not working. When they sing, dance, or talk, however, they are fully involved and involve the viewer with them. When they sing "Marat we're poor, and the poor stay poor" the viewer is tempted even to hum along with them, momentarily convinced of the ironic truths and beauties in their songs if not in themselves. When they step out of character, they become somewhat satanic, repulsive, clowns without appeal. At the same time that such characters are patently actors, however, other "inmates" cannot distinguish between themselves and their roles. Jacques Roux supposedly plays himself—the extreme leftwing idealistic disciple of the real Marat. He stands against Marat's revolutionary position, measuring it just as other inmates provide a measure for Sade (for example, one inmate begins shouting, "I am a mad animal!"). Where does the border between sanity and madness lie? Is a view any more compelling if the speaker "believes" it? (Certainly it is more terrifying.)

Brook and Weiss force the viewer to ask where artifices are biased. Is the debate between Sade and Marat over the meaning of history "fixed"? Marat speaks his lines in a play by Sade, and Sade, while arguing his own ideas, has control over the machinery of his play, and therefore can show a thorough critique of Marat. Are we being forced to identify partially with Sade? What would the play have been like had it been Marat's? Who controls the overall presentation? Weiss, an avowed Marxist? Or Brook, whose politics we don't know? Brook has Sade speak directly to the camera; he seems far more interested in Sade than in Marat. He has even, one discovers later, cut Marat's personal history and put a nightmare in its place, and lent Sade lines about "presenting the great ideas of our time and their opposites"—from a Weiss interview. Just what is the point of view of the filmed play? Obviously, the liberalism of the asylum director, Coulmier, is ridiculed. (Neither Marxists nor radical individualists can stand liberals.) But is the filmed play Brook's? Or Weiss's? Or are they battling just as Sade and Marat battle over ideas? Weiss ends his play with Roux screaming: "When will you learn to see? When will you learn to take sides?" Brook ends his film with the inmates out of control, raping and assaulting their keepers, trying to escape their prison, and shouting "freedom!"

---

* This speculativeness is enhanced by the viewer's knowledge that the inmates are, in turn, played by perfectly sane actors.

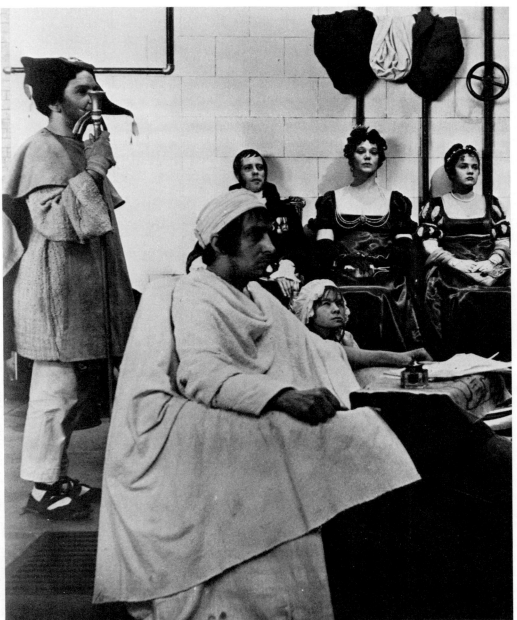

15–8. *Marat/Sade* (1966, Peter Brook). (a) The herald; Marat; Marat's mistress;   (a)
the Coulmiers; (b) Bright, even hard to watch, *Marat/Sade* repels the viewer who
would involve himself, forgetting that this is a film; (c) Is Sade's pain less real for
being imaginary?

(b)

(c)

As in all anti-fiction, one must ask at every level not whether, but in what ways, the work's issues are juggled. Because contradictions are obvious between each two levels of the work (and Brook does draw attention to the contradictions with his camera work), naïve empathies—the aesthetics of trust—are impossible. What one is left with is unraveling one's own mind. Or, more correctly, minds, because the point of anti-fiction is to help the viewer confront not only the work but also his own mutually contradictory reactions.

Is *Marat/Sade* merely an intellectual game, an exercise in ambiguities? Hardly. The work is startling, involving, even revolting at times. One cannot help but react, involving oneself both intellectually and emotionally in the work. There is less distance between *Marat/Sade* and the six-o'clock news than between straight fictions and our contemporary lives. The issues at stake in *Marat/Sade* are no less alive now than in 1793 or 1808. Because the work confronts what the viewer will enter when he leaves the theater, it calls upon mental and emotional resources that straight fiction often ignores. Further, it does not patronize the viewer, saying, as straight fiction does, "Relax! Forget who you are. Sit still while we show you how this situation 'really' is. Become a child for two hours." Rather, it assumes that the viewer is adult, intelligent, fully capable of seeing and judging. *Marat/Sade* demands alertness, demands a mental dialogue between the viewer and the work, demands that the viewer not sit back and be allowed to be told what to think. *Marat/Sade* is as involving as straight fiction, but at a different level of maturity. It involves in a different way, demanding a different kind of consciousness.

What can *Marat/Sade* add to cinema's repertory? What does it do that nonadaptations have not? Anti-fiction cinema often incorporates other media, and asks questions about levels of artifice. But thus far, even the films of Godard have shied away from trusting the viewer in the way that *Marat/ Sade* does. Anti-fiction is always somewhat didactic in purpose: it asks the viewer not only to see, but to see through, to think. But in Kluge's, Sjoman's, Rocha's, and even Godard's films the didacticism functions at the level of a lecture rather than in terms of a discussion. Though a film maker like Godard shows the viewer how to question advertising, novels, news reports—fictions of all kinds—he also asks the viewer to agree with him. He borrows anti-fiction techniques from theater, but mainly from the theater of Bertolt Brecht, who made his own viewpoint directly obvious, and who controlled the ambiguities he asks the audience to contemplate. The difficulty with such didacticism is that it allows the spectator to pigeonhole the viewpoint of the work and therefore to restrict his own involvement to appropriate responses. When I watch a Brecht play or a Godard film I use the Marxist side of my mind for a couple of hours. It is good exercise and (as in straight fiction) I am apt to learn a lot. But because I have not been forced to talk back mentally while watching, I can leave the theater pleased that certain issues have been clarified, have a cup of coffee, and resume my private life. The Brecht or Godard work functions like a lecture; now that I know what to think about "that," I can forget it and resume my pursuits in other areas, areas (like my job or my children) utterly resistant to pigeonholing. Essentially the Brecht-Godard model of current anti-cinema is bad teaching: it does not follow you out of the theater into the street.

The Brook-Weiss model is more sound. It forces the viewer to question the relationships among all roles, all artifices; it leaves the viewer puzzled, forced to resolve its ambiguities and his own ambivalences on his own time. The obvious artifices and ambiguities break down the barriers between the theater and the world outside. Further, the viewer's own complexity and inner contradictions (the deepest parts of his personality?) become part of his viewing role. He cannot leave that role on leaving the theater, the film-exercised part of his consciousness shoved to the side. There is more at stake than two hours of imaginative empathy in the dark.

King Lear *and the Theater of Cruelty*

Marat/Sade contains undercurrents of both the theater of cruelty and the theater of the absurd, but stops short of embodying either movement. It confronts its audience but does not attack it; it recognizes absurdities but does not make them its central subject. It is radically optimistic about its audience's ability to see reasons, solutions, "alternative[s] to the staged disaster," and thus lacks the despairing tone essential to "cruel" and "absurd" art, both of which stemmed from nihilistic strains in the avant-garde movement of the last century. Brook's *King Lear* is a better example of a film based on the theater of cruelty.

The theater of cruelty, as expounded in Antonin Artaud's *The Theater and Its Double,* is the theatrical branch of the "anti-public" art of the avant-garde movement. From the symbolist poets of the nineteenth century on, avant-garde artists have regarded it as part of their duty to *"épater le bourgeois"*— to shock the middle class. Deviating from the traditional view that art is *for* its public, the avant-gardists (and particularly the futurists, dadaists, and surrealists) created an art that is *against* its public, designed to offend, shock, and affront the mainstream of society. The high point of the effort perhaps occurred when the audience of Luis Buñuel and Salvador Dali's film *Un Chien Andalou* rioted; the film was meant to be an incitement to kill. The dadaists framed toilet seats and called it art; they attacked both the received values of the public and the public itself with astonishing vigor. Derived in part from the example of the Marquis de Sade, "cruel" art did not merely offend; it offended deliberately. And the movement is still with us. What began, and continues, in the avant-garde seems to be reaching into the feature film, albeit in adulterated form. There is, apparently, an audience for sado-masochistic art in which the audience takes the masochistic role.

Artaud articulated the principles of the theater of cruelty, but he committed suicide before getting the opportunity to apply them, and thus left the job for others. In one recent New York "happening," an "artist" had his audience climb ladders in a gallery, electrified the gallery's flooded floor, and left the audience stranded all day. In Tony Conrad's "flicker" films, viewers watch stroboscopic flashes of white light; viewer discomfort becomes the films' "content." In Pier Paolo Pasolini's grisly *Salo: 120 Days of Sodom* (adapted very loosely from Sade's novel) the audience watches feces being eaten for perhaps five or ten minutes. What is the purpose? Apparently it is (as Artaud recommended) to get down to the core of an audience's capacity for disgust, to explore its deepest revulsions. The theater of cruelty focuses the viewer's attention on his own corporeality, on his capacity for disgust with himself. The audience becomes the victim of the work. One does not ask why someone would show feces being eaten; one asks what foul thing in oneself makes one put up with watching it and not simply walk out. Rage against the work converts into rage against oneself.

Two distinctions must be made. The theater of cruelty is not simply mimetic, an attempt to "show things as they are." An art that shows war, violence, or corrupt behavior in order to get its audience to face realities unflinchingly has ostensible didactic functions, often becoming a cry for social change. The theater of cruelty is too perverse to be called a request for social change. And it differs dynamically, if not morally, from sadistic theater. A carnival freak show, a bullfight, the public executions and bearbaitings that amused our ancestors—all are forms of sadistic theater, in which the viewer takes pleasure in watching other beings suffer. Sadistic theater ranges from pornography on one end to tragedy on the other. One distinguishes between types of sadistic theater on the basis of the reasons for suffering and the possible affinities between those who suffer and ourselves, but pleasure in others' pain seems a common ingredient. Shakespeare understood only too well that he had to compete with bearbaiting and public executions, as Jan Kott points out:

> If *Titus Andronicus* had six acts, Shakespeare would have had to take the spectators sitting in the first row of the stalls and let them die in agony, because on the stage no one, except Lucius, remains alive. Even before the curtain rose on the first act, twenty-two sons of Titus had died already. . . . Thirty-five people die in this play, not counting soldiers, servants and characters of no importance. At least ten major murders are committed in view of the audience. And most ingenious murders they are. Titus has an arm chopped off; Lavinia has her tongue and hands cut off; the nurse gets strangled. On top of that we have rape, cannibalism and torture. . . . *Titus* is by no means the most brutal of Shakespeare's plays.[8]

Teachers often jokingly refer to the problem of Shakespeare's endings as that of "getting rid of the bodies." But Shakespeare was not punishing his audience by showing them violence. Instead he was catering to the taste of his age and its desire for entertainment.

Yet, as the example of Peter Brook's *King Lear* shows, what is a theater of sadism in one age can become a cinema of cruelty in another. However bloody Shakespeare's plays were, the physical distance between spectator and player and the conditions of theatrical presentation undercut their corporeality. Violence that is repulsive in close-up is easy to watch at a distance. What the imagination can "complete" it can put into acceptable forms—witness the traditional movie Western's "blood at a distance" convention. The chief difference between Shakespeare's world and our world is not in its savagery. Even television news cannot compete with public executions for sheer brutality. Death by bomb or machine-gun is nothing to a severed head rotting on a pike, stinking as well as providing public spectacle; professional football is nothing compared with bearbaiting. The difference between Elizabethan cruelty and the cruelty of our time is rather in the element of personalness. Sade, Artaud, Weiss (in *Marat/Sade*, which Brook also directed), and innumerable other thinkers have reflected on the way violence and death have become impersonal; one's fate has become something not owned but imposed by abstract forces. It is from this point that Brook's film proceeds.

In the world of Shakespeare's play, Lear brings on his own demise. He is arrogant, pompous, blind to his daughters' real natures. Gloucester brings on Edmund's revenge by comments at the play's outset. The cruelty of Goneril, Regan, Edmund, and even of Cornwall is directed personally. The sufferings of Lear, Gloucester, Kent, and Edgar are fully their own. And thus the "redemption" of Lear through Cordelia's love is "adequate"—a personal redemption for personal crimes. It is all in the family, the central, smallest, and most intimate of society's units. But personal violence—and thus personal redemption—is not descriptive of our age. Therefore Brook cut the play's opening, turned attention away from Cordelia, made Edgar an everyman to witness his father's and Lear's downfall. The result is an impersonalized film, in which Shakespeare's language is made to serve something other than the stages in Lear's narrative move toward personal redemption. Lear, Edgar—and the viewer—become involved in trying to comprehend the incomprehensible.

In Shakespeare's play, cruelty is redeemed not only personally but through the beauty of Shakespearean verse. Brook minimizes this beauty. The opening line of Brook's film is "Know." First heard, it sounds like "no," the ultimate negation, the sign of both nothingness and existential rebellion. Then, as Paul Scofield (Lear) continues to speak, it signifies "knowledge," the antithesis of negation. The opening pun signals Brook's terms. He will analyze the relationships between negation, rebellion, and knowledge in terms that force direct confrontation. What does Brook force us to admit that we know? The film's opening shots introduce the viewer to a cold, barren, unfriendly physical reality; beneath the externals of clothing and social circumstance, Brook's characters are all cold, naked wretches. Scofield's face introduces us to unfeeling arrogance: authority is not gentle (15–9). Nor are those, such as Cornwall, who want authority any better than those who have it. Patrick Magee's

15–9. *King Lear* (1971, Peter Brook).

Filmways, Inc.

15–10. *King Lear.*

Filmways, Inc.

Filmways, Inc.

15–11. *King Lear.*

Cornwall, standing next to Lear, is merely a contrast between shrewdness and sadism, between pure, selfish arrogance and disdain (15–10). Goneril, Regan, and Edmund are no better: their game is duplicity, sadism, and sexual satanicalness. Lear's knights are hoodlums. Cornwall's face is that of a Mafia captain who gets pleasure from his "enforcement" work. The worst that Brook will show is what we really know: man's cruelty to man, reflected in Gloucester's crusted, bleeding eyes (15–11).

Against all this, Brook sets Shakespeare's language and his "wisdom." And Brook questions whether anything—any wisdom, any beauty, even art itself—can redeem the negations that we "know." *Lear* becomes a studied ritual sacrifice, the only approach to which is through our ability to comprehend what it means. Shakespeare's lines in this context become not lines performed, but tentative reflections and verdicts on the action. The final verdict of the film, expressed more through Edgar's blank stare than through Shakespeare's language, is one of fatigued incomprehension. Acted out, the fable is mad; even Shakespeare's language cannot make it otherwise. Brook's *King Lear* shows us more than Lear, or Shakespeare's *Lear,* can comprehend.

What Brook does with Shakespeare is similar to what a modern critic or philosopher does with a thinker from the past, excerpting and analyzing a strain within the total work, building on it and judging its contemporary relevance. Brook's work dissects Shakespeare and what Shakespeare has become for many, a source of insights. Philosophy has long abdicated its role of explaining us to ourselves. The myth of the wise philosopher, so carefully nurtured by Socrates and Plato, died in 1932 when Martin Heidegger, probably the most intelligent philosopher of this century, agreed to work for Hitler. Who is still considered wise? Probably—and only—artists like Shakespeare. Brook's film tests the wisdom not only of a play but of a line of thinking. Brook asks his audience to think, to compare Shakespeare's "subject" with the terms he uses to describe it; he asks—no, insists—that his audience "know." The result is a brutal, uncomfortable cinematic experience. But it is also a startling "new" vision of what cinema can be and what it can be used for.

In films such as *Marat/Sade* and *King Lear* Brook says we must examine two things: our culture and our selves. He goes for the guts and the mind as well as for the imagination and the eye. He asks uncomfortable questions. He attacks every verity in our culture, from Shakespeare to reason itself. He attacks *us*. And the only way to respond is to strike back, to think, to act so that Brook's vision stands as a challenge rather than a condemnation. If Brook is right about reality, about culture, and about art, we are in trouble. Brook makes his audience think. And people who think are dangerous. They are capable of anything, even of not lying to themselves.

Bertolt Brecht once wrote that there are three stages in life. There is defeat. There is new action. And there is the space between the two. What happens in that space determines whether new action will result in another defeat, and, if so, whether that defeat will be as stupid and unnecessary as the last one. Art exists in the interval between defeat and new action. And it exists, if it is honest, to explain old defeats and hypothesize about what kinds of action might avoid at least the same kinds of defeat. Only if art is honest can it be of any use to us. And if it is honest it will make us uncomfortable, make us analyze not only our situation but ourselves. Brook's anti-cinema exists between defeat and the future. Those are its terms, and it is honest about them. Can we respond with equal honesty? On that question, the future of anti-cinema depends.

And, perhaps, the future of the cinema and the future of our world as well.

NOTES: CHAPTER FIFTEEN

[1] Susan Sontag, *Styles of Radical Will* (New York: Dell, 1968), p. 118.

[2] Norman N. Holland, *The Shakespearean Imagination* (New York: Macmillan, 1964), p. 29.

3 Stig Björkman, Torsten Manns, and Jonas Sima, *Bergman on Bergman: Interviews with Ingmar Bergman*, trans. Paul Britten Austin (New York: Simon & Schuster, 1973), p. 251.

4 Charles Thomas Samuels, *Encountering Directors* (New York: Capricorn Books, 1972), p. 197.

5 Ibid., p. 203.

6 Geoffrey Reeves, "Finding Shakespeare on Film: From an Interview with Peter Brook," *Tulane Drama Review*, 11, 1 (1966):118.

7 Peter Weiss, *Marat/Sade* (New York: Atheneum, 1965), p. 106.

8 Jan Kott, *Shakespeare, Our Contemporary* (Garden City, N.Y.: Doubleday Anchor Books, 1966), p. 345.

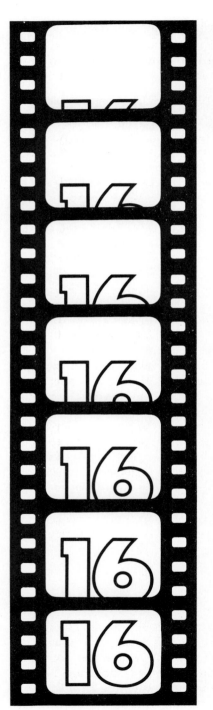

CREATIVITY AND COMMUNITY
Reflections on the Independent Cinema

The cinema is a speculative art form. The viewer, sitting in a darkened theater, engages his eyes and ears, his emotions, imagination, and cognitive power in speculating along with the events on the screen, events that ideally should tell him something about himself, his world, and the act of seeing. Yet the most damning question that can be asked concerning commercial cinema is whether most movies are even worth speculating about. Certainly from the standpoint of theater, literature, painting, philosophy, or serious aesthetics most commercial movies are banal and trivial; even if one treats them as vehicles of popular myths or argues that they stimulate primitive areas of the brain, it remains difficult to justify taking seriously the speculative activity that is central to most popular films. What difference does it make if a make-believe shark munches on a few bathers or an oversized mechanical gorilla climbs New York's tallest building or a fictional bank robber gets away with the loot? Most films are built on idle speculations, escapist artifices, and (if one tries to speak seriously about what they have to say) lead to silly talk. One makes a fool of oneself by attempting to justify just what it was that engaged one's mind totally during two hours in the dark watching a popular film—which is perhaps one reason why most viewers remain staunchly silent after they leave theaters.

Why are most movies trivial? The reason is simple. The mainstream cinema is made by and for the middle class and for those who aspire to the middle class. And the dreams of the middle class are of a piece with their lives, preoccupied with petty comforts and trivial visions of a better life. A more expensive car, a second television set, new draperies are hardly the stuff on which great art can build. And although the culinary aesthetic of the cinema can speak to middle-class values more effectively than any medium except television, what is spoken about is, after all, consumerism, the consumption of the irrelevant and unnecessary. Further, as Herbert Gans has pointed out, because popular art is a matter not of what people want but of what they will put up with, the popular cinema does not so much reflect the dreams of the middle class as it does the middle-class habit of accepting the second-rate, of making do with shoddy consumer goods. Frozen dinners, clumsy automobiles, uncomfortable furniture, and Hollywood movies—these are the convenience goods of our culture. There is no way to treat them as a serious source of values and at the same time maintain one's intellectual conscience.

The miracle of cinema history has been that Hollywood has not expunged independent cinema. Rather, independent cinema has thrived as a guerilla art form, especially during the 1920s and since World War II, using the medium of film (a medium which, because it is industrially based, could not exist except as a form of high-volume mass consumption) for purposes opposed to the values of Hollywood and Hollywood's audience. One turns to independent film makers as justification for treating the cinema as a serious art form, an art rich in worthwhile speculations and important statements. It is to the independent cinema that one turns whenever one asks about the medium's potentials. In this final chapter we will briefly look at some salient discoveries of independent film, some directions being explored by contemporary independent film makers that are ignored by popular film, and the precarious conditions on which the survival of independent cinema depends.

ARTISTIC SUBCULTURES

Very little art of any significance is created in a social vacuum. The cinema, which is usually created by groups rather than individuals and is aimed at audiences rather than lone appreciators, is especially dependent on social considerations: on existing communities that foster and encourage new directions in art. This situation is not, of course, entirely unique to the cinema. The phenomenon of modernism, for example, depended on the existence

of artistic subcultures, both social subcultures and subcultures of related interests. As André Malraux pointed out in *Museum Without Walls*, "All of
our great solitaries, from Baudelaire to Rimbaud, were also men who spent a
good deal of time in the literary cafés; even the rebellious Gauguin attended
Mallarmé's gatherings, and Mallarmé was a close friend of Manet's as
Baudelaire had been of Delacroix."[1] In the cinema, one rarely finds innovators
working alone. The cinema's important advances are usually the results of
movements, of groups working together; the cinema does not advance by
ripples but in waves and bursts of energy. The film makers who discovered
and explored cubist and surrealist forms of cinema in the 1920s were part of
the artistic subcultures of Paris and Berlin; they knew each other and participated in their subculture's common cause—to effect a complete aesthetic
revolution. Rossellini, De Sica, and the other Italian neorealists had the sense
of being part of a movement; so did the New Wave film makers in the France
of the late 1950s—Truffaut, Malle, Godard, Resnais—and the Czech film
makers of the Prague Spring of 1968. Even the cinema's loners—Bergman,
Bresson, Fellini, Antonioni—have worked with the encouragement of small
groups of backers and friends. And the American avant-garde since World
War II, despite its iconoclastic individualism, has flourished as a widespread
subculture of artists who know one another's work (and often one another);
who are encouraged by *cognoscenti* and supported by distributors such as
Cinema 16 and the Creative Film Society, who view independent films as a
cause worth making sacrifices for. Important cinema depends on the existence
of communities, both actual social communities and what Malraux has called a
community of interests. Such communities are the *sine qua non* of any
consideration of film as a serious art form and of any consideration of the
cinema's potentials as an art form.

A cinema made only by major studios, aimed only at a mass, middle-class
audience, is equivalent to a literature made up only of best sellers, a music
made up only of popular songs, a theater consisting merely of Broadway hits.
Independent films are the brains and soul of the cinema. A primary motivation behind independent film making has always been the desire to find what
can be done in the medium of film. Commercial film makers have given the
cinema its economic and industrial base and its large body of conventions. But
it is to independent film makers that we owe a sense of the potentials of the
art.

FORMAL EXPERIMENTS

The 1920s Avant-Garde

The sense that film could do things impossible in other media underlay early
film art and surfaced in full force during the 1920s. This vision of new
frontiers informed the political and formal avant-garde in Russia, the avant-

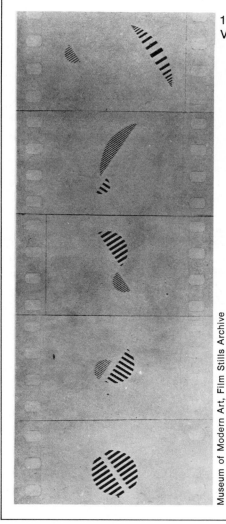

16–1. *Diagonal Symphony* (1924, Viking Eggeling).

Museum of Modern Art, Film Stills Archive

garde of Eisenstein and Dziga Vertov. But it is perhaps most interestingly apparent in the experiments of painters who turned to the cinema.[2] In Berlin, Hans Richter and Viking Eggeling began as early as 1920 to extend their explorations of the scroll (in which transformations of shapes could be set out) into film. Eggeling's *Diagonal Symphony*, hand-animated between 1920 and 1922, was the most impressive result (16–1). A film of transforming shapes composed into breathtaking sequences, *Diagonal Symphony* remains not only one of the most beautiful films ever made but also one of the most important, because it shows that narrativity—the speculative temporal process of film viewing—can take place without story content or mimetic subject mat-

(a)

16–2. *Anemic Cinema* (1926, Marcel Duchamp).

(b)

ter. The importance of this discovery cannot be underestimated: it is the filmic equivalent of discovering that musical notes can be beautiful even if not accompanied by or contained in singing. The accompanying stills give some idea of the kind of transformations on which the film was built.

A second, perhaps equally important discovery was made by cubist painters who turned to film in Paris. Modernist painting requires viewers to make perceptual and imaginative leaps or acts of completion. Given fragmented forms, the viewer synthesizes and integrates them in his mind by an extraordinarily active process of seeing and imagining. Cubist painters such as Marcel Duchamp and Fernand Léger discovered that a similar activism could be imposed on viewers of films that extended cubism in a temporal direction. Duchamp's *Anemic Cinema* (1926) takes spiraling forms, which can be seen as leading either inward or outward, and puns as its basis; the images rotate hypnotically (16–2).

More complex is Fernand Léger's *Ballet mécanique* (1924), the one cubist film masterpiece. Léger's film was photographed rather than animated. The images are of mechanical objects (saucepans, bits of typography, gears) and of ordinary events made mechanical (a woman climbing stairs, over and over again); bursts of light images alternate with dark ones. There is no story, no action-logic; rather, a logic of objects, rhythms, and shapes stands in its place. The frame blow-ups on pp. 270–271 indicate how the stream of images looks; the first, from the film's "logo," links the later images with the tradition of cubist painting (16–3).

The moves toward abstraction, signaled by Eggeling's *Diagonal Symphony*, and toward fragmentation, evident in Léger's *Ballet mécanique*, were, of course, extensions of modernist movements in painting. Yet, as is typical of new developments in the cinema, once the abstract experimental film had been born, it survived on its own terms. After the seminal explorations of the 1920s, experimental film makers could build on the discoveries of film makers such as Eggeling and Léger without a detailed knowledge of the visual arts movements of which Eggeling and Léger were a part.

Recent Formal Experiments

Recently, for example, the abstract experimental film has flowered as a tradition in its own right.[3] Made aware of early experiments (through the proselytizing of artists such as Hans Richter and Amos Vogel), film makers began working in experimental film as a genre of its own. Some important modern experimenters have worked in virtual isolation from the artistic centers of our time: three among them are the Whitney brothers and Norman McLaren. James and John Whitney were potters and painters before developing an interest in computer films. But with the aid of computers (John Whitney was artist-in-residence at IBM for several years), the Whitneys extended experiments such as Eggeling's into complex directions virtually unthinkable without the help of sophisticated technical equipment. For example, in the follow-

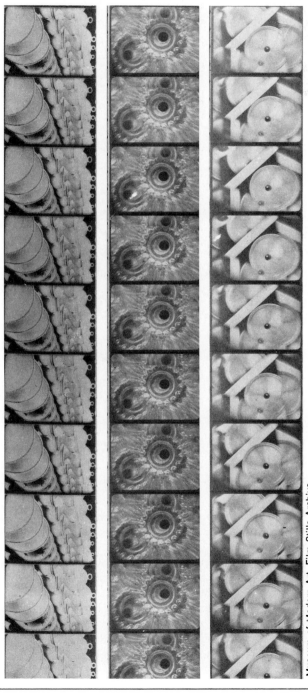

16–3. *Ballet mécanique* (1924, Fernand Léger).

(c)

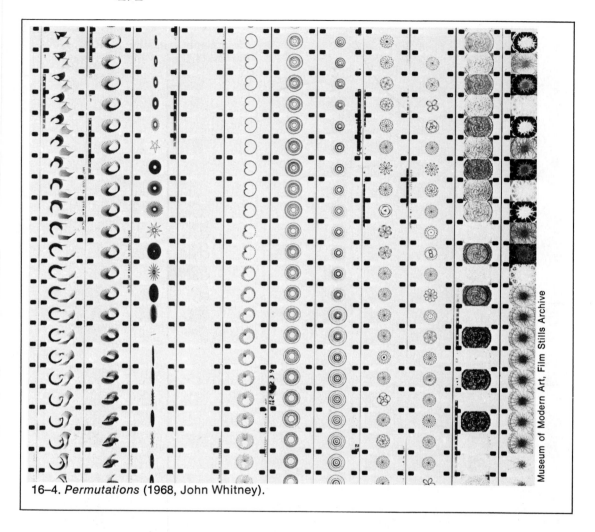

16–4. *Permutations* (1968, John Whitney).

Museum of Modern Art, Film Stills Archive

ing stills from John Whitney's *Permutations*, the transformations of shapes—
Eggeling's essential subject—result in far more complex images than Eggeling
could have ever hoped to achieve (16–4).

The purely formal transformations explored by Whitney suggest possibilities for films with mimetic subjects. Norman McLaren's work for the Cana-
dian Film Board has often involved partial animation. For example, in his *Pas
de Deux,* two dancers, initially photographed in a starkly lit but still realistic
style, become transformed through rephotography into almost iridescent
forms, their movements telescoped, accordioned, and cadenced by stroboscopic repetitions of images. The result is what may be the most visually
beautiful film ever made (16–5).

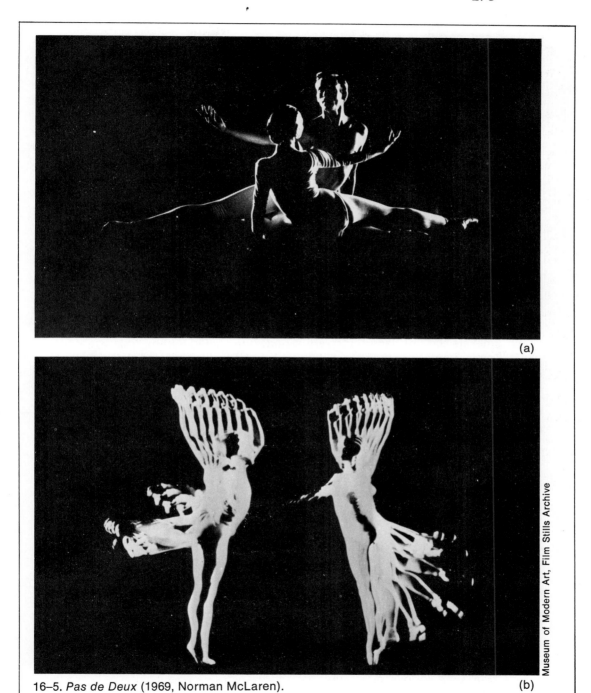

(a)

(b)

16–5. *Pas de Deux* (1969, Norman McLaren).

Museum of Modern Art, Film Stills Archive

The Whitneys and McLaren are but three of hundreds of contemporary experimenters in film's possible visual forms. Others, of equal importance, are Harry Smith (*Smithfilm*), Jordan Belsen (*Phenomena, Samadhi*), Patrick O'Neill (*7362*), and Scott Bartlett (*Moon 69*), each of whom has, outside of the bounds of the feature film, extended the visual possibilities of the cinema in unexpected and important directions. Made with money from personal sources and from grants distributed by cooperatives and small commercial operations, and seen mainly in museums and on college campuses, contemporary abstract films have become an important part of film art—albeit a part rarely seen by the general public. They exist as the product of a small, dedicated film subculture devoted to film as a personal rather than a public medium. Socially and aesthetically, the abstract film resembles traditional art forms, particularly modernist ones, more than it resembles the products of the film studio.

THE CINEMA OF REBELLION

As with form, so with explorations of complex, often discomforting social realities: the commercial cinema has been almost ridiculously fearful of offending its audience, of requiring anything new or difficult. Commercial film makers did not dare, until very recently, to show anything that could not be done in public without breaking the law. Whatever is unsafe has usually been ignored: politics, sexual intimacy and human variation, birth, new ideas, even the human body. During the entire Vietnam War, when the cinema's young

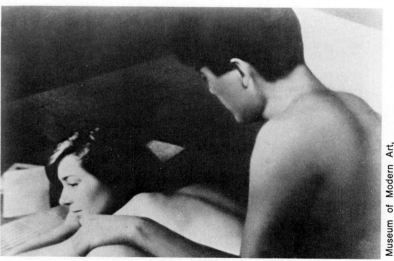

16–6. (a) *Hiroshima, Mon Amour* (1959, Resnais)

Museum of Modern Art,
Film Stills Archive/Contemporary Films/McGraw-Hill

audience was out protesting the war, not a single antiwar feature came out of Hollywood. To be sure, antiwar films were made—*M*A*S*H*, for example—but their focus was never on Vietnam. If they spoke of war, they spoke indirectly and without courage. Although voyeurism and a quest for secrets finally revealed is essential to film's dynamic, the kinds of secrets commercial films have shown have been so safe and conventionally acceptable that the feature film has been, in the main, the most cowardly and timid art form in history, and probably the most socially and intellectually regressive as well. To see the cinema's potentials for social statement, one must look to independent film.

For example, in Hollywood films until the mid-1960s, the maximum explicitness of sexual content did not go much beyond kissing, and political content was nil. The move toward breaking taboos about showing people's bodies and dealing with sexuality began with independent films such as Roger Vadim's *And God Created Woman* (1956), in which Brigitte Bardot shows her body, eats a carrot provocatively, and the like. But the commercial cinema absorbed sexuality as a topic more easily than it did politics. It has yet to accept the fact that sexuality is a political question, and politics a sexual one. Thus in 1959, Alain Resnais, in his independently produced *Hiroshima, Mon Amour*, caused a sensation by showing two *outré* topics: forgivable adulterous love and the victims of Hiroshima. Resnais's independent film was more honest and intelligent than anything that came out of Hollywood in 1959, but it was still a commercial feature. Compare Resnais's circumspect, cautious treatment of the body and human sexuality (16–6a) with what Buñuel, in his patron-financed *L'Age d'Or*, was able to do in 1930, or what

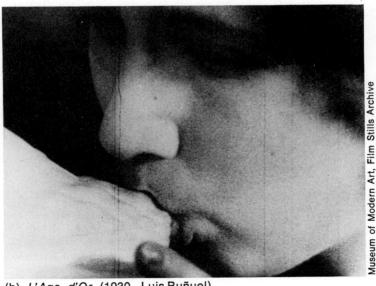

Museum of Modern Art, Film Stills Archive

(b) *L'Age d'Or* (1930, Luis Buñuel).

Dusan Makaveyev, in 1970, was able to do in *WR: Mysteries of the Organism* (with subverted Yugoslavian government funds), and one gets a clear idea of how restricted even the independent commercially produced film is. Buñuel's heroine, sexually frustrated and excited, deprived of a human lover, attacks a statue, committing "toe-latio" on it (see 16–6b on the preceding page). The image has a power to disturb far beyond its "content," because it attacks assumptions about sexuality central to middle-class society.

Both Buñuel and Makaveyev go beyond "merely" sexual statements, of course; both film makers are deeply if perversely political. Buñuel's *L'Age d'Or* questions authority in politics and religion and is a savage attack on middle-class mentality. Makaveyev, coming from a socialist background, attacks puritanism in several contexts. He equates Stalinism with sexual as well as political repression, setting up Stalin against Lenin's revolutionary ideals (16–7a). Makaveyev argues that repression leads to violence and murder—an argument akin to Buñuel's in *L'Age d'Or* and *Belle de Jour*—and asserts that political and personal aspects of revolution must coincide if rebellion is ever to accomplish anything worthwhile. In the final, surrealistic sequence of *WR*,

16–7. *WR: Mysteries of the Organism* (1970, Dusan Makaveyev). (a)

Makaveyev's heroine, decapitated by a Stalinist athlete, speaks directly to the audience, her head (and a death mask of it) removed from her body in a parody of the usual condition of Western man (16–7b). Makaveyev, like Buñuel, uses the cinema to question not only social institutions but our views of society and reality itself.

Most independent films are not as extreme as Buñuel's and Makaveyev's, yet even a clear-sighted view of personal and social life can be revolutionary, and it is the independent cinema that has most clearly shown the photograph-able world's variety and potentials. The surfaces of our world that commercial film shows are so cosmeticized that the viewer must strain his imagination to make any connection between the real and the hypothetical; Hollywood will not help us see if it can avoid it, because to see clearly is to be disturbed by what one sees. It is impossible to look at even the surfaces of visual life and not want to change the world. As Amos Vogel's *Film as a Subversive Art*—the most intelligent and important book on film to emerge in the last decade —shows, and as the films it discusses show even more clearly, an honest cinema is a subversive cinema, a cinema that changes one's mind as well

(b)

as one's eyes. One cannot look squarely at poverty, at sex, at human atrocity, at dreams, even at everyday reality, and integrate what one has seen into one's imaginative life by a quick, easy daydream upon leaving the theater. One must reexamine one's life instead. And films have more power to do that than any other art, except television. It is no wonder that socialist countries maintain state control of film, and it is no accident that films in capitalist countries are distributed by corporate conglomerates. Film is a dangerous art: reality is dangerous, fantasy is dangerous. Art changes the imagination, and the person who imagines is dangerous indeed. As dangerous, even, as the person who thinks, though not as dangerous as the one who both thinks *and* imagines.

Jean-Luc Godard is the most seminal figure in contemporary "modernist" feature film. His reworkings of film language showed film makers what is possible in the feature commercial format. Since Godard (after *Alphaville* and *Weekend*) gave up commercial forms, he has lost what was a fairly substantial audience for his films. The films of the period in Godard's career from *La Chinoise* to—but not including—*Number Two* are arrogant, self-indulgent, and intellectually simple-minded. But *Number Two* is a rebirth: it examines the private lives of two political radicals who live with the husband's parents and with their two children. It is uncompromising in its detailing of the private: of ordinary meals, ordinary sex, of washing up and talking. It dissects coolly though sympathetically the attempts of a family to live honestly and openly, despite everything. It documents a quiet, everyday struggle. But it puts this struggle in context, showing the images from television and posters and advertisements that bombard everyone; it shows the simple and utterly ineffective slogans and ideologies that traditional radicalism uses to counter establishment control over our sources of images. Godard sees the struggle between private life and large social structures as taking on a new dimension because of media such as television. And *Number Two* shows Godard, the film maker in the middle, trying to find in a split culture a form that will integrate the whole. Godard's film says that there may be no such form, that without changes in society integration cannot happen. His film haunts the mind with its pessimistic speculations about the limits of independent art—and of private life—in a media-dominated society.

BREAKING DOWN FEATURE FILM CONVENTIONS

One theme Godard considers, the conflict between everyday life and larger political issues, has been a central theme of recent European films. But Godard's approach has not been emulated by many independent directors (Bertolucci and Kluge are exceptions). Godard places issues in high relief, dramatizing them. A more common approach in contemporary European cinema has been to treat film not as a tool of dramatic advocacy but as a tool of analysis and to treat the cinema as if it were literature, that is, a medium in which reflective, contemplative analyses can take their own time and their own tone so that complex problems can be treated with complexity and nuance. But as film makers have begun to treat film as an analytic tool, two film conventions have come under attack: cinema's two-hour length convention, and its action aesthetic. To limit analysis of a problem to two hours is inevitably to treat the problem shallowly—to overdramatize is to falsify. If new directions in European film are successful in changing viewers' expectations of cinema, the result will be a change in the face of cinema more profound than any that have occurred since the advent of neorealism in the 1940s.

The two-hour convention of cinema is partly a matter of making things easy for viewers, partly a matter of getting two audiences per evening into theaters. But independent film makers have little stake in either reason for the convention's existence, and, because the convention gets in the way of ambitious film making, have challenged it. Few films have done so more successfully than Jean Eustache's *The Mother and the Whore* (1973), which runs three and a half hours, contains little action and a lot of talk, and yet manages to be absorbing during its entire length because of its probing examination of a love triangle consisting of a young man, his somewhat older mistress (the "mother"), and his young girlfriend (the "whore"), who confront one another separately and finally together (16–8).

A remarkable number of recent French, Swiss, and German films have been almost equally long; like *The Mother and the Whore* they rely more on intimate, nuanced acting than on spectacular action for their appeal. Of course, the two-hour convention has been broken, and frequently, by epics, but films like Eustache's or Wim Wenders' *Kings of the Road* (1976) show that the quieter the film, the longer it can last without wearing down its audience. Two and a half, three, even three and a half hours have become common lengths for new independent European films. Do they succeed in doing things impossible in films of shorter length? Often they do, just as novels can be more elaborate than novellas, but the real newness comes from the difference in mood and nuance possible in longer films. Whether there is more than a coterie audience for films as long as *The Mother and the Whore* is questionable. A safe guess would be that the long film will remain an aspect of cinema dominated by the avant-garde.

More important than the challenge to film's conventional two-hour length is the challenge to the action aesthetic of conventional films. A number of directors have mastered the "quiet" form. Among them are Jean Eustache, Jean-Marie Straub, R. W. Fassbinder, Wim Wenders, Alain Tanner, Werner Herzog, and Bertrand Tavernier (see 16–9 a–c, pp. 282–283). All have in common an ability to create and develop characters who hold attention despite the lack of action on the screen; the "quiet" film substitutes emotional and intellectual action for physical spectacle. Beyond a common interest in close observation of carefully developed characters, however, each new "quiet" film maker is different. Tavernier, in films such as *The Clockmaker*, develops a

(a)

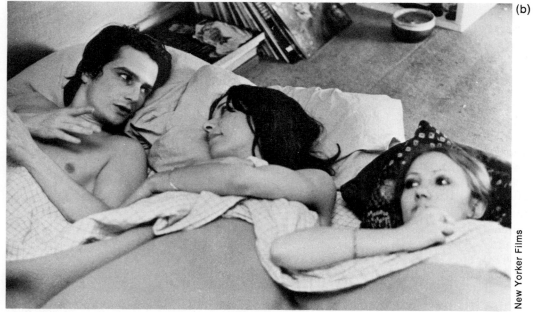

(b)

New Yorker Films

16–8. *The Mother and the Whore* (1973, Eustache).

subtle analysis of the workings of the minds of relatively ordinary people. Tanner, in films ranging from *Charles, Dead or Alive* (1969) to *La Salamandre* (1971) to his recent masterwork, *Jonah, Who Will Be 25 in the Year 2000* (1976), is concerned with the interrelationships between people in small groups as they encounter large historical and economic structures, such as the welfare and jail systems, and the failure of revolutionary hope after the demise of French revolt in 1968. Jean-Marie Straub, like Tanner a Marxist, approaches analysis of character and society through different eyes; essentially he is less concerned with either ideas or emotions than Tanner, more concerned with the materialistic determinants of behavior. R. W. Fassbinder, probably the most prolific film maker in the world (three dozen films in the last dozen years) is harder to categorize: essentially a skeptic, he makes careful, ironic analyses of people who are bound by the fabric of past decisions, the prejudices of society, and their own characters. Watching a Fassbinder film is like watching insects attempting to escape from a spider web; the quietness of the struggle does not diminish its interest. Similarly, in Werner Herzog's films, one sees small people confronting systems with little hope for success; in his best work (*The Cry; The Mystery of Kaspar Hauser* or *Every Man for Himself and God Against All; Strozcek, a Ballad*) there is the same quiet anguish one encounters in Ingmar Bergman's chamber films (*Through a Glass Darkly, Winter Light, The Silence*).

The stranglehold of action on the cinema will not be broken down by a half-dozen or even a dozen directors, of course. But if directors such as Tanner, Herzog, and Fassbinder can continue to work, if they can continue to find an art theater audience for their works, they will have created an alternative set of expectations and conventions which will be able to enrich the alternatives available to the moviegoer.

THE FRAGILITY OF INDEPENDENT FILM

In film, creativity takes money. Films are expensive to make, and experimental films are invariably "bad business." An artist who struggles just to live cannot experiment with film. When money is available, film advances through experiment; when it is not available, experimental film atrophies. In the Paris of the 1920s a good deal of financial support came from the community, especially from patrons such as the Count of Noailles, who financed film projects by Man Ray, Jean Cocteau, and Luis Buñuel. René Clair made *Entr'acte* as an intermission for an experimental ballet. A good deal of other film experiment was supported by a community interested in surrealism and cubism and newness in general. When the Great Depression hit, both money and interest dried up. Some avant-gardists went into commercial film, but most went back to cheaper media such as painting. American affluence since World War II and especially during the 1960s allowed experimental film to flourish again. But most independent film makers have relied on trying to

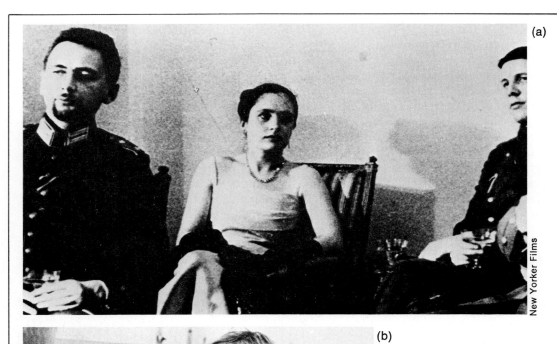

(a)

New Yorker Films

(b)

New Yorker Films

16–9. (a) *Not Reconciled* (1965, Jean-Marie Straub); (b) *La Salamandre* (1971, Alain Tanner); (c) *The Bitter Tears of Petra Von Kant* (1972, R. W. Fassbinder).

(c)

New Yorker Films

make audience support pay for their work. The independent film maker is in the same economic situation as the commercial film maker, but with a single, important difference: his films have a smaller chance of making money.

Very few real cinematic advances have ever paid for their creation, at least since the days of Griffith. *Citizen Kane* broke even, but it is the exception, not the rule. *Last Year at Marienbad* was paid for in part by the French government; everything Alain Resnais has made since has lost money—one of his recent films, *Stavisky*, was subsidized by its star, Jean-Paul Belmondo. The rush of activity in the Prague Spring of 1968, which allowed men such as Milos Forman and Ivan Passer to thrive briefly was government financed. The German government finances the current German film renaissance in which Herzog, Fassbinder, and Kluge work; this is done through taxes (about six cents an admissions ticket) on commercial films. In the completely independent cinema, unlike feature film making sponsored by governments or private sources, there is no chance at all that films will make profits. The cinema, unlike most large industries, has no research and development wing. The hard stuff is done the hard way. And the history of film is dotted with images of men like D. W. Griffith no longer allowed to make films, of men like Orson

Welles struggling to finance the next week's shooting and never having the money to do anything right. It is also filled with near misses: if Ingmar Bergman had not made money with the films immediately following *The Naked Night* (1953), he probably would never have been able to make another movie. The condition of experimental film is the condition of important cinema, but written even more vividly.

Yet the community of the arts involves a great deal more than money. Avant-garde film makers are a cantankerous lot. Cantankerous artistic subcultures almost never exist except in liberal societies and periods. Eisenstein and Pudovkin alike thrived in the "liberal" atmosphere of Moscow in the 1920s; formal experiment in Russia atrophied when the regime became more repressive. The Paris of the 1920s was a haven for rebels. The same could be said for Berlin until Hitler, and for New York, San Francisco, Paris, and Munich in the recent past. Avant-gardes depend on tolerance provided by affluence and liberal urbanity. Will economic uncertainty stop the independent film in the 1970s? A society with other things to worry about rarely encourages the "frivolous" activity of experimental artists.

The great periods of independent film have coincided historically and geographically with the great periods in other kinds of experimental art. The new fiction forms created by James Joyce and Ernest Hemingway took shape simultaneously with the new film forms of artists like Léger. The new musical forms of composers like John Cage took fire at the same time that new forms of dance, theater, and film were being created in the 1960s. One element in artistic advance seems to be the courage that avant-garde communities give artists to be "different." Avant-gardes depend on the ability to hold to avant-garde attitudes. And avant-garde film makers have hardly been exempt from the attitudes described by Renato Poggioli in *Theory of the Avant-Garde* as characteristic of avant-garde artists in all media.[4] Poggioli describes avant-garde artists as being simultaneously elitist and bohemian, as willing to "sacrifice" themselves for those who come later yet inveterately opposed to mass culture. Their favorite myth is that of annihilating the past. Often polemical and always extremist in their art forms, they attempt to find what Ezra Pound called the "brief gasps between clichés." Essentially the avant-garde is a romantic phenomenon, glorifying individuality rather than success.

Contemporary independent film makers seem more aware of their vulnerability than have previous avant-gardes. The flurry of film making activity in Germany during the 1970s often appears to be the response of film makers who fear government subsidies will not last; they must make films quickly before history takes another direction. Those in the documentary film branch of the avant-garde, the so-called cinéma-vérité school of film makers (Frederick Wiseman, Richard Leacock, and Edward Pincus among others) have developed both college and television contacts as a means of support and distribution for their works. Schools such as M.I.T. and New York University have become havens for experimental film activity. And film makers have come to rely on film festivals as a way of publicizing their work. But the dominant mood of independent film makers seems to be one of worry. The economic stagnation of the 1970s does not augur well for either the affluence or the liberalism necessary for experimental art to flourish.

How necessary is the existence of independent film to the development of the cinema? The cinema has survived during periods when there was little independent film activity. But the survival of an entertainment form and the development of an art are two different things. And it is for the latter that independent cinema is important.

The cinema is a speculative art form. It uses what we know and remember as well as our perceptual and imaginative abilities to envision what we have never seen. It depends on artists and audiences being willing to ask "what if?" The questions the cinema asks are limited only by the literateness and openness of film makers and the filmgoing audience. The dialectic between our limited lives and the potentially limitless freedom of our imaginations is the source of cinema. What the cinema can do has not yet been proven. Yet films have begun to explore our realities and our imaginations. If this exploration, just begun, is to continue, the independent cinema must survive.

The history of film is a human history of artists confronting their medium, themselves, and us. And it is a history of our confronting those things, too. That history, for both film maker and audience, is far from finished.

NOTES: CHAPTER SIXTEEN

[1] André Malraux, *Museum Without Walls*, trans. Stuart Gilbert and Francis Price (Garden City, N.Y.: Doubleday, 1967), p. 68.

[2] For a full treatment, see Standish Lawder, *The Cubist Cinema* (New York: New York University Press, 1974).

[3] P. Adams Sitney, *Visionary Film: The American Avant-Garde* (New York: Oxford University Press, 1974).

[4] Renato Poggioli, *Theory of the Avant-Garde*, trans. Gerald Fitzgerald (New York: Harper & Row, 1968). See especially pp. 42–60.

SELECTED
BIBLIOGRAPHY

PART I: HOW MOVIES WORK

Perception and Cultural Communication

Arnheim, Rudolf. *Visual Thinking.* Berkeley and Los Angeles: University of California Press, 1971.

Barthes, Roland. *Elements of Seminology/Writing Degree Zero.* Trans. Annette Lavers and Colin Smith. Boston: Beacon Press, 1968.

Birdwhistell, Ray L. *Kinesics and Context: Essays in Body Motion Communication.* Philadelphia: University of Pennsylvania Press, 1970.

Boorstin, Daniel J. *The Image: A Guide to Pseudo-Events in America.* New York: Harper & Row, 1961.

Eco, Umberto. *A Theory of Semiotics.* Bloomington: University of Indiana Press, 1976.

Gibson, James J. *The Senses Considered as Perceptual Systems.* Boston: Houghton Mifflin, 1966.

Goffman, Erving. *Interaction Ritual.* Garden City, N.Y.: Doubleday, 1967.

———. *The Presentation of Self in Everyday Life.* Garden City, N.Y.: Doubleday, 1959.

———. *Strategic Interaction.* Philadelphia: University of Pennsylvania Press, 1969.

Gregory, R. L. *Eye and Brain.* New York: McGraw-Hill, 1966.

Hall, Edward T. *The Hidden Dimension.* Garden City, N.Y.: Doubleday, 1965.

———. *The Silent Language.* Garden City, N.Y.: Doubleday, 1959.

Hinde, Robert A., ed. *Non-Verbal Communication.* Cambridge: Cambridge University Press, 1972.

Hjelmslev, Louis. *Prologemena to a Theory of Language.* Bloomington: University of Indiana Press, 1953.

McLuhan, Marshall. *Understanding Media: The Extensions of Man.* New York: McGraw-Hill, 1964.

Matejka, Ladislaw, and Irwin K. Titunik, eds. *Semiotics of Art: Prague School Contributions.* Cambridge, Mass.: M.I.T. Press, 1976.

Metz, Christian. *Film Language: A Semiotics of the Cinema.* Trans. Michael Taylor. New York: Oxford University Press, 1974.

————. *Language and Cinema.* Trans. Donna Jean Umiker-Sebeok. The Hague: Mouton, 1974.

Segal, Marshall H., Donald Campbell, and Melville J. Herskovitz. *The Influence of Culture on Visual Perception.* Indianapolis: Bobbs-Merrill, 1966.

Whorf, Benjamin Lee. *Language, Thought and Reality.* Ed. John B. Carroll. Cambridge, Mass.: M.I.T. Press, 1964.

Wollen, Peter. *Signs and Meaning in the Cinema.* Rev., enl. ed. Bloomington: University of Indiana Press, 1972.

How Art Works

Aristotle. *The Poetics.* Several editions available.

Arnheim, Rudolf. *Art and Visual Perception.* Rev. ed. Berkeley and Los Angeles: University of California Press, 1965.

————. *Visual Thinking.* Berkeley and Los Angeles: University of California Press, 1971.

Artaud, Antonin. *The Theater and Its Double.* New York: Grove, 1958.

Auerbach, Erich. *Mimesis: The Representation of Reality in Western Literature.* Garden City, N.Y.: Doubleday, 1957.

Battcock, Gregory, ed. *The New Art.* New York: Dutton, 1966.

Baxandall, Lee, ed. *Radical Perspectives in the Arts.* Baltimore: Penguin, 1972.

Benjamin, Walter. *Illuminations.* Ed. Hannah Arendt. New York: Harcourt, Brace and World, 1968.

Brecht, Bertolt. *Brecht on Theatre.* Trans. and ed. John Willett. New York: Hill and Wang, 1964.

Ellmann, Richard, and Charles Feidelson, Jr., eds. *The Modern Tradition: Backgrounds of Modern Literature.* New York: Oxford University Press, 1965.

Esslin, Martin. *The Theatre of the Absurd.* Garden City, N.Y.: Doubleday, 1961.

Fischer, Ernst. *The Necessity of Art.* Baltimore: Penguin, 1963.

Frye, Northrop. *Anatomy of Criticism.* New York: Atheneum, 1966.

Gans, Herbert J. *Popular Culture and High Culture.* New York: Basic Books, 1974.

Gombrich, E. H. *Art and Illusion.* Princeton, N.J.: Princeton University Press, 1969.

————, Julian Hochberg, and Max Black. *Art, Perception, and Reality.* Baltimore: Johns Hopkins University, 1972.

Goodman, Nelson. *Languages of Art.* Indianapolis: Hackett, 1976.

Hauser, Arnold. *The Social History of Art.* 4 vols. New York: Knopf, 1958.

Holland, Norman N. *The Dynamics of Literary Response.* New York: Oxford University Press, 1968.

Huizinga, Johan. *Homo Ludens.* Boston: Beacon Press, 1955.

Kepes, Gyorgy. *Language of Vision.* Chicago: Theobald, 1967.

Koestler, Arthur. *The Act of Creation: A Study of the Conscious and Unconscious in Science and Art.* New York: Macmillan, 1964.

Kris, Ernst. *Psychoanalytic Explorations in Art.* New York: Schocken, 1964.

Langer, Susanne K. *Feeling and Form.* New York: Scribner, 1953.

Lemaitre, Georges. *From Cubism to Surrealism in French Literature.* Cambridge, Mass.: Harvard University Press, 1947.

Lessing, Gotthold E. *Laocoön: An Essay on the Limits of Painting and Poetry*. Trans. Edward A. McCormick. Indianapolis: Bobbs-Merrill, 1962.

Malraux, André. *Museum Without Walls*. Trans. Stuart Gilbert and Francis Price. Garden City, N.Y.: Doubleday, 1967.

Marcuse, Herbert, et al. *On the Future of Art*. New York: Viking, 1970.

Marx, Karl, and Friedrich Engels. *Literature and Art*. New York: International Publishers, 1947.

Poggioli, Renato. *Theory of the Avant-Garde*. Trans. Gerald Fitzgerald. New York: Harper & Row, 1968.

Read, Herbert. *The Philosophy of Modern Art*. New York: Meridian, 1955.

Scharf, Aaron. *Art and Photography*. Baltimore: Penguin, 1974.

Seldes, Gilbert. *The Public Arts*. New York: Simon & Schuster, 1956.

Sontag, Susan. *Against Interpretation*. New York: Dell, 1966.

Valéry, Paul. *The Art of Poetry*. Trans. Denise Folliot. Princeton, N.J.: Princeton University Press, 1958.

Williams, Raymond. *Keywords: A Vocabulary of Culture and Society*. New York: Oxford University Press, 1976.

Basic Film Theory

Major Theorists

Arnheim, Rudolf. *Film as Art*. Berkeley and Los Angeles: University of California Press, 1957.

Balázs, Béla. *Theory of the Film*. New York: Dover, 1970.

Bazin, André. *What Is Cinema?* 2 vols. Trans. and ed. Hugh Gray. Berkeley and Los Angeles: University of California Press, 1967, 1971.

Burch, Noel. *The Theory of Film Practice*. New York: Praeger, 1973.

Cavell, Stanley. *The World Viewed: Reflections on the Ontology of Film*. New York: Viking, 1971.

Eisenstein, Sergei. *Film Essays and a Lecture*. New York: Praeger, 1970.

———. *Film Form*. New York: Harcourt, Brace, 1949.

———. *Film Sense*. New York: Harcourt, Brace, 1947.

Kracauer, Siegfried. *Theory of Film: The Redemption of Physical Reality*. New York: Oxford University Press, 1960.

Metz, Christian. *Film Language: A Semiotics of the Cinema*. Trans. Michael Taylor. New York: Oxford University Press, 1974.

———. *Language and Cinema*. Trans. Donna Jean Umiker-Sebeok. The Hague: Mouton, 1974.

Mitry, Jean. *Esthétique et psychologie du cinéma*. 2 vols. Paris: Editions Universitaires, 1963.

Nilsen, Vladimir. *Cinema as a Graphic Art*. New York: Hill and Wang, 1973.

Perkins, V. F. *Film as Film: Understanding and Judging Movies*. Baltimore: Penguin, 1972.

Pudovkin, V. I. *Film Technique and Film Acting*. Trans. and ed. Ivor Montagu. New York: Grove, 1960.

Overviews and Anthologies

Andrew, J. Dudley. *The Major Film Theories: An Introduction*. New York: Oxford University Press, 1976.

MacCann, Richard D., ed. *Film: A Montage of Theories.* New York: Dutton, 1966.

Mast, Gerald, and Marshall Cohen, eds. *Film Theory and Criticism.* New York: Oxford University Press, 1974.

Talbot, Daniel, ed. *Film: An Anthology.* Berkeley and Los Angeles: University of California Press, 1967.

Tudor, Andrew. *Theories of Film.* New York: Viking, 1973.

Film Conventions

Braudy, Leo. *World in a Frame.* Garden City, N.Y.: Doubleday Anchor Books, 1976.

Clair, René. *Cinema Yesterday and Today.* New York: Dover, 1972.

Durgnat, Raymond. *The Crazy Mirror.* New York: Dell, 1969.

Everson, William K. *The Bad Guys.* New York: Citadel, 1964.

———. *The Detective in Film.* New York: Citadel, 1972.

Gessner, Robert. *The Moving Image: A Guide to Cinematic Literacy.* New York: Dutton, 1970.

Giannetti, Louis. *Understanding Movies.* 2nd ed. Englewood Cliffs, N.J.: Prentice-Hall, 1976.

Johnson, Lincoln. *Film: Space, Time, Light, and Sound.* New York: Holt, Rinehart and Winston, 1974.

Kerr, Walter. *The Silent Clowns.* New York: Knopf, 1975.

Mast, Gerald. *The Comic Mind.* Indianapolis: Bobbs-Merrill, 1973.

Reisz, Karel. *The Technique of Film Editing.* 2nd ed. New York: Hastings House, 1968.

Solomon, Stanley J. *Beyond Formula: American Film Genres.* New York: Harcourt Brace Jovanovich, 1976.

Taylor, John R., and Arthur Jackson. *The Hollywood Musical.* New York: McGraw-Hill, 1971.

Wood, Michael. *America at the Movies.* New York: Basic Books, 1975.

Wright, Will. *Six Guns and Society: A Structural Study of the Western.* Berkeley and Los Angeles: University of California Press, 1975.

PART II: THE CINEMA IN CULTURAL PERSPECTIVE

Film as a Political, Economic, and Social Institution

Bentley, Eric. *Thirty Years of Treason.* New York: Viking, 1971.

Bogle, Donald. *Toms, Coons, Mulattoes, Mammies and Bucks.* New York: Viking, 1973.

Deming, Barbara. *Running Away from Myself: Dream Portrait of America Drawn from the Films of the Forties.* New York: Viking, 1969.

Guback, Thomas H. *The International Film Industry.* Bloomington: Indiana University Press, 1969.

Haskell, Molly. *From Reverence to Rape.* New York: Penguin, 1974.

Huaco, George A. *The Sociology of Film Art.* New York: Basic Books, 1965.

Jowett, Garth. *A Social History of American Film.* Boston: Little, Brown, 1974.

Leab, Daniel J. *From Sambo to Superspade.* Boston: Houghton Mifflin, 1975.

MacBean, James Roy. *Film and Revolution.* Bloomington: Indiana University Press, 1975.

MacCann, Richard, ed. *Film and Society.* New York: Scribner, 1963.

Mayer, Michael F. *The Film Industries.* New York: Hastings House, 1973.

Mellen, Joan. *Women and Their Sexuality in the New Film.* New York: Horizon Press, 1973.

Sklar, Robert. *Movie-Made America: A Cultural History of American Movies.* New York: Random House, 1975.

Vogel, Amos. *Film as a Subversive Art.* New York: Random House, 1974.

Warshaw, Robert. *The Immediate Experience.* New York: Atheneum, 1970.

Relationships Between the Arts

[Virtually every major film theorist and minor critic has pronounced on the relationships between film and literature. The most useful are André Bazin, Sergei Eisenstein, and Jean Mitry, each of whom comments cogently on literature-film relationships. *Literature/Film Quarterly* is the only journal devoted to relationships between film and the other arts.]

Astre, Georges Albert, et al. *Cinéma et roman.* Special issue of *Révue des lettres modernes.* 36–38 (1958).

Bluestone, George. *Novels into Film.* Baltimore: Johns Hopkins University Press, 1957.

Fell, John. *Film and the Narrative Tradition.* Norman: University of Oklahoma Press, 1974.

Fuzellier, Etienne. *Cinéma et littérature.* Paris, 1964.

Gernsheim, Helmut, and Alison Gernsheim. *L. J. M. Daguerre.* 2nd ed. New York: Dover, 1968.

Grimstead, David. *Melodrama Unveiled: American Theater and Culture, 1800–1850.* Chicago: University of Chicago Press, 1968.

Harrington, John, ed. *Film and/as Literature.* Englewood Cliffs, N.J.: Prentice-Hall, 1977.

Hurt, James, ed. *Focus on Film and Theatre.* Englewood Cliffs, N.J.: Prentice-Hall, 1974.

Jorgens, Jack. *Shakespeare on Film.* Bloomington: Indiana University Press, 1977.

McConnell, Frank. *The Spoken Seen.* Baltimore: Johns Hopkins University Press, 1976.

McLean, Albert F., Jr. *American Vaudeville as Ritual.* Lexington: University of Kentucky Press, 1965.

Magny, Claude-Edmonde. *The Age of the American Novel.* New York: Arno Press, 1972.

Malraux, André. *Museum Without Walls.* Trans. Stuart Gilbert and Francis Price. Garden City, N.Y.: Doubleday, 1967.

Murray, Edward. *The Cinematic Imagination.* New York: Ungar, 1972.

Nicoll, Allardyce. *Film and Theatre.* New York: Arno Press, 1972.

Praz, Mario. *Mnemosyne: The Parallel Between Literature and the Visual Arts.* Princeton, N.J.: Princeton University Press, 1967.

Rahill, Frank. *The World of Melodrama.* University Park: Pennsylvania State University Press, 1967.

Richardson, Robert. *Literature and Film.* Bloomington: Indiana University Press, 1969.

Robinson, W. R., ed. *Man and the Movies.* Baltimore: Penguin, 1969.

Vardac, A. Nicholas. *Stage to Screen: Theatrical Method from Garrick to Griffith.* Cambridge, Mass.: Harvard University Press, 1949.

Overviews of Film History

Cowie, Peter, ed. *A Concise History of the Cinema.* 2 vols. Cranbury, N.J.: A. S. Barnes, 1970.

Dickinson, Thorold. *A Discovery of Cinema.* New York: Oxford University Press, 1973.

Jacobs, Lewis, ed. *The Emergence of Film Art.* New York: Hopkinson and Blake, 1970.

Mast, Gerald. *A Short History of the Movies.* 2nd ed. Indianapolis: Bobbs-Merrill, 1976.

Rhode, Eric. *A History of Cinema.* New York: Hill and Wang, 1976.

Robinson, David. *The History of World Cinema.* New York: Stein and Day, 1974.

Wright, Basil. *The Long View.* New York: Knopf, 1975.

PART III: EXPLORATIONS

Independence in Cinema

Allen, Don. *François Truffaut.* New York: Viking, 1974.

Björkman, Stig, Torsten Manns, and Jonas Sima. *Bergman on Bergman.* Trans. Paul B. Austin. New York: Simon & Schuster, 1973.

Brown, Royal S., ed. *Focus on Godard.* Englewood Cliffs, N.J.: Prentice-Hall, 1972.

Cameron, Ian, ed. *The Films of Jean-Luc Godard.* New York: Praeger, 1969.

———, ed. *The Films of Robert Bresson.* New York: Praeger, 1969.

———, ed. *Second Wave.* New York: Praeger, 1970.

Cameron, Ian, and Robin Wood, eds. *Antonioni.* New York: Praeger, 1969.

Crisp, C. G. *François Truffaut.* New York: Praeger, 1972.

Curtiss, Thomas. *Von Stroheim.* New York: Farrar, Straus & Giroux, 1971.

Durgnat, Raymond. *Luis Buñuel.* Berkeley and Los Angeles: University of California Press, 1970.

Eisner, Lotte. *The Haunted Screen.* Berkeley and Los Angeles: University of California Press, 1975.

———. *Murnau.* Berkeley and Los Angeles: University of California Press, 1973.

Guarner, José. *Rossellini.* New York: Praeger, 1970.

Harcourt, Peter. *Six European Directors.* Baltimore: Penguin, 1974.

Huss, Roy, ed. *Focus on "Blow-Up."* Englewood Cliffs, N.J.: Prentice-Hall, 1971.

Lawder, Standish D. *The Cubist Cinema.* New York: New York University Press, 1974.

Lawson, John Howard. *Film: The Creative Process.* New York: Hill and Wang, 1964.

Leihm, Antonin. *Closely Watched Films: The Czechoslovak Experience.* White Plains, N.Y.: International Arts and Sciences Press, 1974.

McBride, Joseph. *Orson Welles.* New York: Viking, 1972.

Mekas, Jonas. *Movie Journal.* New York: Macmillan, 1972.

Milne, Tom. *The Cinema of Carl Dreyer.* Cranbury, N.J.: A. S. Barnes, 1971.

Monaco, James. *The New Wave: Truffaut, Godard, Chabrol, Rohmer, and Rivette.* New York: Oxford University Press, 1976.

Petrie, Graham. *The Cinema of François Truffaut.* Cranbury, N.J.: A. S. Barnes, 1970.

Rosenthal, Stuart. *The Cinema of Federico Fellini.* Cranbury, N.J.: A. S. Barnes, 1976.

Roud, Richard. *Jean-Luc Godard.* Bloomington: Indiana University Press, 1969.

———. *Straub.* New York: Viking, 1972.

Salles Gomes, P. E. *Jean Vigo.* Berkeley and Los Angeles: University of California Press, 1972.

Samuels, Charles Thomas. *Encountering Directors.* New York: Putnam, 1972.

Sitney, P. Adams. *Visionary Film: The American Avant-Garde.* New York: Oxford University Press, 1974.

———, ed. *Film Culture Reader.* New York: Praeger, 1970.

Sontag, Susan. *Styles of Radical Will.* New York: Farrar, Straus & Giroux, 1968.

Taylor, John R. *Cinema Eye, Cinema Ear.* New York: Hill and Wang, 1964.

———. *Directors and Directions: Cinema for the Seventies.* New York: Hill and Wang, 1975.

Vogel, Amos. *Film as a Subversive Art.* New York: Random House, 1975.

Ward, John. *Alain Resnais or the Theme of Time.* Garden City, N.Y.: Doubleday, 1968.

Youngblood, Gene. *Expanded Cinema.* New York: Dutton, 1970.

INDEX